D0481934

Aerial Hijacking as an International Crime

by Nancy Douglas Joyner

1974
OCEANA PUBLICATIONS, INC. – DOBBS FERRY, N.Y.
A.W. SIJTHOFF – LEIDEN

To C.C.J.

Maintenant, à jamais pour toujours

Library of Congress Cataloging in Publication Data

Joyner, Nancy Douglas, 1945-
A Contemporary concept of piracy in international law.

Bibliography: p.
1. Hijacking of aircraft. 2. Pirates. I. Title.
JX5775.C7J68 341.77 74-8380
ISBN 0-379-00004-0 (Oceana)
90-286-0374-3 (Sijthoff)

Manufactured in the United States of America.

PREFACE

The subject of this study is the historical evolution of the concept of piracy in international law, its relevance to modern-day aircraft seizures, and the degree of compliance exhibited by states which have agreed to international conventions to prevent the unlawful seizure of aircraft.

Moreover, this study is intended to ascertain if piracy on the high seas can be considered analogous to "piracy in the high skies." Evidence of underlying legal and political distinctions is presented to support the conclusions that (1) piracy on the high seas is a crime in the municipal laws of many states, but not in international law; and (2) that aircraft hijacking has been elevated to the status of an international crime through recent international conventions.

Statistical data on all known aircraft hijacking incidents was analyzed to determine whether signatories and/or parties to the "Convention for the Suppression of Unlawful Seizure of Aircraft" signed at the Hague on December 16, 1970, have adhered to the enforcement of this international agreement.

The author wishes to express her deepest appreciation to Dr. Richard B. Gray, Major Professor *par excellence*; to Dr. William Zavoina, for his sincere concern and development of the "Probit" Program at the Florida State University; to Eugene "Andy" Witzleben, for his patience and alacrity in helping whenever needed; to Pam Harrison, a superb typist; to the memory of my dear friend and mentor, Dr. Ross Oglesby; to my family and friends for their loyal encouragement; and, above all, to my loving husband, Chris, a scholar of the highest caliber.

TABLE OF CONTENTS

LIST OF TABLES

Table | Page

LIST OF ILLUSTRATIONS

Figure | Page

INTRODUCTION

For centuries piracy on the high seas has been recognized as a heinous crime detrimental to the interests of all nations. Perpetrators of the crime found themselves unquestionably subjected to the jurisdiction of any state which seized them. Any state making the capture was authorized to take immediate and effective action to prosecute the pirates under the customary international law principle of universal jurisdiction.

In the 1940's, however, a different type of seizure occurred over a new means of transportation, i.e., the hijacking of aircraft. Since early reports of such incidents were referred to as _air piracy_, it was assumed--though not substantiated through written international agreements--that the "pirates" involved could be seized and prosecuted by the state on whose territory the aircraft landed under the recognized principle of universal jurisdiction over pirates as though applied to incidents on the high seas.

As the number of attempts to illegally divert aircraft increased, the use of the term "air piracy" declined and was replaced with a variety of descriptive terms, such as "aerial hijacking," "unlawful seizure of aircraft," or "skyjacking." Moreover, concomitant with the decline of the concept of air piracy was the recognition of universal jurisdiction over the persons who had seized the aircraft. Thus, the failure to prosecute alleged "pirates of the sky" on the part of many nations in whose territory the illegally seized aircraft landed lends credibility to the notion that an analogy of the term piracy as applied to the high seas and piracy as applied to the "high skies" may not be feasible.

It appeared that the customary international law concept of piracy _jure gentium_[1] had certain limitations when applied to the hijacking of aircraft.[2]

Only when the act of piracy had been ". . . committed in a place not within the territorial jurisdiction of any state"[3] did it violate customary international law, which considers the high seas to be the common heritage of all mankind. Consequently, piracy, per se, can not be considered a crime against the law of nations. Rather, the crime must be

---

[1]_Jure gentium_ is the Latin term referring to a law which is common to all nations. Piracy _jure gentium_ violates principles of law and justice as interpreted by all nations. See Charles G. Fenwick, _International Law_ (3rd ed.; New York: Appleton-Century-Crofts, Inc., 1948), pp. 47-48, for an interesting analysis of the term _jus gentium_ as applied to that portion of Roman law applicable to citizens and non-citizens alike.

[2]Traditional piracy referred to plunder of ships on the high seas for private gain by pirates who claimed no allegiance to any nation. See Marjorie M. Whiteman, _Digest of International Law_, Vol. 4 (Washington, D.C.: Department of State, 1965), pp. 648-666.

[3]"Draft Convention on Piracy, with Comments," _The American Journal of International Law, Supplement_, 26 (1932), 760.

defined according to the municipal law of the prosecuting state. Customary international law only confers upon the state the extraordinary jurisdiction to prosecute and punish sea pirates. It does not obligate the states to exercise that jurisdiction, nor does it interfere with piratical acts which may take place within the asserted and recognized territorial waters of the state as exemplified by municipal law.

In the case of an unauthorized seizure of aircraft, nations in whose sovereign territory the aircraft landed did not always feel an obligation to prosecute the captured hijackers. Several reasons can be postulated for their reluctance to prosecute aircraft hijackers as pirates. First, the traditional concept of piracy appears to be an inadequate description of the series of events which tend to shroud an incident of aircraft seizure. Second, there are no recorded instances of plunder for private gains of one airborne aircraft claiming no national registry against another which flies a flag of state registry. Third, if such an action were to take place, it must necessarily occur outside the airspace of any sovereign territory, i.e., in the "high skies."[4]

---

[4]As in the case of the high seas, airspace not above a sovereign territory is considered _communes omnium_, for the common use of all nations. Nicholas M. Matte, _Aerospace Law_ (London: Sweet and Maxwell Limited, 1969), p. 15.

In the 1950's, the majority of hijackings occurred for the purpose of securing political asylum, e.g., American aircraft to Cuba, or what Oliver Lissitzyn calls "hijacking for travel purposes."[5] Since the alleged purpose of the hijacking was attainment of political asylum and was not _animo furandi_ (robbery for private gains), the receiving state asserted its sovereign right to grant asylum to political refugees,[6] regardless of the manner in which they entered that state's territorial boundaries. In such cases, many states displayed unwillingness to prosecute the hijackers and refused to surrender fugitives to other states, despite treaty provisions which required surrender.

---

[5]Oliver J. Lissitzyn, "International Control of Aerial Hijacking: The Role of Values and Interests," _American Journal of International Law_, 61 (September, 1971), 83.

[6]Article 14 of the "Universal Declaration of Human Rights," adopted by the U.N. General Assembly on December 10, 1948, states that everyone has"the right to seek and enjoy in other countries asylum from persecution." However, "this right is qualified in that it may not be invoked in the case of prosecutions genuinely arising from non-political crimes or from acts contrary to the purposes and principles of the United Nations." G.A. Res 217 (III) A.

Later, on December 14, 1967, the General Assembly unanimously proclaimed in its "Declaration on Asylum" that "it shall rest with the state granting asylum to evaluate the grounds for the grant of asylum." U.N. Doc. A/6912.

It should also be noted that a U.N. Declaration, unsupported by a treaty, lacks binding force in international law. See L. C. Green, "Hijacking and the Right of Asylum," in Edward McWhinney, ed., _Aerial Piracy and International Law_ (Dobbs Ferry, N.Y.: Oceana Publications, Inc., 1971) for pertinent comments on the General Assembly Resolutions on asylum.

A second type of hijacking involving kidnapping, injury of some kind, the detaining of passengers and crew, or the destruction of property, appeared in the late 1960's and early 1970's. The purpose of such an act often entailed international blackmail, usually to foster a political movement, as evidenced by recent hijackings of aircraft to the Middle East.[7]

The difficulty in analogizing between air piracy and piracy on the high seas as crimes against the law of nations arises from the relationship between the act of seizing an aircraft (usually regarded as theft if not designated a more serious crime in municipal law) and the act of political flight in search of asylum (an act to which nations often appear sympathetic). A thorough analysis of the conceptual evolution of piracy and its analogy to air piracy is essential if the status of aircraft hijacking as an international crime is to be ascertained.

More than four decades have passed since the first recorded successful aircraft seizures. While this is a relatively brief time for the formation of customary

---

[7]Members of the Popular Front for the Liberation of Palestine (PFLP) successfully seized a Trans World Airline and Swiss Air Jet Liner and forced them to land on the Jordanian desert near Khanna. The Palestine guerrillas demanded the release of Palestinian prisoners being held in various Western nations in exchange for the release of the hostages aboard the hijacked planes. See New York Times, September 13, 1970, p. 1, ff, for a description of the hijacking and the tension-wrought events which led up to the eventual release of the hostages.

international law (which usually evolves slowly and gradually over a long, though unspecified period of time), it appears that the promulgation of two major international conventions (*viz.*, the Tokyo Convention of 1963 and the Hague Convention of 1970) and the substantial number of states ratifying the resultant multilateral treaties may reflect strong communal attitudes to re-instate universal jurisdiction over aircraft hijackers.[8]

Clarity of the conceptual evolution of piracy in international law requires a framework of analysis. This study focused on the interpretation of international law as a system of hierarchically derived norms formally acknowledged by sources cited in the Statute of the International Court of Justice.

Article 38 of the Statute of the International Court of Justice (ICJ) can be viewed both as sources of international law and as steps in the law-creating (legislative) process of the international legal system.

---

[8]Article 4 of the Hague Convention (1970) for the "Suppression of Unlawful Seizure of Aircraft," specifies that each Contracting State may establish its jurisdiction over the offense (as defined in Article 1) if the offense is committed on board an aircraft registered in that state, if the aircraft lands in its territory with the offender still aboard, if the offense is committed on board an aircraft leased without crew to a lessee who has his principal place of business or permanent residence in that state, or in cases where the alleged offender is found in the state's territory.

Several states may well become involved in establishing jurisdiction over the offender, thus approaching in principal a lesser form of universal jurisdiction. See *infra*, pp. 24-26.

The mode of analysis used to develop the evolution of the concept of piracy consists of the following stages:

1) international conventions;

2) international custom;

3) general principles of law recognized by civilized nations;

4) judicial decisions and the teachings of most highly qualified publicists (as subsidiary sources).[9]

---

[9]International conventions consist of written agreements between nations of either a multilateral or bilateral nature and represent the primary stage of development in the international legal process; international customs refer to the slow and gradual process of formulation of legal rules reflecting a considerable degree of consensus in community demands; general principles of law recognized by civilized nations is a more nebulous term derived from the Roman words, _jus gentium_ (law of the people). It should be interpreted as ". . . those principles which govern or are included in domestic legal systems throughout the world and can serve as sources by analogy for international legal norms." See William Coplin, _The Functions of International Law: An Introduction to the Role of Law in the Contemporary World_.(Chicago: Rand McNally and Co., 1966), p. 11.

The Soviet Union, for example, does not recognize "general principles of law" as a separate step in the international legislative process. Rather, Soviet jurists consider it as an encompassing category for any agreements accepted by a majority of states in the international community. See Richard E. Erickson, _International Law and the Revolutionary State_ (Dobbs Ferry, N.Y.: Oceana Publications, Inc., 1972) for an enlightening discussion of the views of Soviet jurists on "general principles of the law" and customary international law.

Judicial decisions and the teachings of most highly qualified publicists include decisions of national and municipal courts and statements by prominent national and international spokesmen, e.g., the Secretary-General of the United Nations, a prime minister, a foreign secretary, or world-renowned scholars in the field of international law.

Through the use of Article 38 of the Statute of the International Court of Justice, it was determined whether an analogy between piracy on the high seas and piracy in the high skies could be posited, and by doing so, revealed the historical norm of piracy in international law vis-à-vis its contemporary status as an international crime. This analysis is normative, however, only in the sense that it seeks to clarify the evolution of legal standards relating to the concept of piracy. It is not normative in the sense of judging or assessing the rightness or wrongness of interpretative views which nations (via national courts) place upon the concept of piracy.

When the conceptual evolution of piracy and the status of aerial hijacking as an international crime was discerned, statistical data on all known aircraft seizure attempts was analyzed to ascertain the degree of compliance of individual nations to the norm of air piracy which has been established through the international law-making process.

Since international law maintains no central enforcement agency or universal sovereign to effect compliance with established international norms, it relies upon voluntary compliance of participating states to advance international order. Richard A. Falk indicates that

> . . . norms of international behavior are secured by considerations of self-interest (the preferred course of action), habits of compliance, and reciprocity

> (mutuality of rights and duties to achieve stability of expectation). . . . In those circumstances in which conditions of self-interest and reciprocity do not exist (and neither do central guidance nor community solidarity), all efforts at legal regulation tend to falter, especially where the stakes are high.[10]

A typology of hijacking attempts, motives of the perpetrators of the crime, and disposition of the perpetrators by states was established to test the degree of compliance by states following the initialing and ratification of the two major international conventions on the unlawful seizure of aircraft, namely the "Convention on Offenses and certain Acts Committed on board Aircraft" in Tokyo, September 14, 1963 (hereinafter referred to as the Tokyo Convention) and the "Convention for the Suppression of Unlawful Seizure of Aircraft," signed at the Hague, December 16, 1970 (hereinafter referred to as the Hague Convention).[11]

The repetition of hijacking episodes since 1961 and the flagrant disregard for the safety of civilian passengers

---

[10]Richard A. Falk, ed., The International Law of Civil War (Baltimore: Johns Hopkins Press, 1971), p. 6.

[11]A third major international convention on aviation, "Convention for the Suppression of Unlawful Acts against the Safety of Civil Aviation," was signed in Montreal on September 23, 1971. The Montreal Convention is primarily concerned with acts of violence, such as sabotage, which pertain to the destruction of aviation facilities, rather than lawful aircraft seizures per se (see *infra*, pp. 216-229.

has led to a "mounting escalation of . . . political intensity"[12] which culminated in the signing of the Tokyo and Hague Conventions. A thorough analysis of recorded aircraft seizures and the disposition of the hijackers via municipal law served as the measurement of nation-state compliance to the provisions of the international conventions designed to decrease the frequency of such incidents.

The following hypotheses concerning both sea piracy and air piracy were posited:

a) While still considered a crime subject to universal jurisdiction of states, piracy no longer poses a threat to maritime interests on the high seas.

b) Major determinants of piracy on the high seas differ from major determinants of air piracy.

c) The criteria of sea piracy when considered in terms of municipal law differ from the criteria of sea piracy when considered in terms of international law.

d) The criteria of air piracy when considered in terms of municipal law differ from the criteria of air piracy when considered in terms of international law.

e) As the frequency of air piracy incidents increases, the status of air piracy as an international crime has a proportional increase.

---

[12]Edward McWhinney, "International Problem-Solving and the Practical Dilemma of Hijacking," in Edward McWhinney, ed., Aerial Piracy and International Law (New York: Oceana Publications, Inc., 1971), p. 15.

f) As the status of air piracy as an international crime increases, the number of international attempts to codify regulations of the problem increases.

The procedure for gathering data for this study was an extensive analytical review of the pertinent literature. Government documents, Department of State bulletins, Reports to Congress, International Civil Aviation Organization (ICAO) Bulletins, League of Nations Official Records, and United Nations documents were utilized. Legal and technical journals, with particular emphasis on the American Journal of International Law and other major international and comparative law journals, were employed.

Current statistics on the contemporary concept of piracy in international law were obtained both through written correspondence, personal interviews with, and documents from State Department and Federal Aviation Administration officials in Washington, D.C. involved in the drafting of United States' proposals for international conventions on the unlawful seizure of aircraft. Additional source data was secured through use of the New York Times Index and International Legal Materials: Current Documents.

The traditional concept of piracy was explored through Whiteman's Digest of International Law, Hackworth's Digest of International Law, Moore's Digest of International Law, writings of distinguished jurists in international law, such as Hugo Grotius, James Brierly, and Lord McNair, and the *British Yearbook of International Law*.

CHAPTER 1

TRADITIONAL PIRACY ON THE HIGH SEAS: A PRE-TWENTIETH CENTURY VIEW

In order to discern whether or not a contemporary concept of piracy on the high seas is analogous to piracy in the high skies, it is necessary to review the evolution of piracy _jure gentium_ from its pre-twentieth century character to the present. Though piracy was traditionally conceived of as indiscriminate robbery on the high seas, a more comprehensive and detailed analysis reveals a sharp disagreement among eminent jurisconsults of international law concerning the elements of piracy _jure gentium_. Such disagreements revolve around the legal facets of piracy in international and municipal law, problems of jurisdiction and the right to approach a vessel suspected of piracy, speculation as to whether or not piracy is a "political crime," and conditions of war or peace which may alter the status of persons committing piratical acts.

The customary laws of piracy which have evolved over centuries of international experiences pose serious legal and practical difficulties when applied _en masse_ to aircraft hijackings. Many of the nuances encountered in the development of the laws of piracy on the high seas reappear in international attempts to define and control traditional piracy before a thorough analysis of contemporary aspects of the problem and its relationship to aircraft seizures can be determined.

Though international law has developed as a code of conduct using treaties, conventions, and diplomatic agreements to govern the relations of nations, it often directs itself to the practices of individuals whose actions violate the very essence of international goodwill and frustrate efforts of nations and their citizens to live together in peace and harmony.[1] A prominent example of an "international personality" who has received considerable attention from international law is the pirate. The normal hazards and perils of commerce on the high seas, e.g., lack of fair weather, assumed a lesser degree of importance than the malicious conduct of pirates on the high seas whose presence was a menace to all concerned.

While freedom of the high seas is a general principle of law which nations have agreed upon for centuries, this time-honored principle became seriously endangered as long as men of ill repute manned the ships which stripped unsuspecting vessels of their valuables and possessions. Thus

---

[1]See Hersch Lauterpacht, "Positions of Individuals in International Law," Transactions of the Grotius Society, 29 (1944), pp. 1-33.

the imposition of an international standard of conduct aimed at dissipating the menace of piratical acts can be considered one of the earliest attempts of the international community towards preserving the common heritage of the high seas for all mankind.[2]

Marjorie Whiteman indicates that a variety of opinions concerning piratical acts finds historical counterparts in the legends of various maritime nations:

> Sea-robbery has not been dishonorable in all ages. Indeed at times pirates of a sort have been regarded as local heroes ,[3] and political communities of considerable power have authorized and commended piratical enterprises. Nevertheless in all times of generally developed international trade, the private foreign pirate has been treated as an enemy of law and civilization by sea-faring mercantile communities.[4]

Early Attempts to Define Sea Piracy

Perhaps the most salient feature of pre-twentieth century attempts to define piracy has been the prevalence

---

[2]Hugo Grotius, The Freedom of the Seas, trans. by Ralph Magoffin (New York: Oxford University Press, 1916), pp. 35, 44, 61. Grotius indicates, "it is clear therefore to everyone that he who prevents another from navigating the sea has no support in law."

[3]Paul Whang, commenting on the activities of ubiquitous pirates who plundered ships on the South China coast, and then retreated into Bias Bay, concludes: "For decades, atrocities perpetrated by the pirates of this famous rendezvous have been related on the front pages of the world press, and books of fiction featured with tales of romance, mystery and heroism have been published to add fame to this otherwise obscure inlet of the China Sea." Paul K. Whang, "Anti-Piracy Measures," The China Weekly Review, 66 (September 2, 1933), 24.

[4]Whiteman, Digest, p. 651.

of the word, "robbery." Authorities, viz., judges on Admiralty courts and founding scholars in the field of international law such as Henry Wheaton, clearly asserted that robbery constituted a primary element of piracy. Accordingly, one who stole at sea was unquestionably a pirate.[5] Charles Fairman recounts that: "When the Merchant of Venice was reckoning the hazards to which Antonio's ships were subject he recalled that along with the perils of waters, winds, and rocks there were water-thieves and land-thieves," adding, "I mean pirates."[6]

As early as 1696, Sir Charles Hedges, Judge in the British High Court of Admiralty, conceded that "piracy is only a seaterm for robbery, piracy being a robbery committed within the jurisdiction of the Admiralty."[7]

Over a century later, Justice Story of the United States Supreme Court presented a definition of piracy which

---

[5]For example, in the course of his judgment in the 1718 piracy trial of Bonnet and others, Judge Trott of the Vice-Admiralty Court of Charlestown, South Carolina defines piracy to be a robbery committed upon the sea and a pirate to be a sea thief. Bonnet's Trial, 15 Howell's State Trial 1231, 1234 (1718).

[6]Charles Fairman, "A Note on Re Piracy *Jure Gentium*," *American Journal of International Law*, 29 (July, 1935), p. 508 (Hereinafter, *The American Journal of International Law* is cited as *A.J.I.L.*).

[7]Regina v. Dawson (1596), 13 Howell's State Trial, 451, 454.

suitably encompassed the case under adjudication:

> Whatever may be the diversity of definitions, in other respects, all writers concur, in holding, that robbery, or forcible depredations upon the sea, _animo furandi_, is piracy.[8]

In cases where entire ships were plundered, justices found little difficulty in branding the culprits as "pirates" and applying severe penalties, usually the death sentence. Piracy merely absorbed the guise of a felony (i.e., robbery) committed at sea. Such a conceptualization of piracy fell short when applied to an aborted attempt to commit piracy. Thus it was once thought that ". . . an attempt to commit piracy could not constitute the crime of piracy because piracy is a felony as distinguished from a misdemeanour."[9] It appeared that one had to be successful as a "sea thief" in order to be prosecuted for piracy.

In the case of _Regina_ v. _Dawson_ (1696) the inconsistency of the previously held view that piracy must be equated with a felony as opposed to a misdemeanour was succinctly put forth:

> Conversely,
>
> When it is sought to be contended, as it was in this case, that armed men sailing the seas on board a vessel, without any commission from any State, could attack and kill everybody on board another vessel, sailing under a national flag, without committing the crime of piracy unless they stole, say, an article worth sixpence, their

---

[8]United States v. Smith (1820) cited in James J. Lenoir, "Piracy Cases in the Supreme Court," _Journal of Criminal Law, Criminology and Police Science_, 25 (1934), 541.

[9]Fairman, "Re Piracy _Jure Gentium_," p. 509.

> Lordships are almost tempted to say that a little common sense is a valuable quality in the interpretation of international law.[10]

Further attempts to operationally define piracy have tended to be either too wide or too narrow in scope. While several writers, viz., Hall, Calvo, Lawrence, and Liszt, ". . . oppose the usual definition of piracy as an act of violence committed by a private vessel against another with intent to plunder,"[11] there does not appear to be any comprehensive definitive view of piracy which a majority of writers accept as authoritative. James J. Lenoir asserts that the status of piracy ". . . in legal theory has never been stated and its actual definition in substantive law is still open to argument."[12]

Whiteman on the other hand, believes that the most inclusive definition of all acts which may be deemed piratical consists of the following:

> . . . piracy must be defined as every unauthorized act of violence against persons or goods committed on the open sea either by a private vessel against another vessel or by the mutinous crew or passengers against their own vessel.[13]

This definition requires further elaboration in that it fails to indicate whether such unauthorized acts of

---

[10] Ibid.

[11] Whiteman, Digest, pp. 648-9.

[12] Lenoir, "Piracy Cases," p. 532.

[13] Whiteman, Digest, p. 649.

violence constitute a crime against the law of nations, municipal law, or both.

Piracy Jure Gentium

The passage of the 1536 "Offenses at Sea Act" in England was the first legislation to establish ". . . an accepted rule that piracy in any form was contrary to all rules of seafaring trade and that the pirate was thus the common enemy of all nations."[14] However, unless a more precise description is presented, piracy, viewed as any crime committed at sea, may well pervade the entire spectrum of the maritime criminal code. While criminal acts at sea receive less than a favorable glance in the eyes of international law, only certain types of activities on the high seas fall within the purview of piracy *jure gentium* (i.e., law of the people) and rate condemnation in international law.

In order to constitute piracy *jure gentium*, the act of violence must be sufficient in degree, e.g., robbery, destruction by fire, or other forcible depredations, such as grave injury to persons or property; it should be committed on the high seas as opposed to acts committed within the territorial jurisdiction of any state; and

> . . . the offenders, at the time of the commission of the act, should be in fact free from lawful authority,

---

[14]Henry Wheaton, *Elements of International Law*, ed. by George G. Wilson (Oxford: Oxford University Press, 1936), p. 163. See Appendix A, *infra*, p. 269.

> or should have made themselves so by their deed, or as Sir L. Jenkins says . . . out of the protection of all laws and privileges, or, in the words of the Duc de Broglie, 'qui n'ait ni feu ni liew:' In short, they must be in the predicament of *outlaws*.[15]

Henry Wheaton offers the following elements to elaborate upon the traditional concept of piracy *jure gentium:*

> I. It is not necessary that a purpose to depredate on property, beyond such as belongs to one nation or one class of persons or one individual, should be proved or artifically presumed.
>
> II. The motive need not be *lucri causa* nor need the acts and intent square themselves to the English common-law definitions of *animus furandi*, or malice. It is enough if the *corpus delicti* exists; and the *animus* be one which the law of nations regards as criminal, and hostile to the rights of persons and property on the high seas.
>
> III. Although the act and intent may be sufficient to constitute piracy, all nations have not jursdiction to try it, unless it was committed beyond the exclusive jurisdiction of any nation. To put it in such predicament, the act must have been committed not only on the high seas, but beyond that kind of jurisdiction which all nations concede to each nation over vessels sailing the seas under at once its *de facto* and *de jure* authority and responsibility, and in the peace of all nations. Crimes, therefore, of whatever character, committed on board by inmates of such vessels, are not justiciable of all nations. But, if such a vessel passes into the control of the robbers or murderers on board, and the lawful authority is in fact displaced, and she becomes an outlaw, any nation may seize the vessel and try the criminals. So, if persons on board any kind of sea-craft, not in fact under any national authority and responsibility, and acting in defiance thereof, board a duly authorized vessel sailing the peace of all nations, and commit robbery or murder on board, and depart, leaving the vessel to its regular authorities, they may still be tried as pirates by any nation in whose jurisdiction they may be found; although the cruisers of a foreign

---

[15]Wheaton, *Ibid*.

> nation, by reason of the rule against international interference, could not have taken them out of such a vessel, if, after their acts were completed, they had been secured by the authorities of the vessel and confined in her, to be taken to port for trial.[16]

It is apparent that the concept of piracy denotes many shades of meaning when used both as a derogatory term indicating an odious crime or when used strictly as a legal term. The core of the controversy lies in the fact that piracy covers a spectrum of subject matter when considered from the viewpoints of authorities in the international realm as well as that of municipal lawyers.

Piracy in Municipal Law and International Law

A sharp distinction appears between piracy under the law of nations and piracy according to municipal law, or local law of a given nation. Indeed, a state may punish few crimes as piracy against the law of nations. It may also prosecute a wider range of criminal acts which do not come under the rubric of international law but which satisfy requirements for piracy under its municipal code. For example, the criminal law of England stipulates that every British subject is, *inter alia*, deemed to be a pirate who gives aid or comfort upon the sea to the King's enemies during a war, or who transports slaves on the high seas.[17]

---

[16] *Ibid.*, pp. 163-4. See also United States v. Pirates, 5 Wheaton (U.S.) 184, 196 (1820), and United States v. Palmer, 5 Wheaton (U.S.) 144, 151 (1820).

[17] James F. Stephen, *A Digest of the Criminal Law* (London: Macmillan and Co., 1877), Arts. 104-114.

Fairman attributes the confusion among the international and municipal laws of piracy to a "misapprehension" of the 1536 English Offenses at Sea Act. He contends that, prior to the passage of this act, pirates were tried in the Court of the Admiralty according to the course of the civil law. Since this procedure proved to be a handicap towards prosecution, the Act provided "that all treasons, felonies, robberies, murders, and confederacies hereafter to be committed in or upon the sea . . ." should be tried according to the common law applicable to those offences when committed upon land.[18] However, it must be realized that a state cannot enforce its statutory laws concerning offenses at sea on persons other than its own subjects; nor can it punish foreigners on the high seas for allegedly committing piratical acts, unless these acts fall within those designated as piracy against the law of nations.[19]

While international law is couched in municipal codes and requires the adjudication of municipal courts for interpretation and enforcement (particularly in countries which espouse the common laws), the international law of piracy may occasionally be misconstrued to accommodate the state's conception of piracy. Punishment of the crime of piracy, as defined either by the law of nations or through

---

[18]Fairman, "Re Piracy Jure Gentium," p. 509.

[19]John Bassett Moore, A Digest of International Law, Vol. 2 (Washington, D.C.: Government Printing Office, 1906), p. 951.

municipal legislation, must be applied according to the statutory provisions of the capturing state.[20] John Bassett Moore, while Judge of the Permanent Court of International Justice, made the following remark in the case of the Steamship _Lotus_:

> In the case of what is known as piracy by the law of nations, there has been conceded a universal jurisdiction, under which the person charged with the offence may be tried and punished by any nation into whose jurisdiction he may come. I say 'piracy by law of nations,' because the municipal laws of many States denominate and punish as 'piracy' numerous acts which do not constitute piracy by law of nations, and which therefore are not of universal cognizance, so as to be punished by all nations. Piracy by law of nations, in its jurisdictional aspects, is _sui generis_. Though statutes may provide for its punishment, it is an offence against the law of nations, and as the scene of the pirate's operations is the high seas, which it is not the right or duty of any nation to police, he is denied the protection of the flag which he may carry, and is treated as an outlaw, as the enemy of all mankind - _hostis humani generis_ - whom any nation may in the interest of all capture and punish. . . .[21]

Thus, it is not through the force of international law that acts which are designated as piracy by the municipal laws of a state are punished. Hall maintains that the jurisdiction of a state to prosecute criminal matters as

---

[20]"The legislative authority of a state may doubtless enlarge the definition of the crime of piracy, but the states must confine the operation of the new definition to its own citizens and to foreigners on its own vessels." Clifford, J., in Dole v. New England Mutual Marine Insurance Co., 2 Cliff. 394, 417 (1st Circ., 1864).

[21]John Bassett Moore, J., in the Steamship _Lotus_, Publications of the Permanent Court of International Justice, Series A, No. 10 (1927), pp. 70-1.

deemed by its criminal code generally extends to the following matters:

> (1st) To the punishment of all offences against its municipal laws, by whomsoever committed, within its territory; (2nd) To the punishment of all such offences, by whomsoever committed, on board its public or private vessels on the high seas and on board its public vessels, and, in some case, on board its merchant vessels in foreign ports; (3rd) To the punishment of all such offences by its own subjects, wheresoever committed; (4th) To the punishment of piracy, and other offences against the law of nations, by whomsoever and wheresoever committed.[22]

It is imperative, then, to devote careful attention to the proper nation-state jurisdictions over public and private vessels, since they form a binding link between piracy *jure gentium* and piracy as presented in municipal law.

Universal Jurisdiction on the High Seas

In essence, piracy does not constitute a breach of legal fiats under the law of nations. Rather, it is an offense against the municipal law of respective states. The status of piracy in international law entails two legal facets: firstly, international law abhors the practice of piracy as a crime *jure gentium*[23] and condemns pirates as

---

[22]Henry W. Halleck, *International Law*, Vol. 1 (3rd ed.; Philadelphia: G. S. Appleton, 1866), pp. 232-5.

[23]The term international law is of relatively recent origin. Until the middle of the 17th Century, it was known as *jus gentium*--"the Law of Nations" or "Universal Law." Y. A. Korovin, *et al.*, *International Law*, trans. by Dennis Ogden (Moscow: Foreign Languages Publishing House, n. d.), p. 7.

hostis humani generis;[24] and secondly, international law delegates to nation-states the extraordinary jurisdiction to apprehend and punish pirates who are lawfully captured on the high seas.

Customary international law interprets the offense of piracy jure gentium to be within the jurisdictional scope of sui generis[25]--specifically referred to as universal jurisdiction. Customary international law, formulated by a consensus of the municipal laws of states over long though unspecified periods of time, dictates that pirates assume the character of hostis humani generis, the common enemies of all mankind, because they violate the general principle of international law that the high seas are the common heritage of all peoples. While hostis humani generis cannot be equated with the traditional concept of piracy jure gentium, it does suggest that such a description of piratical activities serves as ". . . a rhetorical invective to shew the odiousness of that crime."[26]

---

[24]While hostis humani generis (enemy of the human race) may be used to describe activities of persons who are pirates in international law, it is not a synonym or definition of piracy. See James L. Brierly, The Law of Nations (Oxford: The Clarendon Press, 1928), p. 154.

[25]Sui generis is a Latin term denoting "one of a kind." Judge Moore indicates that "Piracy by the law of nations, in its jurisdictional aspects, is sui generis." John Bassett Moore in the Steamship Lotus Case, op. cit., p. 70.

[26]Wheaton, International Law, p. 163. In the context of Wheaton's remarks, "shew" may be read as "show."

The casting of piracy in this light provides a linkage between a nation's interest in providing safe travel on the high seas for its subjects and the means of assuring other states that pirates, if apprehended on the high seas, will be punished regardless of their national character. Though the ordinary limits of national jurisdiction prior to the twentieth century were governed by geographical boundaries three miles from the coast line into territorial waters,[27] universal jurisdiction confers upon states an equal or common opportunity to seize pirates at the scene of their operations, i.e., the high seas. Even if it is ". . . not the special right or duty of any state to police" the high seas, it may well be within the interest of the state and other states that the offender be "denied the protection of the flag which he may carry . . . and . . . treated as an outlaw."[28] This is well stated in Wheaton's

---

[27]In 1800, Franz L. von Cancrin stated that "the most recent opinion is to the effect that a people possesses so much of the adjacent sea as can be dominated by cannons or guarded by men of war." Though it was generally accepted that the range of a cannon from a shore was fixed at three miles, or one English league, not all states adhered to this practice. During the early 1800's, France, for example, claimed a distance of ten leagues from its southern coasts. See Stefan A. Riesenfeld, Protection of Coastal Fisheries Under International Law (Washington, D.C.: Carnegie Endowment for International Peace, 1942), pp. 31-124 for an interesting analysis of the evolution of the cannon-shot rule and the objections to setting a fixed distance of the territorial sea in international law.

[28]Moore, Digest, pp. 951-2.

succinct description of the generally accepted principle of universal jurisdiction vis-à-vis piracy _jure gentium_:

> It is true, that a pirate _jure gentium_ can be seized and tried by any nation, irrespective of his national character, or of that of the vessel on board which, against which, or from which, the act was done. The reason of this must be, that the act is one over which all nations have equal jurisdiction. This can result only from the fact, that it is committed where all have a common, and no nation an exclusive, jurisdiction, i.e., upon the high seas; and, if on board ship, and by her own crew, then the ship must be one in which no national authority reigns. The criminal may have committed but one crime, and intended but one, and that against a vessel of a particular nation; yet, if done on the high seas . . . he may be seized and tried by any nation.[29]

A Counter-View of Universal Jurisdiction

Jurisdiction can be said to refer to those ". . . situations in which a state may lawfully take action with respect to things, persons, and events, from those situations in which it is not the one which may lawfully do so."[30] The question of jurisdiction concerns whether a state "may take certain physical action to exercise its authority . . . [or] whether the particular state may lawfully ascribe the character of legality or illegality to particular actions or events."[31] In essence, a state's jurisdiction extends over both its nationals and its territory.

---

[29]Wheaton, _International Law_, p. 163.

[30]William W. Bishop, Jr., _International Law: Cases and Materials_ (Boston: Little, Brown and Co., 1962), p. 439.

[31]_Ibid_.

Piracy *jure gentium* poses a dilemma to both these facets of a state's jurisdiction. When a pirate perpetrates his criminal activities on the high seas, he becomes, under the law of nations, an enemy of the human race, subject to punishment by any or all states. Yet, while a state's jurisdiction may be expanded to include the lawful capture of pirates on the high seas, the ability to capture and the legality of the capture is subject to qualifications. Such qualifications include a serious questioning of the validity of special (*viz*, universal, common or equal) jurisdiction of states in the disposition of pirates *jure gentium*, the restriction of a state's exercise of jurisdiction over its nationals, and the possible discrepancies between international law and municipal law in adequately defining piracy as an international crime.

Jurisdiction over Public and Private Vessels

Emerich de Vattel, a prominent Swiss diplomat and adroit scholar of international law, concluded over two centuries ago that the jurisdictional domain of a nation reaches out to all of its possessions——including vessels of a nation on the high seas as portions of its territory. Furthermore, the jurisdiction which a nation maintains over its public and private vessels on the high seas is exclusive and reinforced by municipal laws which designate the punishment of crimes committed aboard maritime vessels.[32]

If a nation's jurisdiction extends to its ships upon the high seas and to its nationals for the enforcement of violations against municipal codes, then it becomes a question of both practice and academic interest as to what incentives would prompt a state government to surrender its vested interest to protect or punish those who travel under its jurisdiction. In the same context, are pirates considered pirates _jure gentium_ if they descend from the high seas into the territory of a state, then return to the open waters to pursue piratical activities?

In an attempt to clarify these legal niceties, Paul Stiel, a late nineteenth century authority on piracy, strongly averred that ". . . piracy is not a special ground of criminal judicial jurisdiction under the Law of Nations."[33] His view is couched in the municipal practice of many European states which called for the prosecution of foreigners for offenses committed in their respective states. Examples of such criminal codes include the principle of passive personality--a rather weak basis of jurisdiction in

---

[32]See Hugo Grotius, _De Jure Belli ac Pacis Libri Tres_, trans. by Francis W. Kelsey (Indianapolis: The Bobbs-Merrill Co., Inc., 1923), pp. 436-7.

[33]Paul Stiel, _Der Tatbestand der Pirateris_, cited in Joseph Bingham, "Harvard Research on Piracy," _A.J.I.L. Supp._ 26 (1932), 761.

international law, in which a state claims jurisdiction over a non-national (foreigner) for injuries inflicted to the state's nationals.[34] Or, a state's criminal jurisdiction may be extended on the grounds of the protective principle, i.e., a foreigner's activities are deemed injurious to the national interests of the state. Counterfeiting of currency, for example, may not harm the interests of the state in which the counterfeiter operated, but it is a source of definite harm to the state which the bogus money is directed.[35]

In every instance, when the passive or protective personality principles are asserted, the state must present the *corpus delecti* before its municipal tribunals for trial and punishment. The state may not, however, violate the territorial integrity of another state to capture the alleged criminal. Only if amiable relations exist between the state in whose territory the alleged criminal is found

---

[34]See The *Lotus* Case, Permanent Court of International Justice, P.C.I.J. Series A, No. 10 (1927).

[35]In U.S. v. Arjona, the court ruled that "The law of nations requires every national government to use 'due diligence' to prevent a wrong being done within its own dominion to another nation with which it is at peace, or to the people thereof; and because of this the obligation of one nation to punish those who within its own jurisdiction counterfeit the money of another nation has long been recognized. Vattel, in his Law of Nations, . . . uses this language: 'From the principles thus laid down, it is easy to conclude, that if one nation counterfeits the money of another, or if she allows and protects false coiners who presume to do it, she does that nation an injury.'" 120 U.S. (1887) 484.

and the state whose citizens or interests have been harmed will the general principle of reciprocity (or treaty agreement requiring the return of the individual for an indicated offense) be honored.[36]

Piracy: Loss of National and Territorial Jurisdiction?

In the case of piracy on the high seas, it has been said that pirates and their vessels ". . . lose *ipso facto* by an act of piracy the protection of their flag State and their national character;"[37] thus, all nations, under customary international law, maintain the right to seize and prosecute the offenders. There is considerable disagreement, however, as to whether or not both the pirate and the vessel on which he sails lose their national character.

If it is held that both the pirate and his ship become "denationalized" as a result of an act of piracy, certain legal consequences result from the state which assumes a common jurisdiction over the accosted pirate and his vessel. Under the law of nations, a state is authorized to perform the following acts:

> (1) to seize the pirate ship and its officers, crew and contents and other piratical property and booty

---

[36]W. E. Beckett, "The Exercise of Criminal Jurisdiction over Foreigners," *British Yearbook of International Law, 1925* (Hereinafter cited as *B.Y.I.L.*) (New York: Oxford University Press, 1926), pp. 44-60.

[37]Hersch Lauterpacht, *Oppenheim's International Law* (8th ed.; London: Longmans, Green and Co., 1955), pp. 608-9.

> outside foreign territorial jurisdiction, (2) to direct the consequences of such a seizure, and (3) to prosecute and punish pirates under the law of the prosecuting state.[38]

While it is true that a state may be authorized to perform these acts under customary international law, it is misleading to assume that either the pirate or the vessel becomes totally "denationalized" as a legal consequence of the act of piracy on the high seas. Nations do not readily give up jurisdictional rights, substantiated under customary international law, over both nationals and vessels, whether public or private. In essence, two established principles of the law of nations, viz, the universal jurisdiction over piracy jure gentium and the state's jurisdiction over nationals and vessels, appear to be in conflict. This perplexing situation remains unsolved unless a state has explicitly indicated through diplomatic correspondence, treaty, or a long history of consistent behavior (which supports the principle of universal jurisdiction) a total approval of the right of all other states to prosecute its nationals or seize its vessels which engage in piratical acts.

Fairman has importantly noted that "Criminal law is a field where expansion without positive authority might seem least consistent with sound public policy."[39] In this

---

[38]Hersh Lauterpacht, cited in Whiteman, Digest, p. 650.

[39]Fairman, "Re Piracy Jure Gentium," p. 508.

regard, it would be a grave breach of good faith on the part of nations were they to prosecute pirates when the nation to whom the pirates once claimed allegiance insisted upon the right to try (though not necessarily the exclusive right to seize) these pirates in its municipal court.

Consequently, while piracy jure gentium extends the right of common or universal jurisdiction to all nations, it does not, in turn, mutually exclude the state's customary basis of national and territorial jurisdiction. Whiteman concludes that:

> Certainly a state does not lose its claim of allegiance or any of its ordinary legislative, executive or judicial jurisdiction against its national because he has committed piracy on the high sea. Certainly also, it has a right to intercede diplomatically in his behalf to protect his person and property interests against illegal treatment by another state, although it admits that he is a pirate. Likewise if the pirate ship had a national character before it was engaged in piracy, its participation in piracy does not withdraw it from the ordinary jurisdiction and rights of its flag state without the state's consent. The ordinary jurisdiction, because of the piracy, no longer excludes the common jurisdiction on the high sea, but it may still exist and be otherwise unaffected.[40]

In addition, the principle of international law known as "hot pursuit" may come into effect and directly alter the right of a nation to claim sovereignty over pirates who are its nationals or the vessel which flies the nation's flag. "Hot pursuit" refers to the continuous chase of a vessel from a port or within the territorial

---

[40]Whiteman, Digest, p. 650.

waters of a nation by the authorities of that nation into the high seas for the purpose of apprehending the alleged offenders.[41] Thus, if a pirate from State A flying the flag of State A enters the port or territorial waters of State B for the purpose of committing a piratical act, the authorities of State B may engage in hot pursuit to stop and arrest the alleged criminals even if the chase extends into the high seas. State B would then maintain a "first priority" to try the offenders for piratical acts which violate its municipal law.

Should the situation be reversed, however, i.e, that the chase began in the high seas, but extended into the territorial jurisdiction of another state, a different set of guidelines, reflecting both international and municipal law, became applicable. If, for example, a pirate is chased on the open sea by a vessel belonging to State A, but is not apprehended until he is within the territorial maritime belt of State B, the right of the pursuers to ". . . follow, attack, and arrest the pirate there" is substantiated.[42] However, the pursuers must give the suspected pirate up to the authorities of the littoral state (State B), since the

---

[41]For a comprehensive discussion of "hot pursuit," see "Harvard Research in International Law, Territorial Waters," A.J.I.L. Special Supplement, 23 (1929), 358; Moore, Digest, Vol. 2, p. 985; and Nicholas M. Poulantzas, The Right of Hot Pursuit in International Law (Leyden: A. W. Nijthoff, 1969), pp. 3, 345-8.

[42]Lauterpacht, Oppenheim's International Law, pp. 608-9.

chase was ended in its sovereign territory. The authorities of the littoral state are then in the position to try the alleged criminals either for a violation of the laws of piracy *jure gentium* or of its municipal law of piracy (if applicable), or it may return the alleged pirates to officials of State A who initiated the chase. State B, then, is most likely to opt first for the former, and secondly, for the latter choice, that of granting custody of the alleged pirates to State B. In either case, the state whose nationality the pursued may have claimed or the flag state of the vessel he sailed would not maintain a first priority of jurisdiction in such an incident.[43]

Right of Approach for Suspected Piracy: Times of Peace

In times of peace, the flag which is flown by a ship, whether private or public, evidences the nationality of the vessel. While the flying of a flag appears only to be a symbolic gesture of identification, it is indicative

---

43"For a crime committed in port a vessel may be chased into the high seas and there arrested, without a suspicion that territorial rights have been violated, while to chase a criminal across the borders and seize him on foreign soil is a gross offense against sovereignty." See Theodore D. Woolsey, *International Law* (New York: Charles Scribner's Sons, 1892), p. 58.

It should also be noted that the chase of a criminal across a border refers to both the land boundaries and territorial waters claimed by a sovereign state.

of the theory of territorial sovereignty that a vessel represents a seaward extension of the state's jurisdiction over its territory.[44]

Although a warship may claim the right to verify the authentic nationality of any merchant ship which it may encounter on the high seas, the right of approach (*vérification du pavillon* or *reconnaissance*) in peaceful times is subject to only one qualification--the repression of piracy *jure gentium*. Any other acts of interference with merchant vessels on the high seas are strictly forbidden by the customary principles of international law guaranteeing the right of ships to sail freely under peaceful conditions.[45]

Thus, it ". . . has been officially asserted that 'In the single instance of piracy shown beyond reasonable doubt' may the cruiser visit and search a vessel flying a foreign flag."[46] Should the captain of a vessel demand verification of a foreign flag ship on the high seas which is suspected of piratical acts, and such a seizure proves to to be legally ungrounded, ". . . his government may have to

---

[44]Robert Rienow, *The Test of the Nationality of a Merchant Vessel* (New York: Columbia University Press, 1937), pp. 143-4.

[45]Grotius indicates: "Jure gentium inter quosvis liberam esse mercaturam;" that is, "By the law of nations, the right to trade is free to all persons." Grotius, *On the Freedom of the Seas*, p. 61.

[46]Rienow, *Test of Nationality*, p. 144.

accept substantial responsibility for any interference."[47] On the other hand, if substantial proof is uncovered to support a charge of piracy _jure gentium_, the nationality of the vessel may well be an asset to the capturing vessel, particularly if active interference with a foreign flag had been authorized by treaty between the states of the captured and capturing vessels, respectively.[48]

Flags of a Pirate Ship

Though it has been indicated that the nationality of a ship flying a foreign flag may be challenged on the high seas if suspected of piracy _jure gentium_, Oppenheim contends, ". . . that a pirate may also have a properly evidenced right to a flag is frequently overlooked."[49] Consequently, the question which then arises is: Under what conditions may a pirate ship rightfully (though not

---

[47]Herbert A. Smith, _The Law and Custom of the Sea_ (London: Stevens Publishers, 1959), pp. 64-5.

[48]Rienow, _Test of Nationality_, pp. 144-5.

The treaty of 1841, signed by Great Britain, Russia, Austria, and Prussia, declares that participation in the African slave trade is an act of piracy and a mutual right of search is granted. See Georg Schwarzenberger, "The Problem of an International Criminal Law," in _International Criminal Law_, ed. by Gerhard O. W. Mueller and Edward M. Wise (South Hackensack, N.J.: Fred B. Rothman and Co., 1965), pp. 24-5.

[49]Lassa F. L. Oppenheim, _International Law_ (London: Longmans and Co., 1905), p. 321.

necessarily lawfully) fly a foreign flag other than the "skull and crossbones" associated with the "picturesque" traditional pirate?

The concept of piracy *jure gentium*, previously defined as an offence of depredation on the high seas, may be cautiously extended to (1) such acts which are not authorized by any sovereign state; (2) perpetrators of such acts which accept commissions (official authorization to perform such acts) by more than one sovereign; or (3) piratical acts performed under the colors of a sovereign state which exceed the authority of the commissioned agent. Each of these definitional extensions of piracy *jure gentium* concern the right of a pirate ship to fly a foreign flag and must be presented with careful qualifications.

In the first instance, pirates neither claiming allegiance to any sovereign nor flying a foreign flag pose virtually no difficulty in the extension of universal jurisdiction to their crime *jure gentium*. Rather than consider the pirates and vessel as "denationalized," it is more reasonable to assess the pirate as "stateless," i.e., not claimed as a national by any state, and the vessel as "no flag flown" or "no nationality," since the term nationality is often attributed to the ties, e.g., documentation and registration, which form a binding, genuine link between vessel and state.[50] The hoisting of a "skull and crossbones" does not alter the "stateless" or "no flag flown" status of the pirate and vessel, respectively. It merely provides a more visible means of overtly indicating the intent of the pirate ship to attack vessels indiscriminately on the high seas.[51]

Secondly, the concept of piracy jure gentium may be extended to include punishment of individuals who accept commissions by more than one sovereign when the involved states are at war with one another. Thus, if privateer A accepts commissions from States A, B and C which are enemies in war, it would appear obvious that his status of "privateer," which implies that he is responsible to one sovereign whose rules of war must be obeyed exclusively and to whom the "hiring" state is responsible, drastically reverts to that of pirate. Hautefeuille reveals ". . . that a privateer taking commissions from two sovereigns, though they be allies in the war, is a pirate."[52] Nonetheless, it is questionable whether such a deceitful practice would constitute piracy jure gentium, though it may well reflect a violation of municipal laws of piracy or perhaps that of

---

[50]Green H. Hackworth, International Law (Washington, D.C.: Department of State, 1941), Vol. 2, p. 724.

[51]For an interesting discussion of the concept of statelessness, see Paul Weis, Nationality and Statelessness in International Law (London: Stevens and Sons, 1956), pp. 1-338.

[52]Wheaton, International Law, p. 162.

fraud. Phillimore, on the other hand, ". . . treats such acts as dangerous and to be discountenanced, but not as necessarily piracy."[53]

Thirdly, Wheaton has indicated that the

> . . . officers and crew of an armed vessel, commissioned against one nation and depredating upon another, are not liable to be treated as pirates in thus exceeding their authority. The State by whom the commission is granted, being responsible to other nations for what is done by its commissioned cruisers, has the exclusive jurisdiction to try and punish all offences committed under color of its authority.[54]

Consequently, while a commission may be granted to an individual or individuals in time of war by State A to cruise against the vessels of State B, such commission would not authorize the plunder of vessels registered in State C. Should the possessor of the commission exceed his authority by committing an act of robbery on the high seas against a vessel from State C, the privateer must answer to responsible

---

[53]In addition to Phillimore's comment, Wheaton also indicates:

> The offense of depredating under commissions from different sovereigns, at war with each other, is clearly piratical, since the authority conferred by one is repugnant to the other; but it has been doubted how far it may be lawful to cruise under commissions from different sovereigns allied against a common enemy. The better opinion, however, seems to be, that although it might not amount to the crime of piracy, still it would be irregular and illegal, because the two co-belligerents may have adopted different rules of conduct respecting neutrals, or may be separately bound by engagements unknown to the party.

[54]*Ibid.*

parties of the state from which the commission was issued, since it is responsible for _all_ acts committed by the privateer.

Rebels on the High Seas: "Political" Acts of Piracy

The right of a pirate ship to fly a foreign flag must be qualified on both legal and political grounds. When broadly defined, customary international law grants the right of all states to punish pirates _jure gentium_, though it does not contend that it is the duty or responsibility to actively seek the apprehension or punishment of pirates. Moreover, it has been indicated that belligerent states may issue commissions to individuals to commit piratical acts against the warring parties. Only when the privateer had exceeded his authority by depredating vessels of a nation not party to the belligerency was the privateer-turned-pirate subject to the municipal law of the commissioning state, and his deeds then branded as acts of piracy. While the law of nations may abhor such a practice, political interests dictating the punishment of a privateer who has disobeyed the orders of the commissioning state must outweigh the wishes of the offended third state in retaining a first priority jurisdictional right to punish the privateer.

With the gradual evolution of laws of war, however, the pirate became excluded ". . . from the privileges, rights and powers of a belligerent. Hostilities waged by and against him were not war."[55] By the middle of the nineteenth century, the granting of commission to privateers to perform piratical acts became a moot question. Attention turned to the political question of whether ". . . rebels in arms, cruising on the high seas against the property of a parent state, are pirates."[56]

Though laws relating to the acts of rebels on the high seas remain unsettled, the following propositions are offered by Wheaton as suggested principles reflecting the treatment of rebels by the parent state:

> I. The courts of a State must treat rebellion against the State as a crime, and the persons engaged in it as criminals. If the acts are depredations on commerce protected by the State, they may be adjudged piracy <u>jure gentium</u> by the courts of the State. It is a political and not a legal question, whether the right so to treat them shall be exercised.
>
> II. The fact that the State has actually treated its prisoners as prisoners of war, exchanged prisoners, respected flags of truce, etc., or has claimed and exercised the powers and privileges of war as against neutrals, does not change the abstract rule of law, in the Court. If the State presents such persons to the

---

[55]In addition, the development of alien rights worked to the disadvantage of the pirate. The granting of a broad spectrum of rights to aliens in municipal law afforded the alien nearly equivalent protection of person and property as the general legal protection given to a state citizen. Consequently, the pirate--who was neither a citizen or an alien--remained an eternal foreigner. He, his ship, and goods were outlawed and open to attack and plunder by anyone who came upon them on sea or strand. For an analysis of the old strand law, see Paul Stiel, <u>Der Talbestand der Piraterie</u> (Leipzig: Duncker and Humblot Publishers, 1905), p. 46.

[56]Wheaton, <u>International Law</u>, p. 164.

court for trial, the court must adjudge them criminals. The question whether they shall be so presented is one, not of law, but of policy, which the political department of the State must hold in its hands, and which may be varied from time to time, according to circumstance.

III. If a foreigner knowingly cruises against the commerce of a State under a rebel commission, he takes the chance of being treated as a pirate *jure gentium*, or a belligerent. In point of law, his foreign allegiance or citizenship is immaterial. In this respect, it is immaterial whether the sovereign whose subject he is has recognized the rebel authorities as belligerents or not. It is not the custom of foreign nations to interfere to protect their citizens voluntarily aiding a rebellion against a friendly State, if that State makes no discriminations against them.

IV. If a foreigner cruises under a rebel commission he takes the chance of being treated as a pirate or a belligerent by his own nation and all other nations, as well as by that he is cruising against. If his own nation does not recognize the belligerency of the rebels, he is, by the law of his own country, a pirate. If it does, he is not. In this respect, each nation acts independently of others and for itself; and the courts of each nation are governed by the consideration whether their own political authorities have, or have not, recognized the belligerency.

V. Where a rebellion has attained such dimensions and organization as to be a State *de facto*, and its acts reach the dimensions of war *de facto*, and the parent State is obliged to exercise powers of war to suppress it, and especially if against neutral interests, it is now the custom for the State to yield to the rebellion such belligerent privileges as policy and humanity require; and to treat captives as prisoners of war, make exchanges, respect flags of truce, etc. Yet this is a matter of internal State policy only, changeable at any time.[57]

The aforegoing propositions strongly reinforce the contention that ascertaining the nature of rebellious activities on the high seas by the parent state is a

---

[57]*Ibid*., p. 168.

political question. In many instances, municipal courts will actively seek and utilize the view of its political department in rendering a decision on important pivotal points, viz, the status of the rebels.[58]

This contention is well illustrated by the contrast between the course pursued by the British Government towards the American rebels during the American Revolution (1775-1781) and the attitude of the British toward the Confederate rebels during the War Between the States (1860-1865). In the former case, the British Government was the parent state; in the latter case, the former "rebels" against the British had become the parent state to the Confederate secessionists. It is interesting to note the similarity of opinions in both parent states, via municipal law, in their condemnation of rebellious activities on the high seas as acts of piracy.

In 1777, an Act of Parliament clearly asserted that any activities of the American armies against the British Government were to be considered as treason, piracy, or

---

[58]While it is true that any state can elevate a crime to the status of piracy in municipal law, the courts of the parent state may not be willing to pronounce the crime as an act of piracy jure gentium unless the political climate encourages such a pronouncement.

For example, men cruising against British merchant vessels under a commission from James II (who claimed to be the de jure king) were apprehended and tried as pirates jure gentium. Lenoir, "Piracy Cases," p. 553.

felony, depending upon the location of the crime. The object of the Act was to obtain

> . . . a parliamentary declaration that the legal status of American rebels was that of felons or pirates and to secure a mode of detaining them in custody without recognizing them as prisoners of war, or being obliged to bring them to trial as criminals. In the meantime, between the armies in America, prisoners were treated as prisoners of war, exchanged, paroled, etc.; and it is believed that no persons were judicially tried and punished as criminals during the war; and the recognition of independence disposed of the question.[59]

If any prisoners accused of piratical acts had been brought to trial, there is little doubt that they would have been convicted for piracy under the 1777 Act of Parliament. However, it is questionable whether such prisoners would have been tried for committing piracy *jure gentium*. Such a contention is supported by Wheaton's proposition V.[60] While the parent state may consider the legal status of

---

[59]Wheaton, *International Law*, p. 166.

[60]See page 43, *supra*. Wheaton further argues,

> If it is conceded that a rebel, indicted in the courts of the parent state for piracy under the law of nations, cannot be allowed to set up that his intent was to depredate only *jure belli*, the logical result would seem to be that such courts may declare him a pirate *jure gentium*, unless, to constitute such piracy, and actual intent to depredate irrespective of the national character of vessels is an essential element in the crime.

Note also that the 1777 Act of Parliament only uses the term "piracy." No distinction was made between piracy in British municipal law and piracy under the law of nations.

rebellion to be a crime and the rebels to be criminals, British political policies favored the treatment of the rebels as belligerents and refrained from actively prosecuting detained prisoners.

On April 19, 1861, President Abraham Lincoln issued a proclamation which declared that "any person acting under pretended authority of the States in rebellion and molesting vessels of the United States, would be held amenable to the laws of the Union for the prevention and punishment of piracy."[61] Like the British Act of 1777, President Lincoln's proclamation failed to distinguish between piracy under American statutes and piracy *jure gentium*.[62]

---

[61]An act of Congress of July 13, 1861, entitled "An act further to provide for the Collection of Duties on Imports and other Purposes," gave Congressional approval to Lincoln's proclamation of blockade and authorized the President to close any ports of entry obstructed by blockade. This act also made it lawful for the President to declare, at his discretion, certain sections of the country "in a state of insurrection." 12 U.S. Statutes 256 (1861).

During the trial of the Prize Cases, the Supreme Court indicated that the July 13, 1861 Act of Congress "recognized a state of civil war between the government of the Confederate States and made it territorial." The Prize Cases, 2 Black 635, 903 (1862).

[62]Under the Constitution of the United States (Article I, Section 8), it is provided that "The Congress shall have power . . . To define and punish piracies and felonies committed on the high seas, and offences against the law of nations." In addition, the Federal judicial powers extend "to all cases of admiralty and maritime jurisdiction." (Article III, Section 2).

The first Federal Crimes Act provided for punishment of the offense of piracy. It stipulated that "Whoever, on

In October, 1861, the officers and crew of the _Savannah_, which had been commissioned under Confederate authority, were indicted for piracy and tried in New York by Federal District Judge Nelson. Nelson reasoned that the rebels might be convicted of piracy against Federal Statutes, but he doubted that their crime could be considered piracy _jure gentium_.[63]

The British Crown, which had granted belligerent recognition to the Southern rebels, based its recognition on Lincoln's proclamation of April, 1861, which had authorized the blockade of Southern ports. According to international law, a blockade of ports indicates that a state of

---

the high seas, commits the crime of piracy as defined by the law of nations, and is afterwards brought into or found in the United States, shall be imprisoned for life." Federal Crimes Act of April 30, 1790, 1 Stat. 112, 114.

For a judicial interpretation of this act and the Constitutional provision concerning piracy, see United States v. Palmer _et al._, 3 Wheat. 610, 630 (1818) and United States v. _Smith_, 5 Wheat. 153, 160 (1820).

[63]U.S. v. Baker _et al._ (_Savannah_ Privateers) 5 Blatchford 6, 12; 24 Federal Cases 962 (1861). See also Quincy Wright, "The American Civil War, 1861-65," in Falk, ed., _The International Law of Civil War_, pp. 52-53. Wright cites Judge Nelson as saying that the defendant's indictment ". . . shows if anything, an intent to depredate upon the vessels and property of one nation only, the United States, which falls far short of the spirit and intent which are said to constitute the essential elements of the crime of piracy under international law." U.S. v. Baker, 5 Blatchford (1861); William Marvin Robinson, Jr., _The Confederate Privateers_ (New Haven: Yale University Press, 1928), pp. 141-47.

belligerency exists; i.e., the parent state is at war with the forces in rebellion.[64]

In American politics, the "political" department means the executive department, and the Court apparently had not taken note of Lincoln's blockade proclamation as an act which recognized the belligerency of the Confederacy. Rather, the court reasoned: "Until this recognition of the new government, the courts are obliged to regard the ancient state of things as unchanged."[65]

Thus, the *Savannah* privateers were convicted of piracy against the United States, though not against the law of nations. Wheaton indicates that in a debate in the British House of Lords on May 16, 1861, ". . . Lords Brougham, Chelmsford, Derby, and the Lord Chancellor noted that it was competent for the United States to treat their own citizens cruising under Confederate authority, as pirates; but whether *jure gentium* or under statute law was not distinctly noticed."[66]

Both the laws of the British during the American Revolution and the United States during the War Between the States lend credible support to the contention that piracy

---

[64]Roscoe R. Oglesby, *Internal War and the Search for Normative Order* (The Hague: Martinus Nijhoff, 1971), pp. 44-6.

[65]U.S. v. Baker, *et al.*, *op. cit.*, p. 966.

[66]Wheaton, *International Law*, p. 166.

is defined differently in municipal law than in international law. In addition, while nations may incarcerate the naval forces of internal rebellious groups, they appear reluctant to punish such individuals on the grounds of piracy _jure gentium_.

Historically, municipal courts have relied upon the political (usually executive) department to determine the legal status of rebels. However, once the decision to bring the rebels to court has been made, judges had to rely upon precedent to determine the guilt of the accused. Consequently, though the accused could be found guilty in violation of local statutes of piracy, the condemnation of rebels for piracy _jure gentium_ posed serious problems. The likelihood of proving that the rebels intended to plunder ships on the high seas regardless of national character, or that their intent was solely for private gains, not to capture and destroy _jure belli_, was only minimal.[67]

---

[67]Under the President's Proclamation of April 19, 1861, the United States could treat its own citizens, cruising under Confederate authority, as pirates. However, the actual intent of the individuals to capture and destroy _jure belli_ was a sharp distinction from the concept of piracy _jure gentium_ which implies an indiscriminate plunder on the high seas.

In the trial of Smith in Philadelphia, Judge Grier ruled that he could be treated as a pirate and robber regardless of the fact that his acts were committed under a rebel commission. Following his conviction, President Lincoln transferred him to military custody as a prisoner of war. The question of whether a conviction could be obtained on the grounds of piracy _jure gentium_ remained

Thus, it seems safe to conclude that as the laws of war evolved, the status of rebels engaged in piratical acts slipped from the grip of the law of nations and fell almost completely, into the hands of individual states.

A Review of Pre-Twentieth Century Piracy

In 1973, President Richard M. Nixon forthrightly stated:

> Piracy is not a new challenge for the community of nations. Most countries, including the United States, found effective measures of dealing with piracy on the high seas a century ago. We can--and we will--deal effectively with piracy in the skies today.[68]

If President Nixon is correct in his assertions about piracy *jure gentium*, then a recapitulation of century-old measures dealing with piracy on the high seas should provide the framework for assessing the municipal and international legal problems currently associated with air piracy.

Using Article 38 of the Statutes of the International Court of Justice[69] as a conceptual tool of analysis,

---

unanswered since no additional cases occurred in which the government chose to treat rebels in arms as criminals in violation of U.S. piracy laws. U.S. v. Smith, 5 Wheat. 153, 160 (1820).

[68]Richard M. Nixon, "U.S. Position on Air Hijacking," *Public Information* (Washington, D.C.: Department of State, 1972), Series P-025, p. 3. [Author's emphasis added.]

[69]Article 38 is the guiding text of the Statute of the International Court of Justice, and it is generally

traditional piracy may be clarified and compared to the twentieth century view of piracy and aircraft seizures.

Conventions (Multilateral and Bilateral)

Though piracy on the high seas constituted a grave threat to international shipping and commerce, there are no recorded instances, prior to the Harvard Draft Convention on Piracy in 1932, of any attempts to codify laws of piracy.

Early bilateral agreements concerning piracy were related solely to the elimination of the African slave trade. The denouncement of slave trading as an odious act of piracy received international concurrence in the

---

accepted as an authoritative statement of the sources of international law. In full, Article 38 reads as follows:

> 1. The Court, whose function is to decide in accordance with international law such disputes as are submitted to it, shall apply
>
> a. international conventions, whether general or particular, establishing rules expressly recognized by the contesting states;
>
> b. international custom, as evidence of a general practice accepted as law;
>
> c. the general principles of law recognized by civilized nations;
>
> d. subject to the provisions of Article 59, judicial decisions and the teachings of the most highly qualified publicists of the various nations, as subsidiary means for the determination of rules of law.
>
> 2. This provision shall not prejudice the power of the Court to decide a case *ex aequo et bono*, if the parties agree thereto.

Treaties of Paris, Kiel, and Ghent in 1814, the declaration of the 1815 Congress of Vienna, and an addendum to the treaty of peace concluded in Paris on February 8, 1815.

Further support of the abolition of African slave-trade was seen through multilateral treaties between Great Britain, Spain, and Portugal between 1815 and 1817 and an agreement with Brazil in 1826. An 1845 treaty between France and Great Britain eliminated joint efforts of their naval forces to suppress slave trading off the coast of Africa in favor of a mutual right of search which had been asserted in articles of the 1831 and 1833 treaties, respectively.[70]

Great Britain, Russia, Austria, and Prussia agreed to prohibit the slave trade as a piratical act in the Treaty of 1841 and conceded a mutual right to search flag vessels of their respective nations suspected of violating the convention.[71]

Consequently, the slave trade, rather than piracy as plunder on the high seas, received international attention through the promulgation of bilateral and multilateral agreements denoting it as a crime against the law of nations.

---

[70]Wheaton, International Law, p. 165.

[71]It should be noted that a reservation applicable only among Great Britain, France, and the United States was attached to the Treaty of 1841 which prohibited mutual right of search. Wheaton, Ibid.

Custom

Piracy *jure gentium* is universally recognized as a violation of customary international law; that is, custom dictates that the suppression of piratical acts on the high seas and falls under the universal jurisdiction of all states. Such jurisdiction *sui generis* is applicable only when piratical acts occur on the high seas (not subject to the jurisdiction of any one state) in times of peace. In essence, while not established as an international crime through international conventions, condemnation of piracy on the high seas is firmly entrenched in the customary law of nations. Further, customary international law has represented the highest controlling views on traditional sea-piracy.

General Principles of Law

The early history of international law enunciated the reliance upon broad principles as underlying sources of law. The use of general principles, which combine natural law concepts of basic justice and moral "right" implicit in the nature of things, form the basis of "soft" law vis-à-vis "hard" law, i.e., specific treaties and diplomatic agreements.[72]

---

[72]See Percy E. Corbett, "The Consent of States and the Sources of the Law of Nations," *B.Y.I.L., 1925*, 6, 20.

General principles appear to be "subtle understandings" which undergird the intercourse of nations. Many principles become elevated to the status of customary law through long periods of usage and practice. Regarding the traditional concept of piracy, general principles may be said to consist of:

1. The high seas (i.e., those areas of water outside the territorial or marginal seas) are *res communis*. The freedom of all nations to engage in international commerce on the high seas in times of peace appears to be a firmly established principle of law.

2. In times of peace, each state retains exclusive police jurisdiction over ships flying its flag which are properly in its registry and its nationals who travel on said vessels.

3. The right to search a maritime vessel suspected of piracy *jure gentium* is limited to public vessels of nations, that is, those vessels whose authority derives from a legitimate government.

4. The right of hot pursuit ceases when the pursued vessel enters into the territorial waters of any state other than the territorial waters of the pursuing vessel.

Opinions of Jurists

Two types of piracy exist: statutory piracy and piracy *jure gentium*. The former is defined by individual states and is applicable only to their national courts. The latter is not clearly defined, but generally consists of the following elements:

a) any unauthorized acts of violence committed by a private vessel on the open seas against another private vessel;

b) such acts must be committed with an intent to plunder (*animo furandi*);

c) persons engaged in such acts are considered *hostes humani generis*, enemies of the human race;

d) such acts must be performed indiscriminately against all sea-going vessels; if confined to vessels of only one nation, such acts are not considered *hostes humani generis* and are punishable by the municipal law of the injured state;

e) acts of piracy *jure gentium* must be carried out for private ends.

While President Nixon correctly asserted that piracy *jure gentium* is not a new challenge for international law, the measures of dealing with sea-piracy must necessarily differ from those which attempt to suppress aircraft hijackings. The slow, sea-going travel of centuries ago can hardly compare with the rapidity of air travel today. Land-locked nations rarely came into contact with traditional piratical activities, unless an accused pirate sought refuge within their borders. Historically, piracy *jure gentium* most directly affected the interests of maritime nations. It should also be noted that the foremost international legal measure used to eliminate piracy was that of universal jurisdiction. To be sure, the knowledge that nations were adhering to the customary law of universal jurisdiction and that municipal courts were willing to try alleged pirates as *hostes humani generis* served as forceful legalistic devices for international apprehension.

The increased use of technological communication devices, especially the wireless, greatly enhanced community efforts to suppress piracy on the seas. Towards the end of the nineteenth century, it appeared that the infrequency of piratical attempts and cases of piracy *jure gentium* before municipal courts signaled the demise of piracy as a widespread criminal activity. However, sporadic attempts of piracy and concern over submarine warfare in World War I resurrected the *raison d'être* of applying the customary law of piracy. Thus a new perspective of piracy *jure gentium*--one greatly influenced by the incipient stages of a technological revolution--was ushered in during the first quarter of the twentieth century. And it is these novel legal ramifications that we must now explore.

CHAPTER 2

A TWENTIETH-CENTURY CONCEPT OF PIRACY

Following the American War Between the States, piracy remained a latent subject in international law until the second decade of the twentieth century. In this interim nations were occupied with balance of power politics in Europe, colonialist ventures, and concluding what Woodrow Wilson mistakenly referred to as "The War to End All Wars." Then, as J. E. G. de Montgomery so concisely noted, "Among the many readjustments of the law of nations that the war of 1914 has necessitated or will necessitate, not the least important is the revision of international practice as to piracy."[1]

While it is true that the international law of piracy required adjustment and revision to conform to contemporary changes in transnational travel, the first attempt to do so in the twentieth century served to confuse, not clarify existing customary law.

---

[1] J. E. G. de Montgomery, "The Barbary States in the Law of Nations," Transactions of the Grotius Society, 4 (1918), 87.

The Washington Naval Treaty of 1922

In 1922, nine nations--the United States, Great Britain, France, Japan, Italy, Belgium, China, the Netherlands, and Portugal--convened in conference at Washington, D.C.[2] Their purpose was to discuss a series of proposed agreements, including limitation of armaments, Pacific and Far Eastern questions, and the use of submarines and noxious gases in warfare. These parties to the conference professed deep concern that existing rules of warfare, governed by the Hague Convention of 1907, did not ". . . adequately cover new methods of attack or defense resulting from the introduction or development . . . of new agencies of warfare."[3]

With particular regard to the use of submarines as vehicles for the destruction of commercial vessels, the five major signatory powers concluded that submarine warfare overtly violated "the requirements universally accepted by

---

[2]For the text of the formal American invitations to the Washington Conference on the Limitations of Armament (1921-22), see Norman L. Hill, The Public International Conference (Stanford: Stanford University Press, 1929), pp. 238-40. For an introspective analysis of the Washington Conference, see Denna F. Fleming, The United States and World Organization; 1920-1933 (New York: AMS Press, Inc., 1966), pp. 79-111. See also A.J.I.L. Supp., 16 (1922), p. 57.

[3]Carnegie Endowment for International Peace, Yearbook 1922, Vol. 11 (Washington: Carnegie Endowment for International Peace, 1922), p. 142. See also James B. Scott, ed. The Reports to the Hague Conference of 1899 and 1907 (Oxford: Clarendon Press, 1917), particularly pp. 709-745 on "Convention (X), for the Adoption to Maritime Warfare of the Principles of the Geneva Convention."

civilized nations for the protection of the lives of neutrals and non-combatants."[4] In order to emphasize the seriousness of submarine warfare, they re-instated the universal requirement of "right of search" to which all war vessels, especially submarines, had to comply, thereby elevating the act of submarine warfare to the crime of piracy.[5]

Article 3 of the Washington Naval Treaty of 1922 provided that:

> The Signatory Powers, desiring to ensure the enforcement of the humane rules of existing law declared by them with respect to attacks upon and the seizure and destruction of merchant ships, further declare that any person in the service of any Power who shall violate any of those rules, whether or not such person is under orders of a governmental superior, shall be deemed to have violated the laws of war and shall be liable to trial and punishment as if for an act of piracy and may be brought to trial before the civil or military authorities of any Power within the jurisdiction of which he may be found.[6]

The reference to piracy in the Washington Naval Treaty, however, can hardly be said to constitute a serious threat to the traditional laws of piracy *jure gentium*. This was acknowledged by an anonymous writer in the

---

[4]Carnegie Endowment for International Peace, *Yearbook, 1922*, p. 142.

[5]It is interesting to note that Germany, defeated in World War I, remained unrepresented at the Conference which primarily sought to regulate the type of submarine warfare at which the Germans were so proficient.

[6]The full text of the Nine Power Treaty may be found in Department of State *Treaty Series*, No. 723; also Henry L. Stimson, *The Far Eastern Crisis* (New York: Harper and Bros., 1936), p. 267. [Author's emphasis added.]

British Yearbook of International Law (1938) who proposed that inclusion of Article 3 in the 1922 Treaty should be viewed purely as a political attempt to extend piracy *jure gentium* to war crimes, including those which may have been performed under superior orders.[7]

The reference to piracy in the treaty, it appears, resulted from rising sentiment among the victorious powers of World War I to brand German submarine attacks during the war as piratical acts *hostes humani generis*. Had the treaty received wide acceptance in the community of nations, drastic changes might have resulted in the traditional elements of piracy *jure gentium*. No longer would piracy consist of an act of depredation on the high seas performed for *private* ends; rather, piracy laws would have been expanded to cover acts of military vessels (public warships) done in fulfillment of superior orders.[8]

As history has revealed, when post-war anti-aggression sentiments reach a high level, victor nations often become "paper tigers," venting their revenge into international agreements to chastise the warfare tactics of the defeated parties. On paper and in actual practice, the inclination of the parties to the Washington Naval Treaty--to equate submarine warfare tactics with acts of piracy--fell

---

[7]Anonymous, "The Nyon Arrangements," *B.Y.I.L.* (London: Oxford University Press, 1938), 19, 200.

[8]D. H. N. Johnson, "Piracy in Modern International Law," *Transactions of the Grotius Society*, 43 (1957), 80-81.

far short as a viable international code. The treaty, which was concluded among only five of the nine convening states, *viz*, the United States, Great Britain, France, Japan, and Italy, was never effectively enforced.[9]

Eight years later, the attempt to incorporate Article 3 of the Washington Naval Treaty into its successor, the 1930 London Naval Limitation Treaty, was rejected. With its deletion, ". . . the idea . . . of incorporating into piracy *jure gentium* inhuman violations of the rules of warfare by naval commanders acting under the orders of their government was definitely abandoned."[10]

The League of Nations: Attempts to Codify International Law

While the Washington Treaty of 1922 cannot be considered a highly significant contribution to the development of an international law of piracy it fell to the League of Nations to assume the challenge of its codification. During the Fifth Assembly of the League of Nations, former

---

[9] *Ibid*.

[10] Anonymous, "Nyon Arrangements," p. 200. Such ideas were abandoned only for the present time. Remnants of the same sentiments re-appear in the "International Agreement for Collective Measures Against Piratical Attacks in the Mediterranean by Submarines," signed at Nyon on September 14, 1937. See Nyon Arrangement, League of Nations Document C. 409. M. 273.1937. VII and G. A. Finch, "Piracy in the Meditteranean," *A.J.I.L.*, 31 (1937), 659-65.

Swedish Prime Minister, Knut Hammarskjold recommended that the Council of the League convene a Committee of Experts to consider codification of international law on questions which seemed "sufficiently ripe" for international regulation. The motion was approved and a committee of jurists, under the Chairmanship of Mr. Hammarskjold, began in Geneva on January 1, 1925, to develop topics of consideration.[11]

Representing seventeen different countries, ". . . the main forms of civilization and the principal legal systems of the world,"[12] the Committee of Legal Experts deliberated for two years before submitting two groups of seven topics which they considered timely for international codification. The first group included piracy.[13]

---

[11]Records of the Eighth Ordinary Session of the Assembly, Meetings of the First Committee (Constitutional and Legal Questions), League of Nations Official Journal, Special Supplement #55 (Geneva, 1927), p. 11.

For an analysis of the purposes which would be fostered through codification of international law, see The Project of a Permanent Court of International Justice and Resolutions of the Advisory Committee of Jurists: Report and Commentary by James Brown Scott. Pamphlet No. 35 of the Division of International Law (Washington: Carnegie Endowment for International Peace, 1920), p. 169.

[12]Records of the Fifth Assembly, Plenary Meetings, League of Nations Official Journal (Geneva, 1924), p. 125.

[13]Ibid. In addition to piracy, the first group included the following topics: nationality, territorial waters, and diplomatic privileges and immunities; and the responsibilities of states for damages done in their territories to the personal property of foreigners. The second group consisted of procedures for international conferences and the drafting and concluding of treaties and, secondly

The special Sub-Committee appointed to scrutinize the legal criteria of piracy clearly wished to sever any association of piracy jure gentium from the dubious text regarding submarine attacks in the 1922 Washington Naval Treaty. Its report to the Committee of Experts stipulated that:

> In addition to piracy by the law of nations, States have occasionally, by treaty or in their internal law, established a piracy by analogy which has no claim to be universally recognized and must not be confused with true piracy; the assimilations in question can only create a sort of piracy under internal law and from the point of view of the countries which make them. The acts dealt with are of a grave nature, it is true, but they do not constitute a danger to the shipping and commerce of all nations indiscriminately. Legislators are justified in taking strong measures in such cases, but the classification of such acts as piracy is a fact which only concerns the State whose laws contain provisions to that effect. From the international point of view, the acts come within the competence only of the country in which they are punishable. No country making a capture can cite them as the basis of a claim to international competence nor can they justify actual capture by a foreign State, unless there is a convention which expressly provides otherwise.[14]

Since the League Sub-Committee confined its inquiry to existing, traditional rules governing the laws of piracy, its final report merely promulgated in a more succinct form

---

the question of the exploitation of products from the sea.

Records of the Eighth Ordinary Session of the Assembly, Meetings of the Committees, Minutes of the First Committee (Constitutional and Legal Questions), League of Nations Official Journal, Special Supplement #55 (Geneva, 1927), p. 11.

[14]"Report of the Sub-Committee of the League of Nations Committee of Experts for the Progressive Codification of International Law," League of Nations Document C. 196. M. 70, 1927V, pp. 118-9.

what substance was already understood to constitute the international consensus of piracy <u>jure gentium</u>. No suggestions for the progressive codification of piracy laws were proffered, and the Sub-Committee concluded:

> Piracy has as its field of operation that vast domain which is termed 'the high seas.' It constitutes a crime against the security of commerce on the high seas, where alone it can be committed. The same acts committed in the territorial waters of a State do not come within the scope of international law, but fall within the competence of the local sovereign power.
>
> When pirates choose as the scene of their acts of sea-robbery a place common to all men and when they attack all nations indiscriminately, their practices become harmful to the international community of all States. They become enemies of the human race and place themselves outside the law of peaceful people.[15]

Having reviewed the Sub-Committee reports on each of the seven legal topics under consideration for codification, the Committee of Experts declared:

> . . . that the need of a convention was not equally urgent in the case of every one of these subjects, and concluded by stating that piracy, and possibly diplomatic privileges and immunities might be temporarily left on one side.[16]

Though the topic of piracy was "left on one side" by the League of Nations, the task of codifying the laws of piracy fell to a prestigious, private organization, Harvard Research in International Law, which was organized

---

[15]Ibid., See also the <u>Marianna Flora</u>, 11 Wheaton (U.S. 1826), 39.ff.

[16]Records of the Eighth Ordinary Session of the Assembly, Meetings of the Committees, <u>Ibid</u>.

in 1927 --the year the League Sub-Committee reports were presented.[17]

Harvard Draft Research on Piracy

While the League of Nations Committee of Experts is representative of an official effort to codify international law, the material contribution of unofficial bodies such as Harvard Research in International Law have developed to the point where they now receive legitimate sanction in municipal court proceedings.[18]

In the court proceedings of In Re Piracy Jure Gentium (1930), use of Harvard Research on Piracy played a prominent role in its settlement. At one point in the hearing, British Lord Sankey inquired of Sir Leslie Scott as to what were the sources of international law. His reply enumerated custom, treaties, and the writings of jurists--the latter having played a significant role. In addition,

> The sources from which international law is derived include treaties between various States, State papers, municipal Acts of Parliament and the decisions of municipal Courts and last, but not least, opinions of

---

[17]Reference should be made to the Division of International Law of the Carnegie Endowment for International Peace which cooperated with the Harvard Law School Research in International Law in preparing drafts and conventions for use at official conferences to codify international law, beginning with the Hague Conference of 1930. See Carnegie Endowment for International Peace, Yearbook, 1932 (Washington: Carnegie Endowment for International Peace, 1932), p. 115.

[18]Carnegie Endowment for International Peace, Yearbook, 1927, Vol. 16 (Washington: Carnegie Endowment for International Peace, 1927), p. 69.

> jurisconsults or textbook writers. It is a process of inductive reasoning. . . . Speaking generally, in embarking upon international law, their Lordships are to a great extent in the realm of opinion, and in estimating the value of opinion it is permissible not only to seek a consensus of views, but to select what appear to be the better views upon the question.[19]

Fairman's analysis of the piracy issue in question clearly evidences that the justices' strong support of the "realm of opinion" came in the form of Harvard Research on Piracy, the "better" view of the question of piracy.

The Judicial Committee for the Harvard Draft Convention on Piracy focused upon one overarching question--the significance of piracy in the law of nations. With only a paucity of cases in modern times, there were ". . . no official determinations which will help an investigator to cut away through the jungle of expert opinion."[20]

---

[19]Fairman, "Re Piracy Jure Gentium," p. 511. "The facts out of which the matter grew were that a number of armed Chinese, cruising in two junks, had pursued and attacked a cargo junk on the high seas. Before the pursuers were able to overhaul their prey they were stopped and taken in charge, brought to HongKong, and there tried for piracy. The full court held that an actual robbery was an essential element of the crime, and the defendants were therefore acquitted." Fairman, Ibid., p. 508. See also A.J.I.L., 29 (1935), 140.

In In Re Piracy Jure Gentium, Lord Macmillan was said to have been impressed with the comprehensive nature of the Harvard Research on Piracy. He referred to it as ". . . this compilation from which we have derived so much help." Fairman, Ibid., p. 511.

[20]Harvard Research in International Law, "Draft Convention on Piracy, with Comment," in A.J.I.L. Supp. 26 (1932), 764. (Hereafter referred to as Harvard Draft Research). For text, see Appendix B. At the time of the writing of the Harvard Research on Piracy (May 30, 1930 to

Harvard Research on Piracy embodies a core of expert opinions on piracy. Not only is it salient as the most comprehensive expression of a modernized customary law of piracy, but it also provides the first reference to attacks from aircraft as potential, logical extensions of piracy from the high seas to the high skies.

The mention of aircraft in a draft convention on piracy alludes to several important distinctions between the early international views of piracy and the present legal interpretations. Drafters of the Harvard Convention on Piracy anticipated that differences of opinion were found in three crucial areas:

> (1) The definition of piracy in the sense of the law of nations.
> (2) The meaning and justification of the traditional assertions that piracy is an offence or a crime against the law of nations.
> (3) The common jurisdiction of all states to prosecute and punish pirates.[21]

In approaching each of these three primary aspects of piracy, the Harvard legal experts indicated at the outset that their attempts to codify an international law of piracy

---

December 22, 1931), only a few recent cases of international piracy were known. Rather, the majority of cases concerned ". . . the status of insurgent vessels or of irregular privateers, and a few municipal law cases. . . ." "Comments," A.J.I.L. Supp. 26, 764.

[21]Ibid., p. 749.

would not adhere strictly to a rigorous rendition of traditional views. Rather, they maintained that:

> . . . common jurisdiction . . . rests on tradition and expediency. It is expediency that should be the chief guide in the formulation of a convention. The use of traditional ideas of the nature of piracy . . . should be tempered and controlled by the realization of the great changes that have occurred through the centuries in the conditions of commerce and travel. . . .[22]

What, then, were the "ground rules" that denoted change under which the Harvard Researchers operated? Certainly, if the modern interpretation of international law towards piracy differs from that of a few centuries ago, such changes would have to be clearly delineated to make any significant impact upon the international community.

Harvard Research Definition of Piracy in The Sense of The Law of Nations

It was of primary import to the authors of the Harvard Research on Piracy that a general workable definition of piracy in international law be promulgated. Careful effort was taken to present an international perspective, as opposed to merely incorporating or comparing various municipal law definitions of piracy. Early in the convention, the rapporteur noted that there is often a

---

[22]*Ibid*., p. 787. See also Myres S. McDougal and William T. Burke, *The Public Order of the Oceans* (New Haven: Yale University Press, 1962), 809.

decided difference between municipal law, or statutory piracy (that includes offenses which occur entirely within the territory of one state) and international law piracy (which takes place outside the territorial jurisdiction of any State).[23]

Consequently, the Draft Convention was predicated on the contention that piracy does not constitute a crime under the law of nations. Thus, rather than attempt to evaluate piracy as an international crime, the drafters of the Harvard Research set forth two basic premises: firstly, that piracy ". . . is the basis of an extraordinary jurisdiction in every state to seize and to prosecute and punish persons. . . .;" and secondly, that ". . . any attempt to codify and modernize international piracy law must define this extraordinary jurisdiction."[24] Upon this realization, one might think the drafters were evasive and neglectful in their attempt to define piracy. However, as Peter Jacobson posits,

> . . . the approach taken by the Harvard Research was to formulate a definition of the facts that constitute piracy and then leave it to the states of the world community to implement that jurisdiction by

---

[23]"Comments," A.J.I.L. Supp. 26, p. 749; Johnson, "Piracy in Modern International Law," pp. 68-69.

[24]"Comments," A.J.I.L. Supp. 26, p. 760. It should be noted that the phrase piracy *jure gentium* does not appear in any of the nineteen articles of the Draft Convention.

> appropriate legislation. Within these limits the extent of the jurisdiction therefore depends on municipal law.[25]

Article 3 of the Draft Convention presents a generalized, though comprehensive definition of international piracy.

> Piracy is any of the following acts, committed in a place not within the territorial jurisdiction of any state:
>
> 1. Any act of violence or of depredation committed with intent to rob, rape, wound, enslave, imprison or kill a person or with intent to steal or destroy property, for private ends without bona fide purpose of asserting a claim of right, provided that the act is connected with an attack on or from the sea or in or from the air. If the act is connected with an attack which starts from on board ship, either that ship or another ship which is involved must be a pirate ship or a ship without national character.
> 2. Any act of voluntary participation in the operation of a ship with knowledge of facts which make it a pirate ship.
> 3. Any act of instigation or of intentional facilitation of an act described in paragraph 1 or paragraph 2 of this article.[26]

To derive meaningful conclusions about the definitional construction of piracy as presented in

---

[25]Peter M. Jacobson, "From Piracy on the High Seas to Piracy in the High Skies: A Study of Aircraft Hijacking," Cornell International Law Journal 5 (1972), 166.

International Law, however, does not obligate states to exercise the jurisdiction. Article 18 of the Draft Convention merely asserts ". . . a general discretionary obligation to discourage piracy by exercising their rights of prevention and punishment as far as is expedient." "Comments," A.J.I.L. Supp. 26, p. 760.

[26]Harvard Draft Research, Article 3.

Article 3, it will be necessary to dissect the article according to: (1) Acts of Violence; (2) The Private Ends Requirement; and (3) The Flag vs. No Flag Requirement.

Acts of Violence

The intricate wording of Article 3 illustrates several discrepancies in the pre-twentieth century concept of international piracy and reveals new variations of piracy which tender the challenge presumed by air travel. While traditional piracy was nearly synonymous with sea-robbery (_animo ferandi_), Harvard Research on Piracy includes additional acts which conjure up visions of violence on the high seas. Thus, to imprison, wound, or murder a person intentionally while traveling outside the territorial jurisdiction of any state (whether on the seas or in the air) would constitute an act of piracy, provided that the concomitant qualifications of Article 3 were met.[27]

The plain and simple meaning of Section 1 of Article 3 also indicates that violent acts committed with intent to perform any of the aforementioned atrocities or ". . . with intent to steal or destroy property for private ends without bona fide purpose of asserting a claim of right . . ."[28] would constitute an act of piracy, provided it occurred outside the jurisdiction of any state.

---

[27]_Ibid._, Section 1.

[28]_Ibid._

If, for example, an individual aboard a private aircraft flying at 27,000 feet above the Mediterranean Sea threatened to kill the pilot, crew, or passengers unless they cooperated in force-landing the ship on the high seas, such intention of violence would clearly be an act of piracy according to the Harvard Research Draft.[29] Fairman supports this hypothetical contention as he comments, "One hazards little in assuming that the Judicial Committee would be prepared to uphold a conviction for piracy in an attack in or from the air."[30]

One obvious difficulty arises in this example: Is it realistic to presume that any incidents of this type will ever occur? Even the earliest attempts to perform violent acts aboard private aircraft show no evidence that such acts commenced outside the territorial airspace of any state and ended in the high seas , within the common jurisdiction of all states.[31] If, however, such an attempt to commit acts

---

[29]Article 1, Section 5 of the Harvard Draft Convention describes the term "ship" as ". . . any water craft or aircraft of whatever size." No mention is made of a distinction between private or public ships (vessels of war).

[30]Fairman, "Re Piracy _Jure Gentium_," p. 509.

[31]This assertion is based on aggregate statistical data gathered from the U.S. Department of Transportation, Federal Aviation Administration, Office of Aviation Medicine, _Master List of All Hijacking Attempts, World Wide Air Carrier, and General Aviation_, updated periodically. (Hereafter referred to as F.A.A. Statistics.)

of violence or depredation had begun external to any territorial jurisdiction, but was then aborted over the "high skies," it is conceivable that the act would be considered piracy under the Harvard Draft Convention. Even so, this occurrence seems highly unlikely. It is also important to consider that when the aircraft lands, it is within the territorial jurisdiction of a state, and definitional problems may again result; e.g., is such an act defined as piracy in the municipal laws of the receiving state? Perhaps even more importantly, Article 3, Section 1, is qualified in that:

> If the act is connected with an attack which starts on board ship, either that ship or another ship which is involved must be a pirate ship or a ship without national character.[32]

---

[32]Harvard Draft Research, Article 3, Section 1.

Also complicating this matter is the existence of national piracy legislation. A collection of existing piracy laws made in conjunction with the Harvard Draft Research on Piracy reveals that many states provide only general references to the subject rather than statutes dealing specifically with it. In addition, states without piracy laws usually have penal codes which cover crimes associated with acts of piracy, viz., robbery or destruction of maritime property. Of over eighty countries surveyed (including members of the British Commonwealth), less than two-thirds of the sample maintained laws dealing with piracy. Germany, for example, had a lengthy penal code describing piracy as robbery at sea, but maintained no criminal law provisions for the punishment of offenders.

For an introspective analysis of municipal piracy codes, see Stanley Morrison, ed., "A Collection of Piracy Laws of Various Countries," A.J.I.L. Supp. 26 (1932), 887-1013.

Since the hypothetical act occurred on board a private aircraft with national registry and since ships not claiming flag registry of any state are rarely found, it appears that the viability of the Harvard Draft Convention leaves grave questions of doubt. Though a conviction for international piracy on the high seas might well be obtained through reference to the Harvard Research on Piracy, it is improbable (if not impossible) that an act of depredation aboard an aircraft flying the high seas could ever fully meet the Harvard description of piracy.

The "Private Ends" Requirement

Article 3, Section 1 of the Harvard Draft Convention stipulates that each of the enumerated acts should be committed ". . . for private ends without bona fide purpose of asserting a claim of right. . . ."[33] Since an explication du texte with emphasis on the words "private ends" does not appear in the draft Convention, it is necessary to probe the intentions of the writers and the historical background under which they labored (traveaux préparatoire) in order to discern a precise meaning of the term.

Hersch Lauterpacht has indicated that piracy, conceived of as organized robbery for personal enrichment, is virtually passé. Rather, he believes that it would be

---

[33] Ibid.

proper for the international community to look upon as piratical ". . . such acts of violence on the high seas which by their ruthlessness and disregard for the sanctity of human life invite exemplary punishment and suppression."[34] Concurrently, the Rapporteur of the Harvard Draft Convention affirmed that historical evidence, if thoroughly canvassed could support either contention-- that piracy must or should not necessarily be prompted by a motive for private gains.[35]

The concern of the Harvard Draft Research primarily focused on the scope of the acts listed in Article 3, not on an in-depth analysis of the personal motives which might precipitate them. Moreover, while the Harvard Research was conducted with full awareness that some unrecognized insurgents (though they claim to operate for political purposes) may still be thought to perform piratical acts, the final draft restated the contention that piratical activities should be undertaken for private (not public) ends.[36]

---

[34]Hersch Lauterpacht, Recognition in International Law (Cambridge: Cambridge University Press, 1947), pp. 307-8. Lauterpacht's contention is probably correct, however, the international community would be unwilling to accept a modification of existing customary law of piracy unless sanctioned by multilateral agreement.

[35]"Comments," A.J.I.L. Supp., 26, p. 790.

[36]Ibid., p. 798; Jacobson, "From Piracy on the High Seas," p. 166.

The re-affirmation of the "private ends" principle in the Harvard Draft serves to exclude many incidents from the customary law category of piracy. Thus, it has been readily argued that hijackings of ships or aircraft in defense of a political organization, whether recognized by other states or not, should not be viewed as committed for private ends. Such an assertion applies to both activities committed in pursuance of a political goal or in opposition to a political regime. In essence, the "private gains" question, which received minimal attention by the Harvard Research, handily provides a "legal scape-goat" for any hijacking attempt on the high seas or in the high skies.[37]

The rash of hijacking attempts from the United States to Cuba and those of Israeli aircraft by members of the Palestine Liberation movement followed long after the writing of the Harvard Draft. Only one hijacking incident had been recorded prior to 1932. This occurred when unsuccessful revolutionaries seized control of an aircraft in Peru in an attempt to flee that country.[38] Since the motive of the hijackers was reputedly "political," the case went unnoticed and had only a modicum of impact on the writers of the Harvard Research. Certainly the cardinal purpose

---

[37]"Comments," A.J.I.L. Suppl., 26, p. 798.

[38]Robert P. Boyle, "International Action to Combat Aircraft Hijacking," Lawyer of the Americas, 4 (Oct. 1972), 461.

of their effort--to modernize the customary law of piracy--could not have been wholly diverted to take into account one single instance of aircraft hijacking which could not, at that time, have been predicted to re-occur.

The Flag vs. No Flag Requirement

The Harvard Draft's definition of piracy poses a difficult requirement vis-à-vis the national character of a ship as determined by the flag it bears. Article 3 indicates that for an act of piracy to be committed, violence which commences on board ship must occur on a ship without national character, or directly involve another ship which possesses no national character, i.e., a pirate ship. This contention extends into Articles 4 and 5 which respectively describe the characteristics of a pirate ship and prescribe that the retention or loss of national character remains in control of the state of registry.[39]

Viewed in the aggregate, Articles 3, 4, and 5 leave major questions unanswered: Can acts of piracy be confined to a single flag vessel, or must the action occur on a ship-to-ship basis? Does mutiny on board ship fall into the piracy guidelines established by the Harvard Research?

Johnson proposes that these questions reflect unsettled "doctrinal controversies of the past."[40] The

---

[39]Harvard Draft Research, Article 4 and Article 5.

[40]Johnson, "Piracy in Modern International Law," pp. 63, 71.

Rapporteur of the Harvard Convention emphasized that such limitations (that an attack must be made from one vessel to another or occur entirely on a pirate ship) find expression in traditional international law which concedes those offenses falling within a state's ordinary territorial jurisdiction to that state.[41] Thus, while the municipal law of a state may well condemn unlawful acts of violence aboard ships flying its flag and brand them as piracy, it may be reluctant to surrender exclusive criminal jurisdiction over the offenders. In 1932, as now, the assertion of a state's sovereign territorial jurisdiction presents a formidable block to international cooperative efforts. Ethnocentric national considerations have often overridden the strongest global attempts to deter acts of violence or depredation.[42]

In particular, mutiny on the high seas, if confined to a single flag vessel and not extended to include those additional acts of violence spelled out in Article 1, constitutes a prime example of a criminal wrong which falls beyond the legal breadth of the Harvard Draft. Accordingly, states may not infer that a common jurisdiction exists to

---

[41] "Comments," A.J.I.L. Supp. 26, p. 798.

[42] For example, internal politics which led to the refusal of the United States Senate to agree to American participation in the League of Nations, was a crucial factor inhibiting the effective functioning of that international organization. See Richard W. Leopold, The Growth of American Foreign Policy (New York: Alfred A. Knopf, Inc., 1962), pp. 385-98.

apprehend and suppress mutiny aboard a ship which, by the law of nations, falls under the sole jurisdiction of the state whose flag it flies. The prevailing opinion of international legal jurists supports the contention that common jurisdiction would only apply if a mutinous act were successful, and ". . . the successful mutineers then set out to devote the ship to the accomplishment of further acts of violence or depredation (of the sort specified in Article 3, and Article 1) on the high seas or in foreign territory."[43]

This appears consonant with the traditional view that piracy, from an international perspective, is a menace to the traffic of all sea-faring nations; it does not merely apply to acts of violence or depredation on the high seas which adversely affect only one ship of a single state, as might occur in the case of mutiny. A single act of piracy is not likely to threaten the interests of the community of nations. However, if such acts continue to be performed on the high seas for private, as opposed to public ends (which espouse a bona fide claim of right), a grant of common jurisdiction may be justified to suppress a growing menace to international trade and commerce.[44]

---

[43]"Comments," A.J.I.L. Supp. 26, p. 810. T. J. Lawrence concludes that, should crew members unsuccessfully revolt against their officers, they would be guilty of mutiny, not piracy. See T. J. Lawrence, The Principles of International Law (New York: D.C. Heath and Co., 1910), p. 233.

[44]Lenoir, "Piracy Cases," p. 533.

The single flag requirement remains a polemical aspect of the Harvard Draft, particularly in the case of mutiny at sea. While piracy may occur on one ship, the criteria for distinguishing international piracy as opposed to municipal piracy seems speculative, at best. Only when instances of piracy result from ship-to-ship contact on the high seas does there appear to be broad international consensus. Excepting the troubled internal waters of the China Seas[45] traditional piracy on the high seas involving plunder of innocent merchant vessels is no longer found.

The desuetude of traditional piracy as a salient concern of the international community in the early twentieth century gave way to a new realization--that of "piratical" attacks from the air. At the writing of the Harvard Draft, unlawful seizures of aircraft had posed a hypothetical phenomena. Even so, it was sustained that ". . . codification of the jurisdiction of states under the law of nations should not be drafted to fit only cases raised by present conditions of business, the arts, and criminal operations."[46]

---

[45]Piratical acts performed by junks seem to be a staple activity in the internal waters of the China Sea.

For a dated description of piracy in Chinese waters see Thomas Steep, "Warriors and Pirates of Modern China," Travel, 59 (June, 1932), 45-46, and Whang, "Anti-Piracy Measures," p. 24.

[46]"Comments," A.J.I.L. Supp. 26, p. 809.

With this forebearance, the possibility of acts occurring from the air which resembled piratical acts on the high seas appeared not to be ". . . too slight or too remote for consideration in drafting a convention on jurisdiction over piratical acts."[47] Notwithstanding the obvious foresight evidenced in the Harvard Draft's recognition of piratical-like acts which might occur in the air,[48] it would be thirty years before the incidents they envisioned became an international reality.

The Demise of Piracy Jure Gentium: A Re-Birth of Common Jurisdiction

Though some writers accented the definitive difficulties of piracy, the problem of territorial jurisdication remained the focal point of the Harvard Research. A reading of the Draft Convention reveals strong emphasis on the legal jurisdictional facets of piracy, while avoiding the pitfalls of "blanket" phrases formerly associated with traditional piracy.

The Harvard Draft omits many of the popular expressions previously cited by eminent writers on traditional piracy. Nowhere in it can be found the terms piracy *jure*

---

[47] *Ibid.*

[48] On the extension of international law piracy to air navigation, see Lenoir, "Piracy Cases," p. 534.

gentium or hostes humani generis. Rather than rely upon such phrases, which often were no more than exaggerated hyperboles, the Harvard Draft formulated a clear, functional rule of common territorial jurisdiction.[49]

As previously cited, the Harvard Research directed attention to three distinctive areas of piracy, viz, a law of nations' definition of the problem, an analysis of the assertations that piracy is a crime and offense against international law, and the common jurisdiction of states to prosecute and punish pirates. In the first case, the Harvard Draft presented a broad consideration of events which might constitute piracy in an international sense. Nonetheless, the underlying assumption was that a legal definition of piracy should rightfully continue to be determined by the municipal law of a state. In the latter cases, the Draft Convention dispelled much of the obtuse folklore shrouding acts of piracy in favor of precise development of territorial jurisdiction under international law.[50]

While acts of violence on the high seas may well offend the dignity of the international community, enumeration of phrases connoting the ruthlessness of piratical

---

[49]See "Comments," A.J.I.L. Supp. 26, p. 759.

[50]Ibid. For an intriguing analysis of pirates in fiction and tradition, see Philip Gosse, The Pirates' Who's Who (London: Dulau and Co., Ltd., 1924).

ventures serves only to exacerbate defense lawyers. Exhuming doctrinal controversies of the past (i.e., trying to equate contemporary acts of piracy with the daring, infamous deeds of buccaneers such as Henry Morgan, Captain Kidd, or the Barbary corsairs), would have been a futile gesture.[51] Conclusively, though it is not specifically stated in the Harvard Draft, the Research's own precepts insist that "piracy is not a crime by the law of nations."[52]

If the Harvard Draft signals the demise of piracy _jure gentium_, one wonders whether the undergirding reasons for traditional cooperation among states to suppress piracy have have also faded into the shadows of the past. Why does international law piracy remain only a special case of state jurisdiction? If a state's jurisdiction can be extended beyond its borders to ships on the high seas and also to aircraft under its registry, then why is it necessary to reaffirm this principle through multilateral conferences?

Jurisdiction in international law forms a two-edged sword consisting of prescription on the one side and enforcement on the other. While a state may possess a ". . . legal power and right to govern"[53] its territory

---

[51]Eric Partridge, "History of Pirates," _Quarterly Review_ 262 (1934), 142-53.

[52]"Comments," _A.J.I.L. Supp._ 26, p. 759.

[53]_Ibid_.

and nationals, its competence to prescribe a rule is qualified by the state's ability to effectuate it. The foundations of international law rest upon the general principle that states occupy a specified geographical area. Within each special limitation states are said to possess "sovereignty," i.e., supreme authority over territory and nationals.[54]

Most assuredly, manifold aspects of international law are still argued in terms of this underlying principle. Recognition of state sovereignty, particularly in regard to jurisdictional rights, has been a major canon of international law since the formation of the nation-state system by the Treaty of Westphalia in 1648.[55] Even experimental, ad-hoc conventions, such as the Harvard Research, must consider the principle of sovereign jurisdiction. For to ignore the presence of national sovereignty is to ignore the reality of the international political system. With this understanding, the Harvard Research presented a politically acceptable document,

---

[54]For elucidating comments on the principle of sovereignty see Georg Schwarzenberger, "Title to Territory," A.J.I.L. 51 (1957), 308 and James L. Brierly, The Law of Nations (4th ed.; Oxford: Clarendon Press, 1949), p. 142, ff.

[55]It was not until the Treaty of Westphalia that ". . . the new states were for the first time recognized in a formal document as the component units of the world's political organization." Amry Vandenbosch and Willard H. Hogan, Toward World Order (New York: McGraw Hill, 1963), p. 12.

in treaty form, which heavily stressed an inter-national approach to jurisdiction over pirates.

The meaning (not definition) of the terms "jurisdiction" and "territorial jurisdiction" are found in Article 1, Sections 1 and 2 respectively, of the Harvard Draft.[56] While jurisdiction in international law concerns the ". . . legal governmental power and right as limited by the law of nations,"[57] territorial jurisdiction is said to include a state's jurisdiction ". . . over its land, its territorial waters and the air above its land and territorial waters. The term does not include the jurisdiction of a state over its ships outside its territory."[58]

Since the Harvard Research proffers no justification for a grant of common jurisdiction should acts occur within national territorial limits, the requirements of Article 1, Section 2 have been cited as ". . . the principal feature and indeed the <u>raison d'être</u> of the traditional law of

---

56 See <u>infra</u>, p. 272.

57 Lassa Oppenheim, <u>International Law, A Treatise</u>, ed. by Hersh Lauterpacht (London: Longmans, Green, 1947), p. 452. There is a difference, however, between national jurisdiction and "property right." While a state may own property within the confines of another foreign state, Oppenheim asserts that "The importance of State territory lies in the fact that it is the space within which the State exercises its supreme authority." Oppenheim, <u>Ibid</u>.

58 Harvard Draft Research, Article 1, Section 2.

piracy."[59] However, not all jurisdiction discussed in the Harvard Draft reflects the traditional view of piracy on the high seas. Modernization of ocean shipping and transportation, coupled with increased use of commercial air travel, necessitated a revisionist approach to jurisdictional delineations under the law of nations.[60]

At the outset, the Rapporteur indicated that the common jurisdiction granted to all nations under international law provided a special ground for the apprehension, prosecution, and punishment of pirates on the high seas. It extends rather than limits the ordinary, well-known state jurisdiction over persons and territory.[61] Thus, the Harvard Draft acknowledges the unilateral legitimacy of a nation-state to seize and prosecute those persons accused of a piratical act, and in doing so, reaffirmed the equal, common jurisdiction of all nations.

The Harvard Draft in Retrospect

An Alleged Piracy Incident--1958

While the Harvard Draft purportedly reflects the accepted notion of traditional piracy on the high

---

[59]McDougal and Burke, *Public Order of the Oceans*, p. 813.

[60]See, for example, "In-Flight Crimes, The Tokyo Convention and Federal Judicial Jurisdiction," *Journal of Air Law and Commerce*, 35 (Spring, 1969), pp. 171-203.

[61]Harvard Draft Research, Article 1.

seas,[62] its applicability as a pertinent contemporary document necessitates (1) a review of a recent incident considered by one government to constitute an act of piracy, and (2) an analysis of some early examples of aircraft seizures. With the exception of the seizure of the Santa Maria in 1961,[63] the Guatemalan-Mexican incident of 1958 serves as the most prominent example of the animosity which may erupt between nations when one erroneously construes an act on the seas as piracy.[64]

As previously discussed, the Draft Convention indicates that piracy consists of:

> Any act of violence or of depredation committed with intent to rob, rape, wound, enslave, imprison or kill a person or with intent to steal or destroy property, for private ends without bona fide purpose of asserting a claim of right, provided that the act is connected with an attack on or from the sea or in or from the air.[65]

---

[62]The Harvard Research represents a comprehensive international view of piracy. However, it should be noted that the Reporter, Joseph W. Bingham of Stanford University, and his fifteen colleagues were all Americans. See "Comments," A.J.I.L. Supp. 26, 739, for the names and affiliation of each of the men who advised on the correlation of the Harvard Draft on Piracy.

[63]The seizure of the Santa Maria occurred three years after the writing of the Geneva Convention on the High Seas. See infra, pp. 106-113.

[64]See Whiteman, Digest, pp. 663-664.

[65]Harvard Draft Research, Article 3, Section 1. [Author's emphasis added.]

It is important to realize that the Rapporteur noted the inclusion of the phrase without bona fide purpose of asserting a claim of right was intended to exclude those cases in which a legitimate claim of right may be in question. In a somewhat casual manner, he concluded, "Perhaps quarrels of fishermen of different nationalities will cause most cases of this type."[66]

The Guatemalan-Mexican incident clearly illustrates the reasons underlying the necessity of the bona fide purpose clause in the Harvard Draft. On December, 1958, the Guatemalan Minister of Defense received orders from his President to implement "Operation Drake," authorizing the bombardment of unlicensed vessels fishing within Guatemalan territorial waters.[67]

The Presidential Decree declared:

> In view of the presence of pirate fishing vessels that are plowing our territorial waters without license and, in disregard to (of) warnings that have been given them by the Air Force, treading on our native territory, landing North American and Mexican Pirates, I am communicating through the Minister of Foreign Relations to the North American and Mexican Ambassadors that, beginning on Wednesday, the 31st, the Guatemalan Air Force will bombard and machine-gun until sunk the pirate vessels that by day and night plow our territorial waters.
>
> You will give orders for the Air Force to put into action 'Operation Drake' to initiate without rest, starting Wednesday at 0700, flights by day and night,

---

[66]"Comments," A.J.I.L. Supp. 26, p. 809.

[67]Whiteman, Digest, p. 663.

> using bombs, rockets, and the arms with which the F-51 aircraft are equipped, until an end is put to these bandit pirates and filibusters.[68]

Precisely on the date indicated, Guatemalan F-51 aircraft machine-gunned five fishing vessels within the state's territorial waters. Though none of the fishing vessels displayed a flag of national identification, it was well understood that the vessels and crew were of Mexican nationality. As a result of the attack, three crew members were killed, fourteen suffered injuries, and three vessels and their crews were taken into Guatemalan custody. Because of the incident, diplomatic relations between the two states were severed,[69] and the dispute evoked grave international concern.

Mexican officials vehemently condemned the action of the Guatemalan government and refused to condone the latter's view that the apprehended fishermen be treated as pirates in violation of international law. They accused Guatemala of insensitivity to human life and flagrant disregard for general principles of law and friendship. A Mexican spokesman reputiated the contention that innocent fishermen, peacefully pursuing their occupation (though in a somewhat clandestine fashion) could be considered

---

[68] Ibid.

[69] Translation of the Mexican protest to the Guatemalan Government which appeared in a Mexican newspaper is cited in Whiteman, Digest, pp. 663-4.

"pirates" or "buccaneers:"

> My Government rejects as inadmissible the words 'pirate,' 'buccaneers,' and 'bandits' which are wrongly employed and erroneously used in the before-mentioned order of attack, since piracy is an illicit act of violence against persons or their properties carried out against other ships at sea by a privately owned ship, or, enlarging the concept - by mutinous crews or passengers on their own ship; and it is in such cases when ships of all nations may pursue, attack and capture the pirates at sea and take them to their jurisdiction so that the courts of the country which captured them may pass judgment and decree punishment.[70]

The Guatemalan-Mexican incident resulted from Guatemala's misconstruing of a fundamental element of piracy *jure gentium*--that the act of violence or depredation must take place entirely outside the territorial jurisdiction of a state. In essence, the only violence which occurred had resulted from the enforcement of harsh preventive measures by the Guatemalans. Admittedly, Guatemala may have lacked ". . . the material means needed to exercise the right of visiting, inspecting, and bringing into port the transgressing boats,"[71] but it certainly supplied the air power to attack unarmed fishing vessels.

---

[70]Whiteman, *Digest*, p. 664. See also the *Paquette Habana* (The *Lola*) 177 U.S. (1900) 677. The opinion of the Supreme Court asserted that capture of peaceful fishing vessels, even during times of war, is contrary to customary international law. This contention finds support in Article III of the Hague Convention of 1907 which provides that: "Vessels used exclusively for fishing along the coast or small boats employed in local trade are exempt from capture, as well as their appliances, rigging, tackle, and cargo." 36 Stat. 2396, 2 Malloy, Treaties 2341, 2348.

[71]Whiteman, *Digest*, p. 664.

Though unauthorized fishing within Guatemalan territorial waters may be an infraction of municipal piracy laws, it was not, in any sense, international law piracy under the Harvard Draft.[72]

Incidents of "Air Piracy"- -1930-1958

The harbinger of modern-day aircraft seizures was seen in 1930 when the first recorded aircraft was diverted from its scheduled destination.[73] Not until seventeen years later did the second reported successful aircraft seizure take place--this time to escape from a communist country.[74] Subsequent years reflected a discernible pattern of individuals who took control of aircraft from their state of citizenship to another state whose political regime seemed less oppressive than the former.[75] While it is difficult to document early incidents because of inadequate reporting or lack of knowledge about the intentions and motivations

---

[72]As a result of the good offices of the Chilean and Brazilian Governments, the dispute was settled and diplomatic relations between Mexico and Guatemala resumed. See the American Embassy, Mexico City, to the Department of State, Dispatch No. 312, September 17, 1959, file 612.14/9-1759.

[73]Narinder Aggarwala, "Air Hijacking: An International Perspective," Carnegie Endowment for International Peace, (November, 1971), 9.

[74]Boyle, "Aircraft Hijacking, p. 461.

[75]See Seymour W. Wurfel, "Aircraft Piracy-Crime or Fun?," William and Mary Law Review 10 (Spring, 1969), 820-73.

of the parties involved, Federal Aviation Administration statistics indicate that twenty-two aircraft seizure attempts occurred from 1930 through 1958.[76]

A perusal of the flight plans of aircraft diversions during those years reveals that the seizure of an aircraft ". . . by a desperate political refugee seeking to flee an oppressive regime was an important motivation in early years."[77] Several cases in the late 1940's and early 1950's may be attributed to the political unrest in Czechoslovakia, China, and the Soviet Union.[78] From 1958 to 1962, the majority of cases resulted from the desire of individuals to escape the Castro regime which had overthrown the Batista government in Cuba.[79]

It is interesting to note that no attempts by individuals to divert aircraft occurred during the years which coincided with Hitler's rise to power in Europe or

---

[76]F.A.A. Statistics. Frequency of incidents for these years is shown as follows:

1930:	1	1950:	3
1947:	1	1952:	1
1948:	7	1953:	1
1949:	3	1958:	5

[77]James S. G. Turner, "Piracy in the Air," Naval War College Review, 22 (September 1969), 89.

[78]Alona E. Evans, "Aircraft Hijacking: Its Cause and Cure," A.J.I.L. 63 (October, 1969), 698.

[79]Karl M. Ruppenthal, "World Law and the Hijackers," The Nation, 208, No. 5 (February 3, 1969), 144.

World War II.[80] One might suspect that periods of national political turmoil might be more conducive to aircraft seizure than years of international crisis. For example, while three incidents of aircraft seizure occurred during the first quarter of 1950 and two attempts were reported between 1952 and 1953, none of these appear to bear any relationship to the Korean Conflict.[81] Not until February 16, 1958, did a successful seizure take place involving an aircraft whose flight plan included South Korea and North Korea.[82] Nonetheless, it cannot be determined on the basis of such a paucity of cases that a direct or indirect relationship exists between international conflict and unlawful aircraft seizures.[83]

Each of the twenty-two cases of aircraft seizures between 1930 and 1958 involved the takeover of a single

---

[80]After 1930, no incident of aircraft seizure was recorded until 1947. Boyle, "Aircraft Piracy," p. 461.

[81]In 1952, for example, three Yugoslav crew members on an in-country flight subdued the other flight personnel and diverted the aircraft to Switzerland. A Swiss court refused a Yugoslavian extradition request and granted asylum to the "political" refugees. Robert H. Lynn notes that *In Re Kavic et al.* ". . . is the only internationally reported opinion to deal with air hijacking as a political crime." Robert H. Lynn, "Air Hijacking as a Political Crime--Who Should Judge?," *California Western International Law Journal* 2 (1971), 96; 80 Annual Digest (1952) 371 (Federal Tribunal Switzerland).

[82]F.A.A. Statistics. See *infra*, p. 143, note 90.

[83]See Aggarwala, "Air Hijacking: An International Perspective," p. 9.

plane by ". . . a desperate political refugee seeking to flee an oppressive regime."[84] Interestingly enough, though there is a dearth of information regarding these cases, it does not seem that any significant acts of violence (i.e., the wounding, enslaving, imprisonment, or killing of any persons) were involved.[85]

A final caveat concerning the Harvard Draft Research is in order here. While it can be argued that any aircraft seizure involves robbery (of the aircraft) and threat of violence, such attempts usually begin and terminate within the territorial jurisdiction of some state, thus placing the incidents outside the suggested guidelines of the Harvard Draft.[86] In essence, the Harvard Research--while considered a bold recognition that future piracy-like acts would be confined to aircraft--provides no workable criteria to assess the actual happenings shrouding the seizure of aircraft or an obligation to punish the criminals under the law of nations.

---

[84]Turner, "Piracy in the Air," p. 89.

[85]On November 1, 1958, five men attempted to seize a Cubana Viscount aircraft on a scheduled flight plan from Miami to Veradero. The plan crashed, killing seventeen of the twenty-one passengers aboard. While the tragedy occurred during an unsuccessful diversion to Cuba, it cannot be said conclusively that the disaster directly resulted from the aborted take-over. F.A.A. Statistics. See also Gary Horlick, "The Public and Private International Response to Aircraft Hijacking," Vanderbilt Journal of Transnational Law 6 (1972), 149.

[86]This is predicated upon Article 5 and Article 6 of the Harvard Draft Research. See *infra*, p. 273.

The International Law Commission

While the work of the Harvard Draft did not result in the adoption of a multilateral treaty, the essence of the Research was continued under the auspices of the United Nations International Law Commission (I.L.C.). The Commission, which held its first session in 1949, was charged with the responsibility of reviewing the laws of the high seas and developing a progressive modification of international maritime law in general.[87]

As Rapporteur of the Commission, J. P. A. Francois justifiably acknowledged the contributions of the Harvard Draft Research of 1932. Under his guidance, the Commission labored for seven years before presenting a provisional draft (including articles on piracy) to the United Nations for adoption at the 1958 Geneva Convention on the High Seas. Though the draft followed the basic rationale of the Harvard Research, several pertinent questions (left ambiguous in the Harvard Draft) were clarified in the Commission's report on the provisional draft. Of particular significance is the Commission's attention to the definition of piracy, the number of vessels needed for an act of piracy, and a

---

[87]International Law Commission Report, 10 U.N. GOAR, Supp. 9, at 2, U.N. Doc. A/2934 (1955). Hereafter cited as 1955 U.N. Report.

continuation of the requirement that piratical acts be committed for private ends.[88]

I.L.C. Definition of Piracy

According to the International Law Commission's report of 1956, piracy consisted of the following acts:

> Any illegal acts of violence, detention or any act of depredation committed for private ends by the crew or passengers of a private ship or private aircraft, and directed
> (a) on the high seas, against another ship or against persons or property on board such a ship;
> (b) against a ship, persons or property in a place outside the jurisdiction of any state.[89]

---

[88]In particular, the I.L.C. continued to support the underlying assumption of the Harvard Draft Research that the scope of piratical acts must take place outside the territorial jurisdiction of any state.

The following reservations were presented by the Rapporteur in the Commission's report to the U.N.:

(I) The intention to rob (animus furandi) is not required. Acts of piracy may be prompted by feelings of hatred or revenge and not merely by the desire for gain;

(II) The acts must be committed for private ends;

(III) Save in [a special case now provided in Article 16 of the Geneva Convention on the high Seas] . . . . piracy can be committed only on private ships;

(IV) Piracy can be committed only on the high seas or in a place situated outside the territorial jurisdiction of any state, and cannot be committed within the territory of a state . . .'

(V) Acts of piracy can be committed not only by ships on the high seas, but also by aircraft, if such acts are directed against ships on the high seas;

(VI) Acts committed on board ship by the crew or passengers and directed against the ship itself, or against persons or property on the ship cannot be regarded as acts of piracy.

1955 U.N. Report, p. 6.

International Law Commission Report, 11 U.N. GOAR, Supp. 9, at 28, U.N. Doc. A/3159 (1956) (Hereafter cited as 1956 U.N. Report).

[89]1956 U.N. Report, Ibid.,

The 1955 draft of the I.L.C. provided a similar

Specific acts of violence, as had been enumerated in the Harvard Draft (i.e., to rape, wound, enslave, imprison, or kill), were omitted in favor of a broader committment against "any illegal acts of violence." The inclusion of the phrase ". . . detention or any act of depredation"[90] appeared to be motivated by the desire to cover a wider spectrum of coercive behavior. Each of these modifications fall prey to either broad or liberal interpretations at the discretion of state municipal courts. In the case of piracy on the high seas, traditional concepts of piracy received sufficient recognition to meet most states' approval. However, since the sparcity of aircraft hijackers posed little serious international concern in 1956, the definition seemed to adequately accommodate any incidents of aircraft seizure which might genuinely resemble piracy on the high seas.[91]

---

definition, but worded in a slightly different manner. The earlier report contained the same basic elements, but stipulated that: "Piracy is any of the following acts:

1. Any illegal act of violence, detention or any act of depredation directed against persons or property and committed for private ends by the crew or passengers of a private vessel or a private aircraft:

(a) Against a vessel on the high seas other than that on which the act is committed, or

(b) Against vessels, persons or property in territory outside the jurisdiction of any State."

1955 U.N. Report, at 6.

[90]McDougal and Burke, Public Order of the Oceans, p. 812.

[91]By the end of 1953, only seventeen aircraft hijackings had occurred. No other incidents were recorded

Solution to the Single Flag Requirement

The Commission's definition of piracy does not dispel the notion that such acts might be considered piracy if only one flag vessel were involved. However, unlike the Harvard Research, a study of the debates during sessions of the I.L.C. reveals that only a two-vessel criteria is applicable. According to the Rapporteur, acts committed aboard a single flag vessel could be summarily dismissed as piracy under the law of nations. Though the Commission discussed a Swedish proposal which included a "single flag requirement" in the definition of piracy, the suggestion was rejected. Instead, the Rapporteur indicated:

> In considering as 'piracy' acts committed outside the jurisdiction of any state, the Commission had chiefly in mind acts committed by a ship or aircraft on an island constituting *terra nullius*, or on the shore of an unoccupied territory.[92]

---

after March 23, 1953, until April 10, 1958. F.A.A. Statistics. It is important to note that the Commission rejected the view that mutiny aboard a ship or aircraft would fall within the proposed draft definition of piracy. A comment of the Rapporteur indicated: "The view adopted by the Commission . . . tallies with the opinion of most writers. Even where the purpose of the mutineers is to seize the ship, their acts do not constitute acts of piracy." 1955 U.N. Report, *op. cit.*, at 7.

1956 U.N. Report, *op. cit.*, at 28.

[92] *Yearbook International Law Commission*, Vol. 2, U.N. Doc. A/3159 (1956), pp. 253, 282.

The suggestion that piratical acts might take place on an island *terra nullius* ("no man's land," not belonging to any sovereign state) was fostered by several writers on

Since aircraft hijackings are not committed by one aircraft against another, nor are they likely to occur on land which is terra nullius (i.e., outside the jurisdiction of any state), the I.L.C.'s dismissal of the "single flag act" omits as acts of piracy all incidents of aircraft hijacking which have occurred to date.[93]

Reaffirmation of the "Private Ends" Motivation

Continuation of the "private ends" criteria set by the Harvard Research provoked considerable debate among the members of the International Law Commission. The Soviet and Czechoslovakian delegation to the I.L.C. insisted that acts of piracy committed solely for private ends was contrary to to contemporary international law. Soviet representative Morozov contended that the restriction of the I.L.C. definition of piracy to acts committed for private gains

---

traditional piracy in international law. See for example William E. Hall, A Treatise on International Law (Oxford: Clarendon Press, 1924), p. 314.

[93]While it is true that aircraft hijackers may not make their intentions known to the flight crew until after the plane is above international waters, the landing of an aircraft within a state's territorial jurisdiction places it beyond the definition enunciated by the I.L.C.

See also Article 1, The Chicago Convention, 61 Stat. 1180 (1947), T.I.A.S. No. 1591, 15 U.N.T.S., 295, which asserts the international law rule that state territory includes the airspace above it. Accordingly, an aircraft hijacking which takes place above a state cannot be considered a real act of piracy.

against non-military ships or aircraft violated the

> . . . practice and theory of international law. The so-called Nyon Arrangement of 1937 recognized that the sinking of merchant ships by submarines, contrary to the dictates of humanity, could with full justification be regarded as a piratical act. Similarly, when in September 1940 (1941) the President of the United States of America had ordered the United States naval forces to open fire on German submarines, he had been taking what the Soviet Union delegation regarded as a legitimate measure of defence against piratical attacks carried out contrary to international law. . . .[94]

The exhuming of the submarine warfare-as-piracy controversy, originally generated by the Washington Naval Treaty of 1922, was voted upon unfavorably by the members of the I.L.C. This polemic, of course, bore little, if any relevance to the problem of modern-day aircraft seizures. However, it did reveal that even traditional elements of piracy on the high seas suffered from growing pains of modern naval warfare.[95]

---

[94]Cited in Whiteman, Digest, p. 662. D.H.N. Johnson, however, considers the Nyon Arrangement only as ". . . an ad hoc arrangement for a kind of collective self-defense in peculiar circumstances." It is doubtful that it established a new rule of international law displacing the contention that piracy must be committed exclusively for private ends. Only nine states--the United Kingdom, Bulgaria, Egypt, France, Greece, Rumania, Turkey, the U.S.S.R. and Yugoslavia--signed the agreement. See D.H.N. Johnson, "Piracy in Modern International Law," p. 85.

[95]Jacobson, "From Piracy on the High Seas," p. 167.

It is interesting that by June 30, 1957, ". . . the U.S.S.R. ranked twelfth as a surface maritime merchant shipping Power, but first as an underwater Power equipped with submarines of great destructive ability."

For an analysis of Soviet submarine capabilities and U.S.S.R. developments in nuclear-powered and missile-carrying

The insistency by the Soviet bloc that the "private ends" requirement be deleted and the submarines be considered lawful vehicles of piratical attacks resulted in a compromise proposal. Comments by the Rapporteur noted that one exception was permissible, *viz.*, the provision that piracy can only be committed on private ships.[96] Article 16 of the Convention on the High Seas (Geneva, 1958) acknowledged

> The acts of piracy, as defined in Article 15 committed by a warship, government ship or government aircraft whose crew has mutinied and taken control of the ship or aircraft are assimilated to acts committed by a private ship.[97]

Thus, if a successful mutiny occurred aboard a submarine and the crew continued to commit any illegal acts of violence on the high seas against another ship, such acts would be considered piracy under the Geneva Convention of 1958. The problem of assessing such a phenomena is complicated by the provision that piratical acts must be committed for private ends. Although it is clear that the intention to rob (*animus furandi*) is not required, and

---

submarines at that time, see Hanson W. Baldwin, *The Great Arms Race* (New York: Praeger Press, 1958).

[96]1956 U.N. Report, p. 6.

[97]The Convention on the High Seas, Article 16. U.N. Doc. A/Conf. 13/38, p. 137. See *infra*, p. 279.

piratical acts ". . . may be prompted by feelings of hatred or revenge,"[98] it would be extremely difficult to prove (should such an incident occur) that the motivation of the mutinous crew-turned-pirates was private and not political.[99]

The success of the I.L.C. in resolving political and legal difficulties greatly facilitated the acceptance of the provisions on piracy and other major topics of consideration at the Geneva Conference.[100] The draft articles and

---

[98]1956 U.N. Report, p. 28.

[99]The Case of the Santa Maria, infra, pp. 106-113 illustrates this point.

[100]U.N. Doc. A/Conf. 13/38, Annexes, pp. 132-45. The conference held in Geneva from 24 February until 27 April 1958 under the presidency of Prince Wan Waithayakon of Thailand, was attended by some 700 delegates from 86 countries and from seven specialized agencies, and observers from nine non-governmental organizations. See the Final Act of the Conference, Ibid., pp. 145-7 (Doc. A/Conf. 13/L.58). The conference was convened in accordance with the General Assembly Resolution 1105 (XI) of 21 February 1957, and its work was based on 73 draft articles prepared by the International Law Commission, and on relevant debates of the General Assembly early in 1957. In addition to the four conventions and the resolutions, an optional protocol was adopted by the conference. All countries signing the optional protocol agreed to recognize the compulsory jurisdiction of the International Court of Justice in disputes arising out of the conventions of the Law of the Sea, except with respect to measures for the conservation of resources of the high seas. For the text of the optional protocol see Ibid., pp. 145-6 (Doc. A/Conf. 13/L.57). The four conventions were subject to ratification and all required a minimum of 22 ratifications or accessions to come into force. They were closed for signature on 31 October 1958.

For an introspective analysis of the year-long conference, see Arthur H. Dean, "The Geneva Conference on the Law of the Sea: What was Accomplished," A.J.I.L. 52 (1958), 608-28.

comments presented at the Eighth Session of the I.L.C. provided the basic working papers for the Conference, ". . . except as to the question of land-locked countries placed on the agenda at the last minute by the General Assembly."[101]

The Geneva Convention on the High Seas (1958)

The Geneva Convention on the High Seas of 1958 makes it quite clear that the laws relating to piracy on the high seas are also applicable to piracy in the high skies. Articles 14-22 specifically deal with piracy, whether committed by ships or aircraft.[102] However, while there is some similarity between acts of sea piracy and air piracy, strong legal and technical differences exist. Thus,

> In order to discern whether hijacking of aircraft amounts to piracy as defined by the Geneva Convention on the High Seas of 1958, it is necessary to compare it with piracy under the regime of that Convention.[103]

Though "air piracy" remains a popular term to describe the offense of aircraft hijacking, recent incidents of aircraft seizure do not reflect the legal position on piracy referred to by the Geneva Convention. Moreover,

---

[101]Dean, Ibid., p. 608; International Law Commission Report, U.N. G.A. 11th Session, Official Records, Supp. No. 9 (A/3159); also A.J.I.L., 51 (1957), p. 154.

[102]See infra, pp. 279-80.

[103]Sami Shubber, "Is Hijacking of Aircraft Piracy in International Law?," B.Y.I.L., 43 (1968-69), 194.

application of the piracy provisions in the Geneva Convention to a recent incident of alleged piracy on the high seas (the Santa Maria, 1961) indicates that contemporary examples of sea piracy may no longer exist.[104]

Article 15 of the Geneva Convention serves as the pivotal point for the ensuing provisions on piracy. It defines piracy as consisting of the following acts:

> (1) Any illegal acts of violence, detention or any act of depredation, committed for private ends by the crew or passengers of a private ship or a private aircraft, and directed:
> (a) On the high seas, against another ship or aircraft, or against persons or property on board such ship or aircraft;
> (b) Against a ship, aircraft, persons or property in a place outside the jurisdiction of any State;
> (2) Any act of voluntary participation in the operation of a ship or of an aircraft with knowledge of facts making it a pirate ship or aircraft;
> (3) Any act of inciting or of intentionally facilitating an act described in sub-paragraph (1) or sub-paragraph (2) of this article.[105]

This definition strongly reiterates the contentions of the I.L.C. that: (1) the enumeration of illegal acts of violence shall be determined by municipal state law; (2) that the pirates be motivated by private as opposed to political ends; (3) that the act of piracy involve action from ship-to-ship, aircraft-to-aircraft; (4) that the acts of violence, detention, or depredation take place

---

[104]See the discussion about the Santa Maria, infra., pp. 106-113.

[105]The Convention on the High Seas, Article 15. U.N. Doc. A/Conf. 13/38, p. 137, See infra., p. 279.

outside the jurisdiction of any state, meaning both territorial jurisdiction and the airspace above a state.[106] The duty of states to ". . . cooperate to the fullest possible extent in the repression of piracy" (Article 14) is augmented by Article 19 which re-affirms the universal principle by which states may extend their jurisdiction to apprehend and punish pirates whose criminal arena has been the high seas or high skies.[107]

The *Santa Maria* Incident (1961)

The case of the *Santa Maria* tested the validity of Article 15 of the 1958 Geneva Convention as applied to the take-over of a ship on the high seas.[108] Admittedly, the position of the *Santa Maria* in international law has not been clearly discerned. Authoritative writers in international law, such as Charles Fenwick, assert that the seizure of the *Santa Maria* constituted an act of piracy, though he does not cite conclusive evidence to support his

---

[106]See Haro F. Van Panhuys, "Aircraft Hijacking and International Law," *Columbia Journal of Transnational Law* 9 (Spring 1970), 5.

[107]The Convention on the High Seas, U.N. Doc. A/Conf. 13/38, pp. 136-137. See *infra*., pp. 106-113.

[108]In retrospect, this is true. At the time of the incident (January-February, 1961), the Convention on the High Seas was not yet in force. Ratification did not occur until September 30, 1962.

contention.[109] Whiteman, on the other hand, indicates

> Since the ship was taken over by certain of its own passengers (apparently for private ends), and not by another ship, as at first reported, it was considered that for this, if for no other reason, Article 15 of the 1958 Convention was inapplicable.[110]

A detailed analysis of the seizure of the Santa Maria reveals the tangled nexus of legal, social, economic, and political complications which serve to point up the need for a more precise application of the term "piracy" with respect to international law.

On January 23, 1961, a group of seventy men led by Captain Henrique Galvao, a former Portuguese commissioner and a prominent opponent of the Salazar government, seized the 20,900-ton Portuguese liner, the Santa Maria. The vessel was captured in the West Indies shortly after having left the port of Curacao in the Netherlands Antilles. The Santa Maria, a pleasure-cruising vessel, belonged to the Portuguese Colonial Navigation Company (Companhia Colonial da Navegacão), and carried over 600 passengers. Included among the men, women, and children were passengers of

---

[109]Charles Fenwick, "Piracy in the Carribbean," A.J.I.L. 55 (1961), 426-8.

See also Keesing's Contemporary Archives (February 24-March 4, 1961), p. 17951, which labels the Santa Maria incident as "an act of piracy unequalled in modern times."

[110]Whiteman, Digest, p. 666.

Portuguese, Dutch, Venezuelan, Spanish, and American descent.[111]

Although the vessel was expected to land at Port Everglades, Florida, before its return to Lisbon, Portugal, its voyage was radically changed after the seizure. It appears that Galvao had attempted to follow an east-southeast direction, probably steering towards West Africa. In a special announcement from the vessel on February 2, 1961, Galvao proclaimed that

> . . . the coup was a declaration of political war on Salazar, envisaging 'a revolutionary objective: the reconstruction of Portuguese society on new bases' which would 'open up also overseas the doors of liberty, progress, and independence.'[112]

Before becoming a political exile, Galvao had received a commission in 1947 from the Portuguese government to give an "on-the-spot" report of the conditions of two Portuguese colonies, Angola and Mozambique. According to the Salazar sources, Galvao's report was too unfavorable for publication. When the National Assembly to which Galvao was a member refused to print his account of the colonial maladies, Galvao began his open opposition to the Salazar regime. Although imprisoned in 1951, he escaped eight years later and fled to South America to join General Humberto

---

[111] Keesing's Contemporary Archives, op.cit., p. 17951.

[112] D. C. Watt, Survey of International Affairs, 1961 (New York: Oxford University Press, 1965), p. 416.

Delgado, who had been defeated by Salazar in the 1958 Portuguese presidential election.[113]

Soon after the seizure of the Santa Maria, Galvao's suppressed report of the sordid conditions in Mozambique and Angola appeared in the January 29, 1961 edition of the London newspaper, The Observer. In this publication, Galvao reported severe cases of undernourishment, a high mortality rate, especially among children, and a drastic lack of health facilities. Galvao claimed that the labor forced upon the African population verged upon slavery.[114]

Thus, in his first radio announcement to the outside world on January 24, 1961, Captain Galvao proclaimed that he had captured the Santa Maria

> . . . in the name of the Independent Junta of Liberation led by the General Humberto Delgado, the legally elected President of the Portuguese Republic, who has been fraudulently deprived of his rights by the Salazar Administration.[115]

He acknowledged that all passengers were safe and that most of them had favorably accepted his take-over as a political act. One wonders under those conditions what might have occurred had the passengers strongly objected to Galvao's seizure. The crew, however, did not fare so well as the passengers. The day before his announcement,

---

[113] Ibid.

[114] Keesing's Contemporary Archives, op. cit., p. 17951.

[115] New York Times, January 25, 1961, p. 1.

Galvao had docked briefly at Castries, St. Lucia, in the British West Indies. Here he placed ashore a lifeboat containing eight wounded crewmen and the body of Third Officer Costa. (The injuries had occurred during the ship's seizure when the crewmen on deck were wounded by hand grenades and machine-guns discharged by Galvao's men.) Although most of Galvao's men had boarded ship at Curaçao and had been disguised as passengers, it was also thought that some of Galvao's men were among the original 300 crew members of the *Santa Maria*.[116]

Immediately after the seizure, the Portuguese government requested that American, British, and Dutch ships help search for the *Santa Maria* and recapture her "in accordance with the well-defined terms of international law governing piracy and insurrection on board ship."[117]

When the *Santa Maria* was sighted in international waters by both British and American naval vessels, Galvao radioed that he would be willing to bring the *Santa Maria* to port provided that both he and his crew receive guarantees that they would be treated as political insurgents. Following Galvao's announcement, Rear-Admiral Allen Smith, commander of the U.S. Navy destroyer *Gearing*, went aboard the *Santa Maria* to speak with Galvao. During his talk, Galvao

---

116 New York *Times*, January 24, 1961, p. 1.

117 *Keesing's Contemporary Archives*, *Ibid.*, p. 17951.

reaffirmed his position that he would peacefully surrender the ship and its crew only if he received assurances that he would be treated as an insurgent.[118]

After the Santa Maria was securely anchored in Recife, Brazil, the U.S. State Department announced that the United States had acted under the international laws against piracy. Although General Delgado had proclaimed that the seizure was a political act carried out on his orders, the State Department denied any knowledge of Delgado's demand or Galvao's insistence that the ship be recognized as an international belligerent against Portugal. Regardless of the position taken by the United States, Galvao was immediately granted political asylum by the new president of Brazil, Janio Quadros.[119]

While the case of the Santa Maria conformed with the Portuguese definition of piracy, it fell far short as an incidence of piracy on the high seas as prescribed by the

---

[118]New York *Times*, January 25, 1961, p. 1; Watt, *Survey of International Affairs*, 1961, p. 462.

[119]Had Great Britain and the United States not been sympathetic towards the revolution which Galvao and his followers proposed, the two nations would not have been so concerned about harboring the *Santa Maria* in a Brazilian port and would have delivered it directly to the Portuguese government in Lisbon. *The New Republic*, 144 (February 6, 1961), 8.

1958 Geneva Convention.[120] According to Jacobson, "the facts of the seizure revealed that it was made with the intention of sparking political consequences in Portugal and not for the purpose of private gain."[121]

Certainly, all of the action took place aboard a single ship, and the capture of the Santa Maria rendered it an academic question as to whether or not Galvao and his followers may have intended to commit future acts of piracy directed against other vessels on the high seas. It is interesting to note, however, that China had sought expansion of Article 15 of the 1958 Geneva Convention to include the taking over of navigation or command of a ship by a person or persons aboard.[122] Such a provision would definitely have applied to the seizure of the Santa Maria. However, the provision was withdrawn prior to the voting in the Second Committee, making its relevance to the Santa

---

120The Portuguese Government defined piracy as ". . ". . . forcible seizure of a ship . . . the commission of acts of violence, damages or thefts on any such ship . . . the pursuance on board of activities directly against the Portuguese state." Keesing's Contemporary Archives, p. 17951. However, the two-vessel requirement in Article 15 of the Geneva Convention is noticeably absent from the Portuguese municipal concept of piracy.

121Jacobson, "From Piracy on the High Seas," p. 167.

122The Chinese proposal can be found in U.N. Conference on the Law of the Sea, Second Committee (High Seas: General Regime), Doc. A/Conf. 13/C.2/L. 45, IV, p. 128.

Maria incident and subsequent aircraft hijacking a moot issue.[123]

The Relevance of Aircraft Seizures to the Geneva Convention (1958)

The infrequency of genuine piracy attempts on the high seas coincided with the lack of cases involving the seizures of aircraft that immediately followed the drafting of the Geneva Convention. Federal Aviation Administration (F.A.A.) statistics recorded only three successful and no unsuccessful aircraft hijackings during 1959.[124] Of the three, two involved the flight of persons from the Castro Regime in Cuba, while the other was a successful hijacking to gain entrance into Cuba.[125]

Though the destinations of the parties in the former two cases are diametrically opposed to those in the latter incident, the motivation in each case appears to be political. In addition, the incidents concerned only a single aircraft, thus rendering inapplicable the two-vessel provision of

---

[123] Ibid., p. 84.

But see Oppenheim's "conversion principle" which parallels the Chinese proposal and suggests that the Santa Maria incident, although only one vessel was involved, may be considered piracy since the members of the crew revolted and converted the ship to their own use. Lauterpacht, ed., Oppenheim's International Law, p. 614.

[124] F.A.A. Statistics. See infra , p. 143, note 90.

[125] Ibid.

of Article 15. Therefore, Jacobson concludes:

> While there is disagreement among the authorities on this issue, both customary law and the Geneva Convention on the High Seas exclude, at least by analogy, the application of the law of piracy to hijacking on this ground.[126]

In essence, the act of hijacking an aircraft assumes the character of a "continuous wrong," that is, it begins and ends wholly or partially within the territorial airspace or territory of a state. Even if the actual aircraft seizure occurs over international waters, the landing of the plane will undoubtedly place it within a state's territorial jurisdiction. While the "private ends" and "two-vessel" requirements of the Geneva Convention challenge traditional customary law of international piracy, the territorial aspects of aircraft hijacking completely ignores any bind between international law piracy and aircraft seizures.[127]

Admittedly, the Geneva Convention recognizes an extension of piracy on the high seas to piracy in the high skies. However, the legal ingredients which compose air piracy are not the recipe for aircraft hijacking.[128] With

---

[126]Jacobson, "From Piracy on the High Seas," p. 174-5.

[127]For an analysis of these three critical points of differences between sea piracy and aircraft seizures, see Haro F. Van Panhuys, "Aircraft Hijacking and International Law," pp. 4-7.

[128]Rafat, for example, concludes that hijacking cannot be considered a piratical act simply because it does not have the legal status of piracy. Amir Rafat, "Control of Aircraft Hijacking: The Law of International Civil Aviation," <u>World Affairs</u>, 145 (1971), 9.

the prevalence of hijacking attempts in the 1960's, the void of any relevant customary international law to meet the challenge became patently obvious. Since aircraft hijacking was not a recognized offense under the law of nations, this lack-of-law became a major obstacle to prosecution of the offenders. Without the threat of punishment or refusal of asylum, hijackers could continue to disrupt peaceful commercial air travel.[129] The international community responded to this disability with the most potent instrument of international law--the multilateral convention. It is to these international legal efforts we now turn.

---

[129]McKeithen asserts that hijackings can only be "safely curtailed . . . through international agreement on criminal sanctions to be applied against the hijacker."

R. L. Smith McKeithen, "Prospects for the Prevention of Aircraft Hijacking Through Law," Columbia Journal of Transnational Law, 9 (1970), 61.

CHAPTER 3

TOWARDS A NEW INTERNATIONAL LAW OF AIRCRAFT SEIZURE: THE TOKYO CONVENTION

Existing international law of piracy failed to encompass the series of acts associated with the seizure of aircraft. Though the phenomena of "aircraft hijacking" was often referred to as "air piracy," neither of the two expressions appropriately described the act of unlawfully taking over an aircraft.[1] Thus, the international community faced two difficult, fundamental problems--firstly, to discover a term which was truly descriptive of the act; and secondly, to determine an internationally acceptable solution to the crime.[2]

---

[1]The necessity for distinguishing between the terms "air piracy" and "aircraft hijacking" is discussed in Nicholas M. Poulantzas, "Hijacking or Air Piracy?," _Nederlands Juristenblad_, 566 (1970), No. 20; See also the conclusion of Sami Shubber that aircraft hijacking is a far broader term than piracy. Shubber, "Is Hijacking of Aircraft Piracy?," p. 204.

[2]McKeithen, "Prospects for Prevention," p. 61. For an antithetical view, see Michel Pourcelet, "Hijacking. The Limitations of the International Treaty Approach," in McWhinney, ed., _Aerial Piracy_, pp. 55-58.

While it is true that an international legal definition of air piracy existed under the Geneva Convention of 1958, acts perpetrated prior to and after the Convention only vaguely represented the meaning of piracy as codified in Article 15.[3] On the other hand, to denote aircraft seizures as "hijacking" was also a serious misnomer, both descriptively and legally. Alona Evans reports that

> . . . "hijacking," that relic of the Prohibition Era, is not entirely descriptive of the act, for in common usage hijacking applies to the seizure of a private commercial vehicle or vessel with the intent of theft of its load or cargo.[4]

By the early 1960's it became evident that the unlawful seizure of aircraft was an anomaly, both in international law and in the municipal laws of many states. In the former, classic international interpretations of piracy on the high seas appeared hopelessly inadequate as a basis of possible prosecution.[5] In the latter, an International Criminal Police Organization (INTERPOL) survey revealed that only a few states provided specific statutes to deal with

---

[3]Alec Samuels, "Crimes Committed on Board Aircraft: Tokyo Convention Act 1967," B.Y.I.L. 42 (1967), 276-77.

[4]Evans, "Aircraft Hijacking," p. 696.

[5]See Horlick, "The Developing Law of Air Hijacking," pp. 64-65.

the existing threat of aircraft seizures.[6] The absence of such provisions forced municipal judges to invoke sections of existing criminal codes which, under many circumstances, did not adequately meet the facts of the case.[7]

According to Edward McWhinney, aerial piracy should be viewed as a popular term, not as a strictly legal concept. When asked why the edition of his new book was entitled Aerial Piracy and International Law, McWhinney replied that broadness of terms and purity of translation dictated the use of "piracy" as opposed to "hijacking."[8] The volume resulted from an international conference on aircraft seizures held at McGill University's Institute of Air and Space Law in Montreal, Canada, October 30-31, 1970. Since the meeting was jointly sponsored by the American Society of International Law, the Canadian Branch of the

---

[6]A concise analysis of general preventive measures and recommendations for deterring unlawful aircraft seizures can be found in International Civil Airport Association, Hijacking (Doc. 7111-Gen/15), December, 1971, pp. 22-30.

[7]Ibid., p. 27.

[8]Responses of Professor McWhinney to question of Mr. Larman C. Wilson cited in the discussion, "Panel: New Developments in the Law of International Aviation: The Control of Aerial Hijacking," Proceedings of the A.S.I.L., 65 (September, 1971), 95.

International Law Association, and the Canadian Society of International Law, a number of semantic difficulties arose from Canada's dual French-English native languages.[9] Professor McWhinney noted that

> The term "hijacking" is, in this regard, literally untranslatable into French, where it must be rendered either (rather inelegantly) as détournement illicite or else, more generally and more popularly, as piraterie aériénne.[10]

Thus, the use of the term "air piracy" is limited to three areas. Firstly, it continues to be regarded as a popular expression, particularly by the news media, to emphasize the grave criminal nature of aircraft seizure.[11] Secondly, air piracy may denote the precise wording in some municipal statutes designed to deter local incidences of the crime.[12] And, thirdly, air piracy does constitute an

---

[9] Ibid., p. 95. See also McWhinney, ed., Aerial Piracy, p. 7.

[10] "Panel: New Developments in the Law of International Aviation," p. 95.

[11] See for example, "Pirates in the Sky," Time, Vol. 96, No. 12 (September 21, 1970), and " Israeli Prime Minister Abba Eban Proposes Drive Against Air Piracy," Washington Post, September 15, 1970; p. A-18.

[12] For example, U.S. Congress, Senate, A Bill to Amend the Federal Aviation Act of 1958 to Provide Proper Penalties in the Event of Aircraft Piracy, and for other Purposes, S. 2299, 92nd Cong., 2nd sess., 1972, pp. 7-8; "The Brazilian Hijacking Law," Decree-Law 975 of 20 October, 1969 in International Legal Materials, Vol. IX, No. 1 (January, 1970), pp. 180-184; The Cuban Hijacking Law (see note 103, infra.); For discussions of other municipal legislations to combat aircraft seizures, see New York Times, December 12, 1969,

extension of the traditional international concept of piracy when performed outside the jurisdiction of any nation, thereby conforming to Article 15 of the Geneva Convention on the High Seas (1958).[13]

Referring to the latter case, Haroldo Valladao suggested that:

> . . . si cette convention a marqué un progrès en prevoyant aussi la piraterie aérienne, elle a été très restrictive en donnant la définition de piraterie maritime et aérienne. . . .[14]

Interviews with Department of State officials support Valladao's contention that the term "air piracy" in the 1958 Geneva Convention is too restrictive to be used in connection with the suppression of illegal aircraft seizures.[15] With the exception of federal laws against air piracy,[16]

11: 1 (France); "Luftpiraterie als rechtsproblem," Zeitschrift fur Luftricht und Weltraumrichtsfragen, Vol. 18, (April 1, 1969), pp. 77-80. (German); New York Times, November 27, 1969. 11:5 (Italian); and Washington Post, September 8, 1970, p. A-14 (Denmark).

[13]Haroldo Valladao, "Punition Internationale De L'Actuelle Piraterie Aérienne," in McWhinney, ed., Aerial Piracy, pp. 98-100.

[14]Ibid., p. 99. [Emphasis in original].

[15]U.S. Department of State, Washington, D.C. interviews with a selected group of legal advisers, February 14, 1973.

[16]See: U.S., Congress, Senate, Committee on Finance, Skyjacking, Hearing before the Committee on Finance on H.R. 19444, 91st Cong., 2nd sess., 1970; U.S. Congress, Senate, Anti-Hijacking Act of 1971, Pub. 78-542 0, 92nd Cong., 2nd sess., 1972, S. 2280, S. 2299, S.3815, S. 3871; U.S., Congress, Senate, Committee on Commerce, The Administration's Emergency

the United States has abandoned any international efforts to equate piracy in the air with customary law of piracy on the high seas.[17]

The new crime, it seemed, deserved a more suitable, legally enforcible name and definition. Grappling with semantics became not only a lawyer's pastime, but also a barrier to effective international efforts to suppress the crime. Air piracy could be described and the international instrument calling for enforcement against such an act took effect on September 30, 1962, with the ratification of the required twenty-two states to the Geneva Convention of the High Seas.[18] The problem, however, was simply that the offense recognized under customary international law as "air piracy" was not tantamount to the unlawful acts against aircraft which had begun to occur at increasingly alarming rates.

Since 90% of the crimes from 1958 to 1962 occurred in the Western Hemisphere, _viz._, the United States, the

---

Anti-Hijacking Regulations, Hearings before the subcommittee on Aviation, Senate, on S.39, 93rd Cong., 1st sess., 1973; U.S. Congress, Senate, _A Bill to Amend the Federal Aviation Act of 1958_, 93rd Cong., 1st sess., 1973, S. 39.

[17]Personal Interview with Mr. Clappin, Aviation Affairs, Federal Aeronautics Administration, Washington, D.C., February 15, 1973.

[18]Whiteman, _Digest_, p. 739.

Carribbean, and the North East of Mexico, it could be argued that "aircraft hijacking" posed more of a regional than an international phenomena.[19] Although the initial instance of aircraft seizure occurred in Peru,[20] one official has noted that the

> . . . first real rash of this disease breaks [sic] out in the 4 years 1947 to 1950 during which there were 14 attempts, all in the Eastern Hemisphere. Out of these 14 crimes, 7 were committed in Europe in the year 1948. Nothing in 1951, and only two in the years 1952 and 1953 both of which were also in the Eastern Hemisphere.[21]

By the early 1960's the number of aircraft seizure attempts rose in both the Eastern and Western Hemispheres, while the legal situation of hijacking of aircraft remained obscure. Granted that hijacking of aircraft did not become a genuine threat to world peace until 1970, "by the time the hijacking problem has assumed proportions sufficiently significant to engage the attention of the entire world community, the leading aviation states had already initiated action in ICAO."[22]

---

[19]Remarks by M. A. Rojinsky, Secretary-General of the I.C.A.A. at an Airport Security Seminar in London, November 29-30, 1971, in Hijacking, p. 2.

[20]Boyle, "Aircraft Hijacking," p. 461. Interestingly enough, the pilot of the plane hijacked in 1930 was also the pilot of the first jet hijacked in 1961. See James Arey, The Sky Pirates (New York: Schribner, 1972), p. 57.

[21]Rojinsky, Hijacking, p. 1.

[22]Horlick, "The Public and Private International Response," p. 166.

As early as 1952, the Legal Subcommittee of the International Civil Aviation Organization, a specialized agency of the United Nations, began a study to survey various responsibilities of the aircraft commander vis-à-vis jurisdictional problems of crimes committed aboard aircraft.[23] Its efforts eventually led to a full-scale inquiry into the problems, culminating in the Tokyo Convention of 1963.[24] The Convention represented a fresh international legal approach to cope with aircraft seizures by segregating the legal niceties of "air piracy" in contrast to the implications stemming from traditional "sea piracy."[25]

At the March-April 1962 meeting of the ICAO Legal Subcommittee in Montreal, attention focused on the

---

[23]A specialized agency of the U.N. since 1947, the I.C.A.O. is comprised of 122 states, including Cuba and all states to which aircraft have been diverted except North Korea, East Germany and North Vietnam. Its competence to deal with aircraft hijackings rests in the fact that the I.C.A.O. closely associates itself with all significant aviation organizations, particularly the I.A.T.A. and the F.A.A. See "International Civil Aviation Organization," Yearbook of International Organizations, (1971), 1010-27.

[24]International Conference on Air Law, Tokyo (August-September 1963), sponsored by I.C.A.O. Doc. 8565-LC/152-2. Hereafter cited as Tokyo Convention, and may be found as Appendix D, *infra*, pp. 283-293.

[25]For an interesting discussion of aircraft hijacking as "pseudo-piracy," as opposed to "true piracy," see "Seeking a Definition for Piracy in the Air," ITA Bulletin, 13 (March 30, 1970), 321-4.

rationalization of various state claims to prescriptive jurisdiction over airborne crimes.[26] The problem was manifest in the creation of an international law dealing with aircraft seizures--a law which would clearly define state jurisdiction over those who commit the crime. Jurisdiction remained the core of the hijacking problem for international law.[27]

During the March-April meeting, the United States and Venezuela jointly suggested that items of the draft deal with (1) custody; (2) extradition; (3) punishment; and (4) restoration of control of the aircraft to its commander to ensure a safe continuation of the journey.[28] The former, three proposed sections

> . . . would have required the state in which the plane landed to take custody of the hijacker and, if so requested, to extradite him either to the state of registry of the aircraft or to the state in whose territory the hijacking occurred. If extradition were not requested, the state of landing could try the hijacker under its own laws.[29]

Despite considerable discussion, each of these proposals were deleted at the Fourteenth Session of the ICAO Legal Committee held in Rome, August-September, 1962.[30] The

---

[26]Documents of the Legal Committee, Fourteenth Session, ICAO Doc. 8302, LC/150-2 at 71 (1963).

[27]*Ibid.*

[28]*Ibid.*

[29]McKeithen, "Prospects for the Prevention," p. 63.

[30]Minutes of the Legal Committee, Fourteenth Session, ICAO Doc. 8302, LC/150-1, 149-160 (1963).

remaining section concerning the restoration of control to the aircraft commander and the safety of the passengers, crew, and cargo was retained in the draft convention. Soon thereafter, the Committee recommended the adoption of the Rome reports at an international convention to be held in Tokyo in the fall of 1963.[31]

Unlike the Geneva Convention of 1958 which had defined piracy as a specific area in which international law might effectively operate,[32] the Tokyo Convention on Offenses and Certain Other Acts Committed on Board Aircraft did not confine its subject matter solely to aircraft hijacking. Instead of using the term "hijacker," the Tokyo Convention mentions only "offenders" and relates to all crimes committed on board aircraft.[33] While the Convention does offer several sections which directly reflect the hijacking problem, per se, ". . . its principal emphasis is on assuring that at least one State will have criminal jurisdiction over offenses committed on board a civil aircraft in flight."[34]

---

[31]Ibid.

[32]See Geneva Convention on the High Seas, Articles 14-22, infra, pp. 279-281.

[33]McKeithen, "Prospects for the Prevention," p. 63.

[34]K. E. Malmborg, "Malmborg Sees Advance in Hijack Conventions," Virginia Law Weekly, DICTA, Vol. XXIV, No. 17 (1972), p. 1.

One writer, Sami Shubber, has suggested in the British Yearbook of International Law that certain aspects of the Tokyo Convention relating to hijacking might be viewed as "a special, perhaps a limited, type of piracy."[35] It has been previously stated that the salience of traditional international cooperation to suppress piracy on the high seas stemmed from the universal jurisdiction of states to apprehend and punish pirates.[36] Thus, in order to determine whether the Tokyo Convention resembles piracy *jure gentium*, it is necessary to analyze pertinent sections that might reveal a relationship (if any) between offenses committed on board aircraft and the classic elements of sea piracy under the law of nations.[37]

Purposes of the Tokyo Convention

Unlike Shubber's contention that the Tokyo Convention might reflect a special form of piracy in international

---

[35]Shubber, "Is Hijacking of Aircraft Piracy?," p. 202.

[36]Johnson, "Piracy in Modern International Law," p. 71. See *supra*, pp. 24-27.

[37]Remarks on the Tokyo Convention will be confined primarily to those areas reflecting traditional legal problems associated with piracy *jure gentium*, *viz.*, definition of the crime, jurisdiction of states to apprehend and prosecute the offenders, and determining whether unlawful aircraft seizure is an international crime. See Shubber, "Is Hijacking of Aircraft Piracy?," pp. 199-204.

law, the actual stated purpose of the Convention was ". . . to promote aviation safety through establishment of continuity of jurisdiction over criminal acts occurring on board aircraft."[38] In addition, Robert P. Boyle, Chief U.S. Delegate to the Tokyo Convention, indicated four specific purposes which the Convention was designed to achieve:

> 1. To confirm the jurisdiction of the flag state over offenses committed aboard an aircraft in flight;
> 2. To confer power on the commander in order to enhance safety of flight;
> 3. To define the duties of the state where the aircraft lands after commission of the offense; and
> 4. To deal with hijacking.[39]

Scope of the Tokyo Convention

It can be readily seen from all the above-mentioned purposes that the Convention dealt primarily with the free-passage of the endangered aircraft, not with concrete international solutions to the hijacking problem. Rather than distinctively define offenses aboard aircraft, Article 1 of the Tokyo Convention broadly indicates that the Convention

---

[38]U.S. Congress, House, Committee on Interstate and Foreign Commerce, Implementation of Tokyo Convention, Hearings before a subcommittee on Transportation and Aeronautics, House of Representatives, on H.R. 14301, 91st Cong., 1st sess., 1969, p. 5.

[39]Boyle and Pulsifer, "The Tokyo Convention," p. 328. Turner proposes an additional purpose of the Tokyo Convention, *viz.*, ". . . to define the rights and status of a person detained in a foreign state after commission of an offense." Turner, "Piracy in the Air," p. 101.

applies to:

> a) offenses against penal law;
> b) acts which, whether or not they are offenses, may or do jeopardize the safety of the aircraft or of persons or property therein or which jeopardize good order and discipline on board.[40]

Thus, no attempt is made to define or elaborate upon any act falling under the aegis of the Convention. Municipal law is paramount, and it remains for individual states to determine what constitutes an offense against their own criminal code.[41] Furthermore, subparagraph (b), paragraph 1 of Article 1 states that acts committed need not be defined as offenses under municipal law.[42] The Convention presumably encompasses any act, subject only to one's imagination, which might place the safety of an aircraft in jeopardy.[43]

Admittedly, at this nascent stage of international development towards a law of hijacking, a stringent definition of the crime may have been unwise. However, it

---

[40]Tokyo Convention, Article 1.

[41]For an analysis of the application of U.S. municipal law to aircraft hijacking cases, see John A. Volpe and John T. Stewart, Jr., "Aircraft Hijacking: Some Domestic and International Responses," Kentucky Law Journal 59 (Winter, 1971), pp. 273-305.

[42]Tokyo Convention, Article 1, Paragraph 1, Subparagraph (b).

[43]See Horlick, "The Public and Private International Response," p. 168 and A. I. Mendelsohn, "In-flight Crime: The International and Domestic Picture under the Tokyo Convention," Virginia Law Review 53 (1967), pp. 513-4.

seems unlikely that states would genuinely respect a convention which does not exclude any criminal jurisdiction exercised under national law.[44]

Article 1 is further qualified in several respects. Firstly, the Convention applies only to offenses or

> . . . acts done by a person on board any aircraft registered in a Contracting State, while that aircraft is in flight or on the surface of the high seas or of any other area outside the territory of any State.[45]

Since the Convention considers an aircraft to be ". . . in flight from the moment when power is applied for the purpose of take-off until the moment when the landing run ends,"[46] it is conceivable that bizarre cases of hijacking, such as the "Cooper Incident," in which the hijacker parachuted out of the plane, would be excluded from the scope of the Convention.[47]

Secondly, Article 1, paragraph 4 clearly omits any military, customs, or police service aircraft from the

---

[44]See Boyle, "Aircraft Hijacking," p. 463.

[45]Tokyo Convention, Article 1, Paragraph 2.

[46]*Ibid.*, Article 1, Paragraph 3.

[47]On November 11, 1971, "D. B. Cooper" seized control of a B-727, bound from Portland, Oregon, to Seattle, Washington. After receiving his extortion demands of $200,000 and four parachutes from ground authorities in Seattle, the plane resumed flight, and "Cooper" parachuted out somewhere in route to Reno, Nevada. As of February 1, 1973, the office of Air Transportation Security still classifies him as "fugitive." Federal Aviation Administration, Office of Air Transportation Security, *Chronology of Hijackings of U.S. Registered Aircraft*, Updated February 1, 1973, p. 12.

jurisdictional parameter of the Convention.[48] The omission of military aircraft from the scope of the Convention probably resulted from the same nation-state concern as that regarding piracy on the high seas--that states themselves should maintain jurisdiction over military vessels.[49] However, it should be noted that offenses committed aboard military aircraft are quite nominal as compared to the rising number of offenses occurring aboard commercial planes.[50] And it was the latter, not the former, to which international attention had turned.

Article 2 has likely provoked the most extensive comment of any of the Convention's stipulations.[51] In the case of piracy *jure gentium*, emphasis had been traditionally placed on the requirement that the act of depredation on the high seas be performed for private ends. Motivation of the alleged pirate was determined more through an analysis of intentions for perpetrating the act.[52] In the Tokyo

---

[48]Tokyo Convention, Article 1, Paragraph 4.

[49]Provisions excluding military, customs and police aircraft from aviation conventions are a firmly established principle. See for example, Chicago Convention on International Civil Aviation, Article 3, U.S. T.I.A.S. 1591; 61 Stat. 1180, 1181; 15 UNTS 295, 298.

[50]Thus, Article 1, Section 4 of the Tokyo Convention did not apply to the ". . . attempted hijacking of a commercial jetliner chartered for military airlift . . ." on February 9, 1968. Turner, "Piracy in the Air," p. 101.

[51]See Tokyo Convention, Article 2.

[52]See Harvard Draft Research, Article 3, Section 1, *infra*, p. 272.

Convention, however, states agreed to wide discretion in determining the motivation of the offender. In fact, the latitude of states in assessing the undergirding reasons for the offense is so broad that nearly any offense (excepting those performed by the most notorious of criminals) may be excluded from the scope of the Convention.[53]

Article 2 indicated that:

> Without prejudice to the provisions of Article 4 and except when the safety of the aircraft or of persons or property on board so requires, no provision of this Convention shall be interpreted as authorizing or requiring any action in respect of offenses against penal laws of a political nature of those based on racial or religious discrimination.[54]

Article 4's exception to all political, racial, or religious overtones, coupled with a failure to provide a proper definition of the crime, left the "Convention on Offenses and Certain Other Acts Committed on Board Aircraft" nearly devoid of applicable incidents. It will be recalled that the first recorded aircraft seizure concerned Peruvian

---

[53]Under the principle of "specialty" hijackers may only be tried for the extraditable offense, which must be listed in the treaty as a crime under both the laws of the surrendering and receiving state. Since aircraft hijacking contains elements of many common crimes, such as robbery, kidnapping, or assault, states often extradite known criminals on the basis of the more ordinary crimes, rather than a specific agreement to return "aircraft hijackers" per se. See John P. McMahon, "Air Hijacking: Extradition as a Deterrent," The Georgetown Law Journal 58 (1970), pp. 1137-38.

[54]Tokyo Convention, Article 2. [Author's emphasis added.]

revolutionaries; cases in the late 1940's and mid-1950's were provoked by political turmoil in Eastern Europe; and those of the late 1950's and early 1960's are traced to Fidel Castro's activities in Cuba.[55] Since any of the successful offenders could still be received in the state of landing as welcomed political refugees, the inadequacy of the Tokyo Convention as a "suppressive device" for hijacking becomes patently obvious.[56]

Provision on Hijacking

Chapter 4, Article 11 has been cited as the first codified attempt to specifically qualify hijacking as an international crime. It stipulates that:

> (1) When a person on board has unlawfully committed by force or threat thereof an act of interference, seizure, or other wrongful exercise of control of an aircraft in flight or when such an act is about to be committed, Contracting states shall take all appropriate measures to restore control of the aircraft to its lawful commander or to preserve his control of the aircraft.[57]

---

[55] Ibid., Article 4; Boyle, "Aircraft Hijacking," p. 461.

[56] In his 1969 address to the General Assembly, President Nixon indicated that hijackings could not be curtailed as long as ". . . the pirates received asylum." Department of State Bulletin 61 (1969), 300. Also for an excellent analysis of the political offense exemption and a discussion of Anglo-American, French, and Swiss approaches for granting political asylum, see McMahon, "Extradition as a Deterrent," pp. 1138-44.

[57] Tokyo Convention, Chapter 4, Article 11, Paragraph 1.

Moreover, the second paragraph of Article 11 provides an affirmative obligation for signatory states to permit the passengers and crew of the unlawfully seized vessel ". . . to continue their journey as soon as practicable and . . . return the aircraft and its cargo to the persons lawfully entitled to possession."[58]

Viewed in the aggregate, McWhinney asserts that these two sub-sections form ". . . a legal pleonasm."[59] The obligation to restore aircraft control to the commander and allow the passengers and crew to safely continue their flight already exists ". . . under customary international law, on the analogy of foreign vessels entering the port of another country, in distress."[60]

The limited, special type of piracy formerly alluded to by Shubber, finds expression in Article 11, paragraph 1.[61] Drawing on McWhinney's analysis of the right of entry in distress under customary law and Shubber's contention that the Contracting States obligate themselves to take all necessary measures to restore control of the hijacked aircraft and all personnel aboard, it becomes obvious that emphasis is placed on the safe return of the aircraft, not

---

[58] *Ibid.*, Chapter 4, Article 11, Paragraph 2.

[59] McWhinney, "International Legal Problem Solving," in McWhinney, ed., *Aerial Piracy*, p. 21.

[60] *Ibid.*

[61] Cf. Shubber, "Is Hijacking of aircraft Piracy?," pp. 194-98 and Tokyo Convention, Article 11, Paragraph 1, *infra*, p. 287.

on prosecution of the offender.[62] Rather than allow universal jurisdiction (the crux of internatiional support against piracy jure gentium), the Convention merely calls for "universal coercive measures" to be taken against the hijackers by the signatory states.[63]

Regretfully, no effort is made to describe hijacking as an international crime, nor does the Tokyo Convention grant any kind of universal jurisdiction for the apprehension and punishment of hijackers.[64]

Jurisdiction Over the Offender

While the Tokyo Convention does not require mandatory extradition or punishment of hijackers, it does recognize several categories of possible state responses to seizures. Article 13 asserts that signatory states ". . . shall take delivery of any person whom the aircraft commander delivers pursuant to Article 9, paragraph (1)," which grants the pilot broad descretion in disembarking (in the state of landing) any person seriously suspected of hijacking.[65]

---

[62]Cf. McWhinney, "International Legal Problem Solving;" pp. 21-22 and Shubber, "Is Hijacking of Aircraft Piracy?," pp. 194-198.

[63]*Aviation Week and Space Technology*, Vol. 91, No. 10, September 8, 1969, p. 14.

[64]*Ibid.*; It should be recalled that more forceful sections dealing with custody, punishment, and extradition of the offender were deleted at the Fourteenth Session of the I.C.A.O. Legal Committee meeting in Rome (August, 1962). See *supra*, note 26.

[65]Tokyo Convention, Article 13, Paragraph 1, and Article 9, Paragraph 1.

However, police officials in the landing state need not automatically take custody of the alleged offender. Temporary detention regarding the hijacker is qualified in that officials of the landing state are to be the sole determinants as to whether ". . . circumstances warrant placing the accused in custory."[66]

Should the state of landing assume custody of the offender, it is obligated under Article 13, paragraph 5 to ". . . immediately make a preliminary inquiry into the facts."[67] Once investigated, a report of the circumstances must be presented to the state of registration of the aircraft and the state of nationality of the hijacker.[68]

Though Article 13 ensures courteous notification of the state of aircraft registry and the state of which the hijacker is a national, the state of landing may legally refuse to admit the hijacker. If such an option is chosen, the landing state is only obligated to ". . . return him to the territory of the State of which he is a national or permanent resident or to the territory of the State in which he began his journey by air."[69] At best, such provisions

---

[66]*Ibid.*, Article 13, Paragraphs 1 and 2.

[67]*Ibid.*, Article 13, Paragraph 5.

[68]*Ibid.*; See also McKeithen, "Prospects for the Prevention," p. 64.

[69]Tokyo Convention, Article 14, Paragraph 1.

provide only minimum standards of conduct on the part of the Contracting States. Little foundation is laid for an international punitive system, supported by municipal criminal codes, to deter the hijacking menace.[70]

Assertion of State Jurisdiction

K. E. Malmborg, of the Legal Division, U.S. Department of State, asserts that the primary thrust of the Tokyo Convention is to assure ". . . that at least one State will have criminal jurisdiction over offenses committed on board a civil aircraft in flight."[71] Since Article 3, paragraph 1 recognizes the competency of the state in which the aircraft is registered ". . . to exercise jurisdiction over offenses and acts committed on board," the "law of the flag" seems to be firmly established.[73] Support for the jurisdiction

---

[70]McWhinney attributes the weakness of the Convention to inherent political bargaining. By eliminating the hard-line U.S. approach for punishment of hijackers in favor of a "vaguer," "more modest" draft, the I.C.A.O. draft blended ". . . the worst elements of the two alternative policy choices . . . a convention without teeth in it, and one with very, very few ratifications." McWhinney, "International Problem-Solving," in McWhinney, ed., Aerial Piracy, p. 21.

[71]Malmborg, "Hijack Conventions," p. 1.

[72]Tokyo Convention, Article 3, Paragraph 1.

[73]The "law of the flag" implies that an aircraft forms a ". . . movable piece of national territory." State jurisdiction over the flag aircraft extends to the surface of the high seas or any other area outside the territory of any state." "Crime in the Air," The Economist, August 31, 1963, 723; See also Turner, "Piracy in the Air," p. 101 and Boyle and Pulsifer, "The Tokyo Convention," p. 333.

of the flag state is reinforced in Article 4, which instructs other states (particularly the state in which the offense occurred) not to interfere with the flight of the aircraft in order to secure jurisdiction, unless the offense directly affects its territory or nationals.[74]

In his message to the Senate calling for ratification of the Tokyo Convention, President Lyndon Johnson postulated that

> . . . a positive rule of international law is established between contracting states which provides that the State in which an aircraft is registered is competent to exercise jurisdiction over offenses committed aboard that aircraft when it is in flight . . . however The Tokyo Convention does not establish a rule of exclusive jurisdiction. . . .[75]

Instead, the Convention provides for concurrent jurisdiction reflecting traditional jurisdictional rules of international law.[76]

Thus, while the Convention upholds the operation of the law of the flag, it also alludes to possible assertion of jurisdiction according to the principles of territory, active nationality, protective, and passive nationality.[77]

---

[74]Tokyo Convention, Article 4, Sub-paragraphs a-e.

[75]Lyndon B. Johnson, "Convention on Offenses and Certain Other Acts Committed on Board Aircraft - Removal of Injunction of Secrecy," Congressional Record, September 25, 1968, p. S11450.

[76]*Ibid*.

[77]Turner, "Piracy in the Air," p. 101, Cf. note 73.

Article 4 allows a state whose interests have been directly affected to exercise jurisdiction on the basis of territory or nationality.[78] While a broad, liberal interpretation of the jurisdictional aspects of the Convention approach the customary requirement of universal jurisdiction against sea pirates, lack of a firm committment for punishment of the offender renders Article 3, paragraph 3 and Article 4 basically ineffectual.[79] D. H. N. Johnson confirms this analysis of the jurisdictional provisions in the Tokyo Convention as he posits, ". . . there is a danger that, whereas in the past there has sometimes been insufficient jurisdiction with regard to crimes committed on board aircraft, there may in future be too much."[80]

Extradition

For the purpose of extradition, the Tokyo Convention provides that offenses committed on board an aircraft (in any area not within the territorial jurisdiction of the flag state) should be considered as having been committed in the

---

[78]See Tokyo Convention, Article 4, <u>infra</u>, p. 284.

[79]Cf. Articles 3 and 4 of the Tokyo Convention, <u>infra</u> , p. 284, with the discussion concerning universal jurisdiction, <u>supra</u>, pp. 24-27.

[80]D. H. N. Johnson, <u>Rights in Air Space</u> (Dobbs Ferry, N.Y.: Oceana Publications, Inc., 1965), pp. 78-79.

place in which they occurred and in the territory of the flag state.[81] Article 16, paragraph 2, however, qualifies this provision in that ". . . nothing in this Convention shall be deemed to create an obligation to grant extradition." Consequently, no definite obligation exists between the state in which the aircraft lands and the flag state, unless an extradition treaty is in force between the two parties denoting the crime as an extraditable offense.[82]

In essence, the Tokyo Convention recognizes a legitimate right of the state in which the incident occurred and the flag state to request extradition of the offender. Theoretically, Articles 13-15 provide a pattern which officials of the state in which the aircraft lands may follow: Article 13 suggests that the hijacker be taken into custody and a preliminary inquiry be made; Article 4 further indicates that the offender be expelled at the wishes of the receiving state; and Article 15 calls for

---

[81]Tokyo Convention, Article 16, Paragraph 1.

[82]Customary international law does not impose a duty upon states to extradite offenders. Rather, it is purely a matter of comity or treaty obligation. Such treaties, however, frequently prohibit extradition if the offense is not a crime under the laws of both states. See note 53, supra., p. 131. Gerald F. Fitzgerald, "The Development of International Rules Concerning Offenses and Certain Other Acts Committed on Board Aircraft," Canadian Yearbook of International Law 1963 (Vancouver: University of British Columbia, 1963), p. 250; and Boyle and Pulsifer, "The Tokyo Convention," p. 345.

extradition or prosecution of the offender at the discretion of the landing state.[83] If circumstances warrant and the offender evades each of these Convention provisions, he is virtually assured of liberty. As R. L. Smith McKeithen remarked, "Because of this wide latitude which the Convention gives to Contracting States, . . . [it] recognizes and legitimizes their right to do as they wish with hijackers."[84]

Limitations of the Tokyo Convention

As a first effort towards a law of nations approach to aircraft hijacking, the Tokyo Convention is perhaps more notable for what it omits than for what it includes. On the positive side, the Convention abided by the basic norm of international law respecting jurisdiction among contracting states. It reaffirmed the "law of the flag," a principle sacred to maritime law, but also alluded to concurrent jurisdiction among contracting states whose interests have been adversely affected through offenses committed on board aircraft in flight.[85]

Most assuredly, ratification of the Convention signifies approval of a multi-state approach to promote international aviation safety. Yet the thrust of the Convention--the restoration of aircraft control to the commander and

---

[83] Tokyo Convention, Articles 13-15.

[84] McKeithen, "Prospects for the Prevention," p. 64.

[85] On the "law of the flag" see <u>supra</u>, pp. 78-82.

expeditious continuation of the journey for the passengers and crew--seemed only to reiterate an already established, viable principle of international law.[86] With the deletion of more forceful draft provisions on custody, extradition, and punishment of the offender, the Convention opened for signatures on September 14, 1963, proved to be a very shallow one indeed.

It would be fair to say, moreover, that the Tokyo Convention was neither a hijacking prevention device nor even a hijacking convention per se. Only Article 11 directly relates to the phenomena of hijacking, though it provides no definition or suggestion that the "unlawful seizure of aircraft" might deem recognition as an international crime.[87] While the substance of the Convention dates to Geneva in 1956, hijacking did not rate recognition as a separate category until 1962, when the United States and Venezuela introduced provisions relating to the concept for acceptance in the draft convention. As previously

---

[86]On the analogy of the entry of a vessel in distress, see Moore, International Law, Vol. 2, pp. 339-362; Hackworth, International Law, pp. 277-282; and Harvard Research in International Law, Territorial Waters, A.J.I.L. Spec. Supp. 23 (1929), 299 et seq.; It appears to be an already established principle among states, whether parties to the Tokyo Convention or not, to expedite the speedy return of a hijacked vessel in conformity to the standard set in Article 11.

[87]See Horlick, "The Developing Law," pp. 35-36, and Robert T. Turi, et al., Criminal Justice Monograph, "Descriptive Study of Aircraft Hijacking," Vol. 3, No. 5 (1972), pp. 60-61.

indicated, the proposals were deleted, and it appeared that the international community was not ". . . ready to attempt to deal with the entire problem."[88]

By the fall of 1963, aircraft hijackings had not yet affected a multiplicity of states, and immediate attention to the Tokyo Convention may have seemed less imperative than other pressing international matters.[89] Consequently, the Convention did not go into effect until December 4, 1969, six years after the initial signing, when the required twelve ratifications were deposited with the ICAO in Montreal. Ironically, the United States--the nation most heavily affected by aircraft seizures--claimed the dubious honor of being the twelfth state to become a party to the Convention. During the six years prior to Senate approval of the Tokyo Convention (between September 14, 1963 and September 5, 1969), sixty hijacking attempts occurred involving the United States either as the flag state, the state in

---

[88]Boyle, "Aircraft Hijacking," pp. 462-63.

[89]Many international events of 1962-1964 overshadowed the Tokyo Convention. The Cuban missile crisis, extension of the Sino-Soviet rift, the India-China border hostilities, the Cyprus dispute, the aftermath of President Kennedy's assassination, the internal war in Yemen, and the Nuclear Test Ban Treaty were among them. See Young Hum Kim, Twenty Years of Crises: The Cold War Era (Englewood Cliffs, N.J.: Prentice-Hall, Inc., 1968), pp. 198-255.

which the aircraft landed, or the state from which the seized aircraft ascended. Over half of the incidents (including both successful and unsuccessful attempts) occurred between January 2 and August 29, 1969. The phenomenal increase of hijacking activities during that period may well have been the major incentive for Senate approval of the Tokyo Convention.[90]

Indeed, it is quite probable that increased support of the Convention since the fall of 1969 resulted from the

---

[90]Figures for the number of aircraft attempts vary according to the compiler's criteria. Cf. Evans, "Aircraft Hijacking," p. 698; House Committee on Foreign Affairs, Subcommittee on Inter-American Affairs, Air Piracy in the Caribbean Area, 90th Cong., 2nd Sess. (Committee Print, 1968); F.A.A. Statistics; reports from I.C.A.A., Hijacking; and statistics found in the New York Times Index, January, 1960 through September, 1969. A synthesis of these sources was compiled for this author's data, cited herein as F.A.A. Statistics.

At this point, distinctions should be made in the process of treaty formulation. Gerald J. Mangone provides a useful description as he posits:

> The gravity of international obligations through treaties has traditionally been underscored by procedure, consisting of: signature by a person with 'full powers,' a plenipotentiary; then ratification by the constitutional processes of the contracting states; then an exchange of ratifications between states, or a deposit of the ratification with a state or an international organization. Modern treaties ordinarily require the ratification of a state after its representative has signed the document to make the agreement binding. Other conditions to give legal effect to a treaty may be specified, and in the case of multilateral agreements a minimum number of ratifications may be necessary before the treaty has any binding force.

Gerald J. Mangone, The Elements of International Law (Homewood, Illinois: The Dorsey Press, 1967), p. 88. Thus, signing the agreement is merely initial approval by a national delegate, whereas ratification becomes more significant in that it is formal acceptance by a nation's government.

upsurge of hijacking attempts on both a world-wide and individual state level. Thus, nations previously unaffected by hijacking threats showed little inclination to overtly support the Convention until an incident occurred within their territorial jurisdictions or aboard aircraft registered in their countries. Japan, for example, had maintained no laws respecting hijacking nor had it ratified the Tokyo Convention" . . . until a Japan Air Lines Boeing 727 was forced to fly to North Korea by a band of radicals."[91] Japan promptly affixed its approval to the Convention on May 26, 1970, less than two months after the aircraft take-over by the revolutionary students of the "Red Army."[92]

Though it cannot conclusively be determined that the frequency of hijacking attempts within a state solely account for that state's ratification of the Tokyo Convention, it does appear to catalyze state legislative bodies. Between September 14, 1963 and December 2, 1969, 42 states became signatories to the Tokyo Convention. Of this group, 16 had signed the Convention to the former date. Yet eight of the total 42 signatory states, viz., Colombia, Congo (Brazzaville), the

---

[91]"Anti-Hijacking Proposals Proliferate," Aviation Week and Space Technology, Vol. 93, No. 12, September 21, 1970, p. 27.

[92]The plane was hijacked by the nine students after take-off from Tokyo to Fukuoka. Japanese and South Korean officials attempted to divert the plane to Seoul, but without success. Passengers and Hijackers were held on board for seventy-five hours until an agreement was reached. Then the plane departed for Pyongyang, North Korea with government official Yamamura and the hijackers aboard. Thirty-six hours later, the craft safely returend to Tokyo with all crew and Yamamura. "Fly Me to Pyongyang: Japan Airlines 727," Newsweek, Vol. 75 (April 13, 1970), p. 40.

Holy See, Indonesia, Ireland, Liberia, Pakistan, and Venezuela, are not yet parties to the Convention ". . . in accordance with their constitutional procedures."[93]

Attendance at the Convention, however, does not guarantee a state's ratification, nor does it preclude ratification by other states which choose not to send delegates. Both Articles 19 and 22 invite accession by members of the United Nations or of any U.N. specialized agencies.[94] Theoretically over 150 states and territories would be eligible to accede to the Convention,[95] though it is not likely that some of the smaller states would elect to do so--particularly those which do not currently maintain commercial air facilities.[96] Since hijacking problems

---

[93]As of January 10, 1973, signatory dates for the eight non-party members are as follows:

Colombia: November 8, 1968
Congo (Brazzaville); September 14, 1963
The Holy See: September 14, 1963
Indonesia: September 14, 1963
Ireland: October 20, 1964
Liberia: September 14, 1963
Pakistan: August 6, 1965
Venezuela: March 13, 1964

Data from: U.S., Congress, Senate, _Report of the Senate Committee on Commerce_ on S. 39, Report No. 93-13, 93rd Cong., 1st sess., February 2, 1973, pp. 51-53.

[94]See _infra_, pp. 290-291.

[95]See John Paxton, ed., _The Statesman's Yearbook 1972-1973_ (London: The Macmillan Press, Ltd., 1972), pp. 10-13.

[96]For the international rating and comparison of world airports, see B. J. Hurren, _Airports of the World_ (London: Wolfe Publishing Limited, 1970).

more greatly affect the larger "aviation states," the significance of the Convention lies in the number of these states which became parties, not merely in an overwhelming number of ratifications.

The rate at which states became parties to the Tokyo Convention may be arbitrarily divided into three periods: early, middle-range, and late. By surveying the number of hijacking attempts which occurred prior to the accession of each state, a causal relationship may be suggested between the number of hijackings directly involving a state (i.e., a hijacking aboard a state's flag aircraft, the landing of a seized aircraft within state territory, or the take-off of a hijacked aircraft from the state's soil) and state willingness to become a party to the Tokyo Convention.[97] As of June 11, 1973, only sixty-three states had registered accession to the Convention, and the rate at which official approval was granted seemed alarmingly slow.[98] However, towards the latter period it appears that as the frequency of air hijacking incidents increases, the number of states becoming parties to the Tokyo Convention proportionately increases. Tables 1, 2, and 3 illustrate this point.

---

[97]N.B. The figures used in this analysis are not inclusive of all international hijackings for these designated periods. Rather, they represent the number of hijackings which directly affected nations who were parties and/or signatories to the Tokyo Convention.

[98]U.S., Congress, Senate, Report of the Senate Committee on Commerce on S. 39, p. 53.

TABLE 1

EXPOSURE TO HIJACKING ATTEMPTS AND INDIVIDUAL STATE SUPPORT OF THE TOKYO CONVENTION (AS OF JUNE 11, 1973)
EARLY PARTIES

State	A. Date Became Party	B. Date Became Signatory	Number of Months Between A. and B.	Number of Incidents Between 1960 & B.	Number of Incidents Between A. and B.
Portugal	11/15/64	3/11/64	8	1	0
Phillipines	11/26/65	9/14/63	26	0	0
Republic of China	2/28/66	9/14/63	29	0	0
Denmark	1/17/67	11/21/66	13	0	0
Norway	1/17/67	4/19/66	9	0	0
Sweden	1/17/67	9/14/63	39	0	0

Among the "Early Parties," only Portugal experienced a hijacking attempt prior to its signing of the Tokyo Convention. The incident, which occurred on November 10, 1961, concerned a small group of Portuguese political activists who successfully seized a Portuguese aircraft in order to drop political leaflets over Lisbon. The plane landed safely in Morocco, where the offenders received temporary political asylum.[99] Each of the other five states in the first group signed and ratified the Convention between 1964 and 1967, but apparently had not been directly influenced by any aircraft hijacking incidents occurring between 1960 to the time of ratification.

In the "Middle-Range" category (see Table 2) a slightly different pattern emerged from that exhibited by the "Early Parties." Though Italy and the United Kingdom both signed on September 14, 1963, neither recorded any hijacking attempts between 1960 and that date. However, Italy experienced its first hijacking incident on July 23, 1968,[100]

---

[99]A Portuguese airliner on the regular Casablanca-Lisbon flight was seized in mid-air by five armed men and a woman, all Portuguese supporters of Captain Henrique Galvao (See <u>supra</u>, pp. 206-13). They forced the pilot to circle Lisbon without landing while they dropped leaflets calling upon the population to refrain from voting by helping Captain Galvao in the "war against the Salazar regime." The plane then flew back to Morocco and landed in Tangier. Captain Galvao, with his political supporters who had seized the plane, were subsequently expelled from Morocco on November 17 for "subversive action against a neighboring country," but were able to receive conditional asylum in Brazil. <u>Keesing's Contemporary Archives</u>, Vol. 13 (1961-62), p. 18546.

[100]New York <u>Times</u>, July 23, 1:7.

TABLE 2

EXPOSURE TO HIJACKING ATTEMPTS AND INDIVIDUAL STATE SUPPORT OF THE TOKYO CONVENTION MIDDLE-RANGE (1968-1970)

State	A. Date Became Party	B. Date Became Signatory	Number of months between A. and B.	Number of incidents between 1960 & B.	Number of incidents between A. and B.
Italy	10/18/68	9/14/63	61	0	1
United Kingdom	11/29/68	9/14/63	62	0	3
Mexico	3/18/69	12/24/68	3	1	5
Upper Volta	6/6/69	9/14/63	69	0	0
Niger	6/24/69	4/14/69	2	1	0
United States	9/5/69	9/14/63	72	12	60
Israel	9/19/69	11/1/68	10	1	0
Spain	10/1/69	7/27/64	63	0	1
Canada	11/7/69	11/4/64	60	0	1
The Netherlands	11/14/69	6/9/67	29	1	0
Saudi Arabia	11/21/69	4/6/67	31	0	1
Malagasy Republic	12/2/69	12/2/69	0	0	0
Federal Republic of Germany	12/16/69	9/14/63	75	0	2

Table 2--Continued

State	A. Date Became Party	B. Date Became Signatory	Number of months between A. and B.	Number of incidents between 1960 & B.	Number of incidents between A. and B.
Brazil	1/14/70	2/28/69	11	0	4
Gabon	1/14/70	-	-	-	0*
Iceland	3/16/70	-	-	-	0*
Nigeria	4/7/70	6/29/65	58	0	1
Japan	5/26/70	9/14/63	80	0	1
Ivory Coast	6/3/70	-	-	-	0*
Kenya	6/22/70	-	-	-	0*
Australia	6/22/70	-	-	-	2*
Chad	6/30/70	-	-	-	0*
Belgium	8/6/70	12/20/68	20	0	0
France	9/11/70	7/11/69	14	1	1
Sierra Leone	11/9/70	-	-	-	0*
Panama	11/16/70	9/14/63	74	0	2
Guatemala	11/17/70	9/14/63	74	0	0

Table 2--Continued

State	A. Date Became Party	B. Date Became Signatory	Number of months between A. and B.	Number of incidents between 1960 & B.	Number of incidents between A. and B.
Dominican Republic	12/3/70	-	-	-	1*
Hungary	12/3/70	-	-	-	1*
Ecuador	12/3/70	7/8/69	17	3	2
Switzerland	12/21/70	10/31/69	14	0	2

*denotes number of incidents between 1960 and ratification.

Three months later it became a party to the Tokyo Convention, despite a delay of over five years between the initial signing and formal ratification. On the other hand, only one hijacking took place aboard a British registered aircraft prior to ratification by the United Kingdom (the infamous Tshombe Incident of June 30, 1967).[101] Yet two additional hijackings of August, 1968, involved the Bahama Islands and may have triggered British ratification of the Tokyo Convention on November 29, 1968.[102]

"Ratification fever" also seemed to touch Mexico, the Federal Republic of Germany, Brazil, Ecuador, and Switzerland, each of which were involved in more than one hijacking incident shortly before evidencing the desire to become a party to the Convention. Yet in the cases of Panama and Guatemala, each signed and ratified the Tokyo Convention on nearly identical dates, although the latter was not plagued with any hijacking attempts during the ten-year period from 1960 to the fall of 1970. In addition,

---

[101]The plane carrying the former Congolese Prime Minister was forced by a Frenchman to alter course and land at Algiers. All persons aboard the aircraft, including Tshombe, the pilots and the hijacker, were immediately placed under detention by Algerian security officials. The Algerian government justified this action to conduct official inquiry into the incident. By the end of September, 1967, all persons had been released, except for Tshombe, who was kept under detention until his death on January 29, 1969. Turi, et al., Criminal Justice Monograph, pp. 63-64.

[102]F.A.A. Statistics.

Belgium and France also signed and ratified the Tokyo Convention within a six-month period of one another. Since Belgium (as in the case of Guatemala) recorded no known hijacking incidents during a comparable ten-year span, it appears there may be some "sister-state" influence within regions, viz., Western Europe and Latin America, respectively. However, this cannot be verified to any degree of significance and may well reflect only coincidental internal politics.

Certainly, the United States was most heavily affected by the "hijacking disease" of the 1960's. Aircraft seizures aboard American flag ships and within U.S. territory accounted for the "lion's share" of all successful and unsuccessful attempts. Although the United States was a principal supporter of the Tokyo Convention in its planning stages, it did not become a party until seventy-two months after the initial signing. Several reasons can be postulated for the delay in formal ratification. First, over 96% of the hijacking attempts involved Cuba, i.e., either U.S. flag aircraft were seized at home or abroad with the avowed intent of flying to Cuba; or, foreign aircraft in Cuba were hijacked in an effort to reach American soil. Secondly, the Cuban government consistently refused to enter into any multilateral agreement to control aircraft seizures. Thus, immediate U.S. ratification of the Tokyo Convention would have had no effect upon Cuba (the primary target of U.S. hijackers) since an international agreement is not binding upon a "non-party."[103] Thirdly, the United States initiated secret negotiations with Cuba during the administration of President Lyndon B. Johnson to effectuate a bilateral agreement between the two states.[104] Parenthetically, the completion of this communique may have been anticipated sooner than the actual date on which it was announced.[105]

---

[103]A New York Times report, "Cuba Enacts Anti-Hijacking Law Providing for Extradition of Hijackers to Country of Origin," stated that the United States would remain unaffected since

> . . . laws will be applied only on basis of equality and strict reciprocity, and gives Cuba the right to determine whether hijacker is common transgressor or political refugee. Communique stresses that Cuba will not recognize any multilateral agreements worked out by such groups as U.N. or O.A.S. The move is linked to Cuban awareness of world-wide condemnation of hijackings. . . . U.S. State Department in studying the decree says 1904 extradition treaty with Cuba is technically still in effect, but virtually inapplicable in absence of diplomatic relations.

New York Times, September 20, 1969; 1:6.
On the question of "Non-party" obligations to a treaty, see Harvard Law School Research in International Law, "Law ot Treaties," A.J.I.L. Supp., 29 (1935), pp. 918 et seq.; Case Concerning Certain German Interests in Polish Upper Silesia, P.C.I.J., Judgements, Ser. A, No. 7, 1926, p. 29; Case Relating to the Territorial Jurisdiction of the International Commission of the River Oder, P.C.I.J., Judgements, Ser. A, No. 23, 1929, pp. 19-22.

[104]Personal Interview with Mark B. Feldman, Assistant Legal Adviser for Inter-American Affairs, The State Department, Washington, D.C. February 15, 1973.

[105]Ibid. The signing date of the United States-Cuban Hijacking Agreement was February 15, 1973.

However, the lack of national legislation to effectively implement the Tokyo Convention may have been more decisive than any of the aforementioned reasons suggested for the six-year lag in U.S. ratification.[106] Consequently, additional changes were required in federal criminal codes before the Tokyo Convention could become self-executing under U.S. federal law. According to Alona Evans: "Until the Federal Aviation Act was amended in 1961, prosecution for aircraft hijacking was maintained primarily on the charges of transportation of a stolen aircraft in interstate commerce, kidnapping the person aboard, or obstructing commerce by threats or violence."[107] The Senate did advise and consent to the ratification of the Convention on May 13, 1969, even though a number of more comprehensive changes in the original Federal Aviation Act of 1958, in the amended version of 1961, and in the updating of U.S. extradition treaties to include aircraft hijacking as an extraditable offense were not yet completed.[108]

---

[106]Personal Interview with Knute E. Malmborg, Assistant Legal Adviser for Management, Security and Consular Affairs, the State Department, Washington, D.C., February 13-14, 1973.

[107]Evans, "Aircraft Hijacking," pp. 696-697.

[108]The Tokyo Convention was ratified by President Nixon on June 30, 1969, deposited with the I.C.A.O. September 5, 1969, and entered into force by the United States, December 4, 1969. U.S. Department of State, Aviation: Offenses and Certain Other Acts Committed on Board Aircraft, Treaties and other International Acts Series 6768, Pubn. 0-36-139 (1969), p. 1.

Among the "Late Parties" (see Table 3) to the Tokyo Convention, only two states experienced more than two hijacking attempts aboard their flag aircraft or within their territories, i.e., Poland and Argentina, which ratified the Convention in 1971. Ratification may have been encouraged by seven attempts involving Poland which occurred between October, 1969, and August, 1970,[109] and six attempts which directly affected Argentina,[110] but were diffused between September, 1966, and July, 1970. Although Argentina waited one year after the last hijacking to ratify the Convention, Poland acted within seven months after the August 27 incident to become a party to the Convention.

While sixty-three states became parties to the Tokyo Convention, many states significantly affected by aircraft hijackings have never acceded to it. In particular, three states which signed, but did not ratify the Convention, *viz.*, Venezuela, Colombia, and the Congo, experienced twenty-two, five, and one hijacking attempts aboard their flag aircraft or within their territorial boundaries, respectively.[111] Cuban-related hijacking incidents accounted for 134

---

[109]Regarding the seven attempts affecting Poland, four were successful and three were unsuccessful. Two parties involved in the successful attempts were granted asylum in Denmark and the Bormholm Islands. The remaining parties were prosecuted.

[110]Five of these attempts were successful. Four parties were granted asylum, and one was extradited. The one unsuccessful party was prosecuted.

[111]Based on aggregate collected data. See note 90, *supra* p. 143.

TABLE 3

EXPOSURE TO HIJACKING ATTEMPTS AND INDIVIDUAL STATE SUPPORT OF THE TOKYO CONVENTION; LATE PARTIES (1971 TO June 11, 1973)

State	A. Date Became Party	B. Date Became Signatory	Number of months between A. and B.	Number of incidents between 1960 & B.	Number of incidents between A. and B.
Yugoslavia	2/12/71	9/14/63	77	0	1
Republic of Korea	2/19/71	12/8/65	62	0	1
Singapore	3/1/71	-	-	-	1*
Poland	3/19/71	-	-	-	7*
Finland	4/2/71	10/24/69	18	0	0
Rwanda	5/17/71	-	-	-	0*
Greece	5/31/71	10/21/69	19	3	1
Mali	5/31/71	-	-	-	0*
Burundi	7/4/71	-	-	-	0*
Argentina	7/23/71	-	-	-	6*
Togo	7/26/71	-	-	-	0*
Paraguay	8/9/71	-	-	-	0*

Table 3--Continued

State	A. Date Became Party	B. Date Became Signatory	Number of months between A. and B.	Number of incidents between 1960 & B.	Number of incidents between A. and B.
Zambia	9/14/71	-	-	-	0*
Fiji	1/18/72	-	-	-	0*
Trinidad & Tobaga	2/9/72	-	-	-	2*
Thailand	3/6/72	-	-	-	0*
Senegal	3/9/72	2/20/64	97	0	0
Barbados	4/4/72	6/25/69	34	0	0
Lesotho	4/28/72	-	-	-	0*
South Africa	5/26/72	-	-	-	1*
Cyprus	5/31/72	-	-	-	0*
Libya	6/12/72	-	-	-	0*
Luxembourg	9/21/72	-	-	-	0*
Laos	10/23/72	-	-	-	0*
Costa Rica	10/24/72	-	-	-	2*
Malawi	12/28/72	-	-	-	0

*denotes the number of incidents between 1960 and ratification.

attempts between 1960 and December, 1970. As previously mentioned, the majority of these cases involved the seizure of American aircraft to Cuban soil or foreign aircraft to or from Castro's regime. Even so, Cuba has not yet signed. In addition, three dozen other states recorded incidents of hijacking attempts during that period, including the Soviet Union which registered nine attempts. Thus, while a total of sixty-seven states became either a signatory, a party, or both, thirty-five other states--involving 134 Cuban and over 80 other hijacking attempts--did not accede to the Tokyo Convention.[112]

The preceding tables were designed to provide specific data on individual state exposure to aircraft seizure attempts and the action taken to deter them (i.e., through signature or ratification of the Tokyo Convention). However, little causal relationship was suggested between the rate of a state's accession and the number of incidents affecting its national interests. In each of the three designated periods--early, middle-range, and late--some states did react quickly against "skyjackings" by formally sanctioning the Tokyo Convention (e.g., Portugal, Mexico, and Brazil), while others did not (e.g., the United States, Poland, and the United Kingdom).

Therefore, when viewed from an individual-state perspective, no definitive pattern emerges to support the

---

[112] *Ibid.*

hypothesis that states directly affected by the hijackings will ratify more readily than those which were not. The disparate ratification-incident rates of the United States in contrast to Upper Volta and the Phillipines as opposed to Argentina make this patently obvious.

Nonetheless, when aggregate state practices were graphically projected on an international spectrum against the number of hijacking incidents, a significant pattern developed. Cumulative state support verified the contention that as the frequency of aircraft seizures increases, the number of states becoming parties or signatories to the Tokyo Convention tended to increase proportionately. This aggregate international response is depicted in Fig. 1.

Notice that as the frequency of hijacking attempts increases, especially in 1969 and 1970, a concomitant increase is seen in Tokyo signatory and ratification commitments. The early surge to sanction the agreement was catalyzed by two resolutions, one by the International Civil Aviation Organization in September, 1968,[113] and the other by

---

[113]Dissatisfaction with the Tokyo Convention was expressed by several delegates at the Sixteenth ICAO assembly in September, 1968, held in Buenos Aires. The result was seen in Resolution A16-37, which urged all states to give immediate effect to the principles of Article 11 of the Tokyo Convention. ICAO Doc. 8779, Res. A/16 at 92 (1968). Also see Volpe and Stewart, "Domestic and International Responses," pp. 273, 291. For text of Resolution A16-37, see *infra*, Appendix E, p. 295.

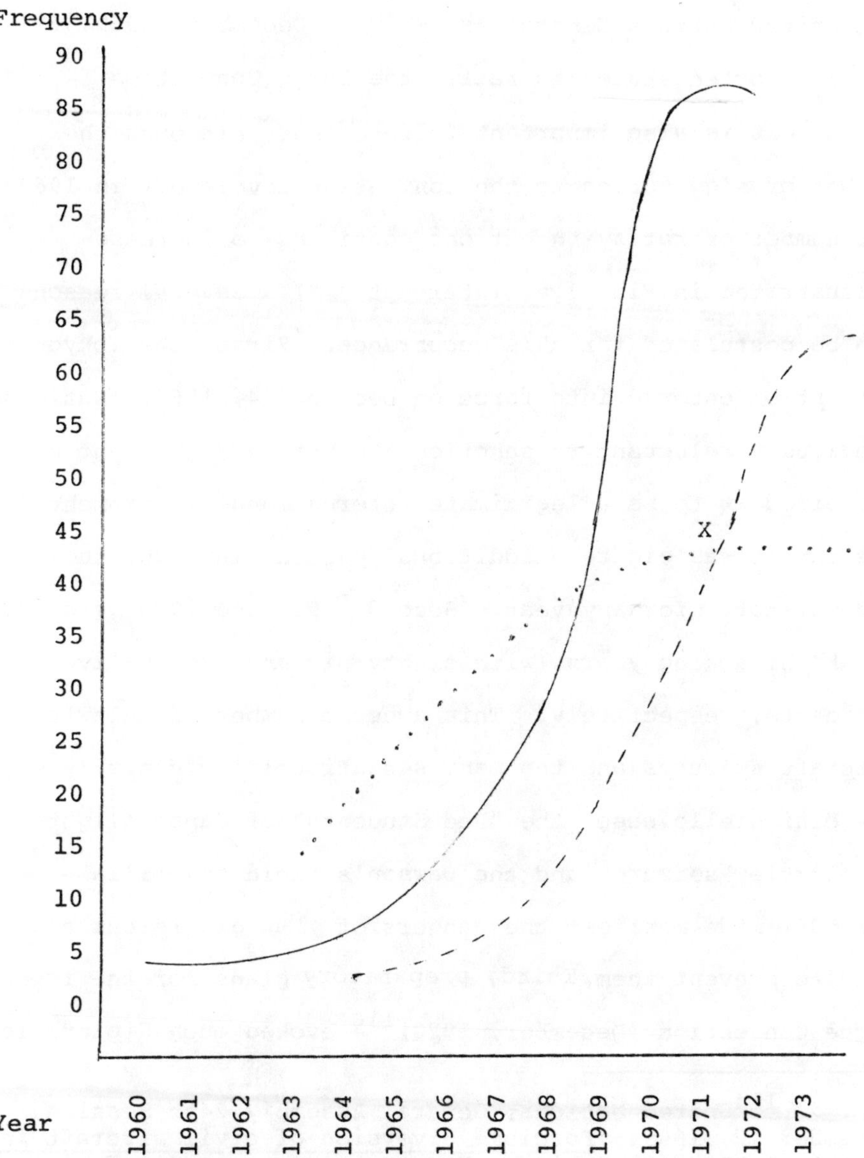

_______Yearly Hijacking Incidents
.......Cumulative Signatories
-------Cumulative Ratifications

x - Intercept point at which cumulative number of parties begins to exceed the cumulative number of signatories.

Fig. 1.--The influence of worldwide hijacking attempts on cumulative state support of the Tokyo Convention (January, 1960-June 11, 1973).

the United Nations General Assembly in December, 1969,[114] which exhorted states to ratify the Tokyo Convention.

It is also important to note that, although the number of signatories to the convention levels off in 1969, the number of ratifying nations continues to increase (illustrated in Fig. 1 at intercept "x"). Several reasons can be postulated for this occurrence. First, the Tokyo Convention entered into force on December 4, 1969. Nations previously reluctant to sanction the untried agreement now perceived it to be a legitimate international instrument.[115] The result was eighteen additional parties in 1970, the highest total for any year. Second, 1969 and 1970 were the "peak" hijacking years, with eighty-six and eighty-five incidents, respectively. This awesome number of unlawful aircraft seizures and the many sensational incidents (e.g., the Minichiello case, the "Red Students" of Japan flight, the Barkley seizure, and the Dawson's Field guerrilla episode) made manifest the dangers of plane diversions and the need to prevent them. Third, preparatory plans for the impendin Hague Convention (December, 1970)[116] evoked much diplomatic

---

[114]United Nations, General Assembly 24th Session, December 12, 1969. _Forcible diversion of civil aircraft in flight_, A/RES/2551 (xxiv). For test, see Appendix F, _infra_, p. 297.

[115]Personal Interview with Ambassador Richard Kearney, U.S. Member, International Law Commission, American Society of International Law National Convention, Washington, D.C., April 14, 1973.

[116]See McWhinney, _Aerial Piracy_, _passim_.

intercourse about the international efforts to suppress "skyjacking."[117] Undoubtedly, this continued diplomatic exposure prompted some late parties to ratify. Fourth, insistent appeals from global transport organizations (i.e., the International Air Transport Association,[118] the International Federation of Airline Pilot Associations,[119] and the International Transport Workers' Federation)[120] pointed up their concern and anxiety for viable solutions. Finally, sundry international resolutions by the ICAO Legal Committee,[121] the United Nations Security Council,[122] the

---

[117] For a general discussion on this, see Charles F. Butler, "The Path to International Legislation Against Hijacking," in McWhinney, ed., Aerial Piracy, pp. 27-35.

[118] New York Times, December 20, 1969; 61:3; Department of State Bulletin, Vol. 62 (January 12, 1970), 31; IATA News Review, April, 1970, pp. 4-5; Washington Post, September 8, 1970, p. A15: 1.

[119] New York Times, December 18, 1969; 93:8; Wall Street Journal, December 22, 1969; 10: 3; Aviation Week and Space Technology, Vol. 92, No. 15 (April 13, 1970), p. 43; Air Line Pilot, Vol. 39, No. 7 (July, 1970), pp. 42-46.

[120] ITF Newsletter, March 1970 supplement; Aviation Daily, Vol. 191, No. 24 (October 5, 1970), p. 188.

[121] ICAO Doc. 8838, LC/157, 35-36 (1969); also see McWhinney, ed., Aerial Piracy, Appendices 7 and 8, and Thomas Buergenthal, Law-Making in the International Civil Aviation Organization (Syracuse, N.Y.: Syracuse University Press, 1969).

[122] United Nations Security Council Resolution 286 (1970), adopted at its 1552nd Meeting, on September 9, 1970.

United Nations General Assembly,[123] the Council of Europe (Consultative Assembly),[124] and the Inter-American Juridical Assembly[125] encouraged formal sanction of the Tokyo Convention by the international community.

Admittedly, the Tokyo Convention provided for the safety of passengers and crew in the event that offences were committed aboard an aircraft in flight.[126] Yet, this agreement lacked efficacy to prosecute offenders and failed to formally recognize unlawful aircraft seizure as a crime against the law of nations. Moreover, the slow pace at which parties ratified the Convention, concomitant with the large number of non-participant nations, mirrored a reluctance to secure a more definite obligation for contracting states to exercise jurisdiction over the alleged hijacker. It remained for a newer, more comprehensive international effort, the Hague Convention, to set forth the criminal nature of aircraft seizure and to provide adequate punitive guidelines under the aegis of international law.

---

[123]United Nations General Assembly Resolution 2645 (XXV), adopted by the General Assembly (on the report of the Sixth Committee (A/8176) on November 30, 1970.

[124]Council of Europe, Consultative Assembly, Resolution 450 (1970), adopted September 18, 1970 (10th sitting) and Recommendation 613 (1970), adopted September 24, 1970 (18th sitting).

[125]Inter-American Juridical Committee, "Draft Convention on Terrorism and Kidnapping of Persons for Purposes of Extortion" for the Organization of American States. Promulgated in Rio de Janeiro, September 26, 1970.

[126]The Tokyo Convention, Article 1, Paragraph 1; Article 6, Paragraph 1; and Article 11, Paragraph 1.

CHAPTER 4

THE HAGUE AND MONTREAL CONVENTIONS: CONCERTED INTERNATIONAL ACTION TO SUPPRESS AIRCRAFT SEIZURES

In 1970-1971 the weaknesses of the Tokyo Convention were translated into the strengths of the Hague and Montreal Conventions. The provisions set forth in the Tokyo Convention had left major questions unanswered regarding custody and prosecution of hijackers. The planners of the new conventions utilized the Tokyo agreement as a vantage point from which an international law of hijacking could be effectively implemented.

The impetus to the new conventions stemmed not only from the bland provisions of the Tokyo Convention, but also from a new upsurge of aircraft seizures, seizures tantamount to international blackmail which posed an even more " . . . urgent and drastic threat to international civil aviation" than in the past.[1]

During the preparatory work, uncertainty arose about the potentially conflicting nature of the newly proposed

---

[1]K. E. Malmborg, Jr., "Address by K. E. Malmborg, Jr.," A.J.I.L. Proceedings 65, No. 4 (September, 1971), 77.

provisions vis-à-vis those agreed upon in Tokyo. Even before the United States became a party to the Tokyo Convention, it made overtures to the ICAO calling for a draft Protocol that would deal solely with aircraft hijacking to secure some provision for mandatory extradition of the offender(s).[2] This Protocol proposal was made to counter unforeseen legal nuances stemming from two separate conventions over essentially the same international problem.[3] However, it was rejected with the assurance of the ICAO Legal Committee and Subcommittee ". . . that states could become parties to both conventions without inconsistent obligations."[4] Nonetheless, a formal memorandum to the ICAO Legal Subcommittee from the International Air Transport Association provided further encouragement for review and revision of the legal status of hijacking, hopefully to elevate it to the level of "an international crime."[5]

Despite opposition from the ICAO Council regarding incorporation of mandatory prosecution into the Tokyo Convention, the Legal Committee was directed ". . . to examine

---

[2]ICAO Doc. LC/SC. SA WD7 (5/2/69).

[3]Report of ICAO Legal Subcommittee on Unlawful Seizures of Aircraft, in International Legal Materials, 8 (March, 1969), 245.

[4]Malmborg, "Address," p. 76.

[5]ICAO Subcommittee Report, Doc. 8838, LC/157; See also Van Panhuys, "Aircraft Hijacking," p. 17.

both the development of model national legislation and the possibility of an international convention dealing with the prosecution of hijackers."[6] Thus in 1968 these two considerations merited careful attention by the ICAO, and in February, 1969, the ICAO Secretariat recognized that certain beneficial "objectives" could be realized from both.[7] Accordingly, the Secretariat noted that:

> The above objectives could be attained either by the enactment of uniform national legislation by the consenting States or by means of an international instrument. Such instrument might well be one which would leave untouched the Tokyo Convention, some provisions of which would remain applicable to certain aspects of the problem of "unlawful seizure," but would contain complementary provisions which, without amending the Tokyo Convention, would fill gaps . . . and would also include other provisions which a proper study of the subject might indicate.[8]

Subsequent meetings of the ICAO Subcommittee on February 10-22, 1969, and September 23-October 3, 1969, supported the latter contention, i.e., that a multilateral

---

[6]Cited in Horlick, "The Public and Private International Response," p. 169; ICAO Doc. 8779, Res. A/16, 92 (1968).

[7]ICAO Doc. 8838, LC/157, 35-36 (1969). These "objectives" included: (1) recognition of unlawful aircraft seizures as a penal offense, subject to the jurisdiction of every state; (2) encouragement of states to establish such jurisdiction; and (3) proposition to states of alternatives for penal measures, <u>viz</u>., extradition, prosecution, or under select circumstances, asylum.

[8]ICAO Doc. 8838, LC/157, 35-36 (1969).

convention would be the more effective means ". . . to see that the state in whose territory the hijacked aircraft has landed will . . . either prosecute the hijacker itself or else extradite him for prosecution in some other state having jurisdiction."[9] The draft convention produced by the Subcommittee was adopted with only minor revisions made by the Legal Committee in Montreal, February 9-March 11, 1970.[10]

The outgrowth of these preparations was a special diplomatic conference which convened December 1-16, 1970, at the Hague to consider the draft proposal. The fruition of this effort was the Convention for the Suppression of Unlawful Seizure of Aircraft, more commonly referred to as the Hague Convention.[11]

---

[9]Cited in Jacobson, "From Piracy on the High Seas," p. 177.

[10]One revision made in the Subcommittee draft was to extend jurisdiction to the state in which the hijacked plane landed. The draft already included jurisdiction to the state in which the hijacker actually leaves the aircraft. Cf. <u>International Legal Materials</u>, 9 (1969), 77. to <u>International Legal Materials</u>, 9 (1969), 669.

[11]Convention for the Suppression of Unlawful Seizure of Aircraft, opened for signature December 16, 1970, ICAO Doc. 8920. Also referenced as T.I.A.S. 7192 and found in <u>International Legal Materials</u> 10 (1971), 133; Department of State <u>Bulletin</u>, 64 (1970), p. 50; also, see note 16, <u>infra</u>. Hereinafter cited as the Hague Convention, and reproduced as Appendix G, <u>infra</u>., pp. 299-305.

In the years since the Tokyo Convention, greater concern over the phenomenon of hijacking had been patently ecognized in the global community. No less than 210 hijacking attempts had been made in this period, with more than 80 of these occurring in 1970 alone.[12] Perhaps the greatest catalyst precipitating active state participation in the Hague Convention was the "Dawsons Field" incident in September, 1970. Four major jetliners were diverted to the Jordanian desert, where they were held by members of the Popular Front for the Liberation of Palestine.[13] This overt act of political blackmail pointed up the need for immediate international cooperation, not only to fill the prosecution voids inherent in the Tokyo Convention, but also to reach viable solutions that would prevent such acts from reoccurring.[14]

Consequently, the roster of participants at the Hague Convention included representatives from seventy-seven states and ". . . observers from twelve organizations interested in international civil aviation." Both the Soviet

---

[12]F.A.A. Statistics.

[13]U.S. Congress, Senate. Aircraft Hijacking Convention, Hearings before the Committee on Foreign Relations, Senate, on Executive A, 92nd Cong., 1st sess., June 7 and July 20, 1971, p. 3, 11.

[14]Ibid., p. 10.

bloc countries and the United Arab Republic sent delegates, although Cuba was noticeably missing.[15]

The Preamble of the Convention indicates the urgency of the conference and its mission:

> The States Parties to this Convention
>
> Considering that unlawful acts of seizure or exercise of control of aircraft in flight jeopardize the safety of persons and property, seriously affect the operation of air services, and undermine the confidence of the peoples of the world in the safety of civil aviation;
>
> Considering that the occurrence of such acts is a matter of grave concern;
>
> Considering that, for the purpose of deterring such acts, there is an urgent need to provide appropriate measures for punishment of offenders. . . .[16]

Designating the Offense

Not unlike the definitional problems associated with "piracy" under international law, the task of providing a universally acceptable definition of unlawful aircraft seizures proved to be a difficult one indeed. Several of the municipal law definitions, particularly those of the United States, Australia, Argentina, and Brazil, encompassed more than the ICAO Legal Committee wished to recognize.[17]

---

[15] U.S. Congress, Senate, Aircraft Hijacking Convention Report together with Individual Views, S. Rept. No. 92-98 to accompany Ex. A, 92-1, 92nd Cong., 1st sess., August 5, 1971, p. 1.

[16] Preamble of the Hague Convention, Suppression of Unlawful Seizure of Aircraft (Hijacking), T.I.A.S. 7192, U.S. Govt. Pub. 69-006-71, p. 4.

[17] ICAO Doc. 8877 - LC/161, p. 36.

For example, the Committee rejected a proposal which would make it illegal for persons to carry firearms or other dangerous weapons aboard an aircraft.[18] It was noted that such provisions should be contained in municipal statutes, such as in the case of the United States.[19]

Admittedly, the definition of the unlawful seizure of aircraft as finally established by the Hague Convention was less vehement than that desired by the United States or the Soviet Union.[20] Even so, it is viable enough to cover any principal or accomplice who contemplates or attempts to seize an aircraft in flight, and is set forth in Article 1:

> Any person who on board an aircraft in flight:
> (a) unlawfully, by force or threat thereof, or by any other form of intimidation, seizes, or exercises control of, that aircraft, or attempts to perform any such act, or
> (b) is an accomplice of a person who performs or attempts to perform any such act
>
> commits an offence (hereinafter referred to as "the offence").[21]

---

[18]*Ibid.* See Jacobson, "From Piracy on the High Seas," p. 178.

[19]49 U.S.C. Section 1472(l). For punishment under United States criminal law, see United States v. Bearden, 304 F.2d 532 (5th Cir. 1962), vacated on other grounds, 372 U.S. 252 (1963) (per curiam), obstruction of commerce charge aff'd, 320 F2d 99 (5th Cir. 1963), cert. denied, 376 U.S. 922 (1964). An excellent analysis of United States municipal provisions to combat hijacking is to be found in Michael C. McClintock, "Skyjacking: Its Domestic Civil and Criminal Ramifications," *Journal of Air Law and Commerce*, Vol. 39, Issue 1 (January, 1973), 29-80.

[20]Malmborg, "Address," p. 77.

[21]The Hague Convention, Article 1. See *infra*, p. 299.

The United States objection to Article 1 was raised because it is ". . . too narrow with reference to the persons contemplated in that it may not include those not aboard the aircraft who assist an offender aboard the aircraft; further, it may not include co-conspirators."[22] Yet, it should be realized that the Hague definition of the questioned offense is far more explicit than that found in the Tokyo Convention. Article 1 of the Tokyo provisions only touches upon broadly stated acts which jeopardize the safety, good order, and discipline on board an aircraft in flight; in contrast, the Hague wording more closely approximates a law of nations definition.[23] The basic elements of the crime are spelled out to conform with most national legislation, without exaggerated interpretation. However, although the unlawful nature of the act is well described, no specific name is given to the crime. It is merely designated as "the offence." Notwithstanding this discernible defect, Article 2 urges that "Each Contracting State undertakes to make the offence punishable by severe penalties."[24] This

---

[22]U.S., Congress, Senate. <u>Aircraft Hijacking Convention</u>, Hearings before Committee on Foreign Relations, <u>op. cit.</u>, p. 50.

[23]Cf. Article 1, The Tokyo Convention, <u>infra</u>, p. 283.

[24]The Hague Convention, Article 2. In reflecting upon the question, "What is a 'severe penalty'?," Oliver J. Lissitzyn pointedly observes:

The Convention does not define it. Legislation and actual decisions in various countries suggest that the

was done to accommodate disparate municipal penalties, in accordance with their national legislations.[25] Yet, it is

---

international standard of severity in such cases is by no means well defined. . . .

The diversity of values and interests is evidently at work. Laws that provide for extremely severe penalties may be counter-productive, by making judges and juries reluctant to convict. It may well be, incidentally, that the very high penalties required by our own anti-hijacking statute may make extradition of some offenders to the United States more difficult. It should be amended by eliminating the death penalty and setting a lower minimum penalty than twenty years. One possible interpretation of the word 'severe' in terms of American law is that it only requires making hijacking a felony rather than a misdemeanor. As you know, a felony may be punishable by as little as one year in prison. Diversity in national standards of severity, furthermore, may be reflected not only in the statutory provisions for penalties, but also in the relative ease of placing convicted offenders on probation or parole. There is, in brief, no assurance that the new convention, even if generally ratified, will result in sufficiently severe penalties in all cases to serve as an effective deterrent. Oliver J. Lissitzyn, "International Control of Aerial Hijacking: The Role of Values and Intersts," A.J.I.L. Proceedings, 65 (September, 1971), 84.

[25]See: "Tribunal de Grande Instance de Corbeil," 1969: Revue Generale De L'Air Et De L'Espace 358 (1969) (French Punishment); "Tribunal of the French Military Government of Berlin, 1970" (German punishment); Juris Classeur Periodique 16.540. Horlick mentions some interesting disparities in national prosecution efforts:

> Of greater significance is the treatment meted out to hijackers who land in Cuba. A considerable body of evidence suggests that since 1969, Cuban treatment of American hijackers has been quite harsh in most cases. One hijacker who stole 1,700 dollars from the passengers of the diverted aircraft was arrested by the Cubans upon landing, and the Cubans returned the money, just as they had done following the only other hijacking-theft. The voluntary return of fourteen hijackers to the United States (via Canada) is evidence in itself of the quality of Cuban treatment of hijackers; more publicity about the conditions of life for hijackers in Cuba hopefully will deter potential hijackers.
>
> Punishment of hijackers has varied elsewhere, from two unsuccessful hijackers whose throats were slit by

of importance to note that national courts have largely been unwilling to sentence convicted hijackers to the maximum punishments prescribed by their own statutes. According to Alona Evans, the sentencing of hijackers has been very "unpredictable."[26] By May, 1971, United States courts had issued only ". . . . one sentence of life imprisonment, one of twenty-five years, and three of twenty years; thereafter there is a variation from twenty years to one year for kidnapping, as well as the two years on a charge of interfering

---

Ethiopian Airlines guards, to Christian Belon, who stepped off the plane that he had diverted to Beirut, announced, "I did it for Lebanon," and was released on bail of $7.50 before the resulting international uproar resulted in new charges being brought against him. Noteworthy is the trend of prosecution of refugee hijackers from Eastern Europe by Western European countries, despite obvious political sympathy. For example, two East Germans were each sentenced to two years in prison by a French military court in West Berlin and two Poles were jailed for 27 months and 24 months respectively by an Austrian court. In addition, charges were brought in Sweden against two hijackers of Greek aircraft, and Raffaele Minichiello was sentenced to seven and one-half years in prison in Italy after his flight from the United States (he was released, however, after eighteen months as a result of various amnesties). Horlick, "Public and Private International Response," pp. 159-160. [Footnotes omitted.] Also see: U.S. Congress, House of Representatives. Hearings on Air Piracy in the Caribbean Area Before the Subcommittee on Inter-American Affairs of the House Committee on Foreign Affairs, 90th Cong., 2nd sess. September 19 (1968); and U.S. Congress, House of Representatives. Hearings Before the House Committee on Foreign Affairs on Aircraft Hijacking, 91st Cong., 2nd sess. (1970), p. 110.

[26]Alona Evans, "Comments by Alona E. Evans," A.J.I.L. Proceedings, 65 No. 4 (September, 1971), 91.

with the crew."[27] To be sure, many cases have been dismissed on grounds of temporary insanity, albeit off-hand passengers' remarks and "jokes" about hijacking while aboard an aircraft in flight have been met with indignation and some arrests.[28]

Other nations' laws evidence more severe punitive measures.[29] A 1970 French statute categorizes hijackings into three types, and designates appropriate penalties for each: offenders convicted of "simple" hijacking, i.e., one in which no violence occurs, may be sentenced from five to

---

[27]Evans, Ibid., p. 90. Of 128 incidents involving United States aircraft since 1961, 35 persons have been convicted of air piracy or related crimes (ten in 1971), and ten persons have been committed to mental institutions. An additional thirteen cases await trial or the outcome of mental examinations, and there have been two acquittals. Another hijacker was shot and killed in a bank robbery after returning secretly to the United States. F.A.A. Release 72-15, January 24, 1972, pp. 2-3, cited in Horlick, "Public and Private International Response," p. 159.

[28]An excellent psycho-analytical treatment of "the skyjacker" is David G. Hubbard, The Skyjacker: His Flights of Fantesy (New York: Macmillan Co., 1971). With regard to "jokes," one scholar noted, "In Boston, a passenger who asked a stewardess 'how long does it take this plane to get to Cuba?' was fined $200 on a charge of disturbing the peace." (New York Times, July 11, 1969, 36:2), cited in Evans, "Aircraft Hijacking," note 2, p. 695.

[29]The Netherlands, Great Britain, Saudi Arabia, and Bulgaria have all chosen to return offenders to the states where seizure occurred or the state of registry——in some instances, without existing extradition treaties. (McKeithen, "Prospects for the Prevention," p. 67). In the Soviet Union, several persons recently tried on charges for plotting or attempting to hijack Soviet aircraft were sentenced to death; however, their sentences were reduced on appeal to a sentence of fifteen years in prison, the maximum imprisonment sentence

ten years imprisonment; if in the course of the hijacking, the offender injures another party, a ten-to-twenty-year prison term will be imposed; finally, should a death come as a result of the aircraft's seizure, the offender is subject to life imprisonment.[30] The grave attitude of the French towards "skyjacking" is well illustrated by the case of two East Germans who seized a Polish aircraft and fled to the French sector of West Berlin in 1969. Political sympathies of the French Military Court were overshadowed by the nature of the crime. The result, two-year prison sentences for the refugees.[31]

Some states have chosen to return hijackers to the country in which the aircraft was seized or to the flag state, even in cases where extradition treaties were not applicable.[32]

---

permitted by Soviet law. Interestingly, they were not charged under a law specifically applicable to hijacking (which is apparently lacking in Soviet legislation), but rather under a law forbidding departure from the country without permission. Lissitzyn, "International Control of Aerial Hijacking," p. 84. Also See Gerhard, O. W. Mueller, and Fre Le Poole - Griffiths, Comparative Criminal Procedure (New York: University Press, 1969), pp. 159-174.

[30]Lissitzyn, "International Control of Aerial Hijacking," p. 84. Also, "French National Assembly Legal Committee Approves New Penal Code Article Making Hijackers Liable to Jail Terms of from 5 Years to Life," New York Times, December 12, 1969; 11.:1.

[31]New York Times, November 21, 1969; 3:3. The incident occurred prior to the French statute's passage (1970), thus explaining the lesser sentence of two years.

[32]McKeithen, "Prospects for the Prevention," p. 67. See note 29, supra. "Extradition treaties, however, are not a practicable solution to the problem of punishing hijackers. Such treaties are negotiated with friendly countries, to

On the other hand, West Germany, Denmark, and Austria have seen fit to grant asylum to hijackers, ". . . apparently with the understanding that they will not be returned to the country from which they came."[33] Nonetheless, in cases involving theft of aircraft (without political implications), or illegal possession of dangerous weapons which endanger the lives of passengers, these same states have denied the right of asylum to the offenders.[34] The end does not justify the means.

Despite the internationally proclaimed illegal nature of hijacking, some nations persist in welcoming "offenders" as heroes. Syria, for example, printed a special stamp in 1969 to commemorate the seizure of a Trans World Airline Boeing 707 jetliner to Damascus. The stamp boldly depicts the aircraft, with its nose section blown off, surrounded by the band of jubilant hijackers.[35] Algeria and

---

which a hijacker is least likely to go, and they are the type of agreement that is most likely to fall into desuetude should relations between the two states become strained." Horlick, "Public and Private International Response," p. 161. Cf. Lissitzyn, "International Control of Aerial Hijacking," pp. 80-85 and McMahon, "Extradition as a Deterrent," pp. 1137-1138.

[33]Evans, "Comments," A.J.I.L. Proceedings, p. 91.

[34]Evans, Ibid. This is to say, while the offenders were not returned to another country, they were prosecuted for the criminal acts performed in the course of the hijacking. In essence, political asylum was granted, but not exemption from prosecution.

[35]R. Hotz, "More on Hijacking," (editorial), Aviation Week and Space Technology, Vol. 91, No. 19 (November 10, 1969), p. 11.

Jordan have also refused to prosecute or extradite hijackers, particularly when the aircraft seizure had political overtones.[36]

Such refusals to prosecute offenders have led the American Society of Travel Agents (A.S.T.A.) to suspend customer travel service to Algeria, Iraq, Jordan and Syria until these nations evidenced a willingness ". . . to take whatever steps are necessary to halt these acts of piracy."[37] Interestingly enough, none of these nations has ever become a signatory or a party to the Tokyo Convention, though it is important to note that Iraq and Jordan have assumed the international obligations of the Hague Convention, both as party and signatory members.[38]

---

[36]Aggregate statistics reveal that Algeria was involved in four hijackings and Jordan in five. An important consideration is that though not excessively great in quantity, these hijackings were extremely sensationalist in nature. See <u>supra</u>, p. 152, note 101; For comments on the impact of national politics vis-à-vis legal reactions of states, see Horlick, "Developing Law," p. 44. It should not be overlooked that Jordan has ratified the Hague Convention (November 16, 1971) and also the Montreal Convention (February 13, 1973). Details of the Montreal provisions are discussed <u>infra</u>, pp. 306-15.

[37]Lawrence Dody, "Anti-Hijacking Drive Gains Impetus," <u>Aviation Week and Space Technology</u>, Vol. 93, No. 16 (October 19, 1970), 27.

[38]U.S., Congress, Senate. <u>Report of the Senate Committee on Commerce on S. 39</u>, Report No. 93-13, 93rd Cong., 1st sess., February 2, 1973, p. 52.

Towards Mandatory Universal Jurisdiction over Hijacking

Reminiscent of Article 3 in the Harvard Draft Research on Piracy, the Hague description of unlawful aircraft seizures is limited to enumerating those acts constituting the offense. This consideration makes manifest a crucial question regarding international law: Does mere definition of the offense, augmented by punitive prescriptions, making hijacking a true international crime? The answer appears to be "no," unless qualified by the traditional rule of universal jurisdiction. The law of nations' interpretation of piracy calls for suppression of the crime by applying common, world-wide jurisdiction. That is to say, an individual person is capable of violating international law, and he is subject to punishment by any nation which captures him.[39]

---

[39]This is an already accepted norm despite the relatively short duration of its universal recognition. It has been since World War II that individual responsibility has assumed an important position in the basis of international law. Coplin notes two categories of development: (1) those which attempt to bring leaders of states under the personal responsibility of international law; and (2) those which seek to guarantee rights to individuals under international law. Coplin, Functions of International Law, p. 29. Most notable in the first category are, of course, the Nuremburg Trials, which declared that leaders of states committing "crimes against humanity," "crimes against peace," and "war crimes" are subject to personal punishment for these acts. It is interesting to speculate if this category might someday be applicable to unlawful aircraft seizures as a "crime against humanity." The second group--

The Hague Convention neither explicitly recognizes aerial hijackings as an offense against customary international law, nor does it specify that states should have universal jurisdiction over offenders. However, the fact that two noteworthy international conventions (the supreme source of international law) have been held to suppress unlawful aircraft seizures indicates that a "conventional" international law is evolving, one which establishes aircraft hijacking as an international crime against the laws of the Contracting States. The lengthy time element required for customary international law is wanting to achieve true universal jurisdiction; but, conventional law has made evident the international consensus that skyjacking is an

---

protection of individual rights---consists of regional developments, such as the European Court of Human Rights, and in universal international law, such as the Convention on Genocide.

On the impact of individual responsibility in international law, see: Philip Jessup, A Modern Law of Nations (New York: Macmillan, 1950), pp. 69-93; Hersch Lauterpacht, International Law and Human Rights (New York: Praeger, 1950), pp. 27-73; and Wolfgang Friedmann, The Changing Structure of International Law (New York: Columbia University Press, 1964), pp. 233-253.

For discussions on the impact of the Nuremburg Trials on international law (including the potential implications for individual responsibility), see Hans Kelsen, "Will the Judgement in the Nuremburg Trial Constitute a Precedent in International Law?," International Law Quarterly, 1 (1947); G. A. Finch, "Nuremburg Trials and International Law," A.J.I.L., 41 (1947), 770-794; and especially Robert K. Woetzel, The Nuremburg Trials in International Law (London: Stevens and Sons, 1960).

illegal act, subject to prosecution under municipal legal codes.[40]

The provisions cited in Article 4 of the Hague Convention assert that jurisdiction may be lawfully exercised by any of four potentially involved states:

> 1. Each Contracting State shall take such measures as may be necessary to establish its jurisdiction over the offence and any other act of violence against passengers or crew committed by the alleged offender in connection with the offence, in the following cases:
> (a) when the offence is committed on board an aircraft registered in that State;
> (b) when the aircraft on board which the offence is committed lands in its territory with the alleged offender still on board;

---

[40] Horlick probes deeper into the evolution of international legal restraints as he contends:

> Real world considerations, however, pose problems for the deterrence plan of assuring punishment through international obligation. For example, a state such as Cuba, even though it recognizes the dangers posed to international aviation (in which it participates), may refrain from punishing even hijackers motivated solely by personal reasons, simply to avoid doing anything considered desirable by a state with which it is on unfriendly terms. Moreover, collusive trials may subject favored hijackers to only a minimal deprivation for their mandatory punishment; in fact, internal politics may prevent altogether the punishment of any hijacker who claims a popular political affiliation. For these reasons, Hijacking also must be made an international crime, so that any state within which an accused hijacker is found could apply the appropriate penalty without regard to the place of the alleged offense. Most hijackers motivated by personal reasons are not interested in spending the remainder of their lives within the social and geographic confines of the state of landing. Universal jurisdiction should also help deter the use of hijacking for political demonstration or for the taking of hostages, because the hijackers, after the initial offense, would be confined to those countries what were strongly sympathetic to their aims.

Horlick, "Public and Private International Response," p. 164.

> (c) when the offence is committed on board an aircraft leased without crew to a lessee who has his principal place of business or, if the lessee has no such place of business, his permanent residence, in that State.[41]

From the above, jurisdiction over the offender is subject to (1) the state in which the aircraft is registered, (2) the state in which the hijacked aircraft lands; (3) the state of a lessee's domicile under a barehull charter, i.e., an aircraft leased without crew. Additionally, Paragraph 2 of Article 4 further extends state jurisdiction so that

> Each Contracting State shall likewise take such measures as may be necessary to establish its jurisdiction over the offence in the case where the alleged offender is present in its territory and it does not extradite him pursuant to Article 8 to any of the States mentioned in paragraph 1 of this Article.[42]

Consequently, any party to the Convention in whose territorial limits an alleged hijacker is found can assume jurisdiction over him, or extradite him according to their stated municipal provisions.

Of especial interest regarding jurisdiction are the provisions sanctioning nation-states' legislation. Article 4, Paragraph 3 declares, "This Convention does not exclude any criminal jurisdiction exercised in accordance with national law."[43] This statement is the same precise wording of Article 3, Paragraph 3 in the Tokyo Convention, and is

---

[41]The Hague Convention, Article 4, Paragraph 1.

[42]*Ibid.*, Article 4, Paragraph 2.

[43]*Ibid.*, Article 4, Paragraph 3.

purposely designed so that municipal status can deal with serious criminal offenses, e.g., murder, assault, kidnapping, or extortion, which might occur during an act of unlawful aircraft seizure.[44] Paragraph 2 of Article 3, in accordance with the general practice of limiting aviation conventions to civil aircraft, provides that jurisdictional directives in the Hague Convention ". . . shall not apply to aircraft used in military, customs, or police services."[45] This assertion is followed by the reaffirmation that local authorities are to deal with unsuccessful seizure attempts that occur solely within the territory of the flag state.[46]

For the jurisdictional provisions granted to the "take-off" state and the landing state to be applicable, both locations must be external to the flag state's territory, i.e., if the hijacked flight occurs wholly within the territorial jurisdiction of the state of registry the incident is excluded from the aegis of the Hague Convention, it being ". . . immaterial whether the aircraft is engaged in an international or domestic flight."[47]

---

[44]Cf. Article 3, Paragraph 3 of the Tokyo Convention, _infra_, p. 284, to Article 4, Paragraph 3 of the Hague Convention, _infra_, p. 309 . Also see note 29, _supra_.

[45]The Hague Convention, Article 3, Paragraph 2. This Article is verbatim repetition of Article 1, Paragraph 4 of the Tokyo Convention. See _infra_, p. 283.

[46]_Ibid_., Article 3, Paragraph 3.

[47]The Hague Convention, Article 3, Paragraph 3. On the issue of "the international character" required of

Since the paramount purpose of the Hague Convention is international suppression of unlawful aircraft seizures, Paragraphs 3 and 4 of Article 3 lend credence to the belief that individual states are competent to justly deal with "skyjackers," albeit the criminal act primarily only affects one state (viz., the flag state).[48] In order to present

---

flights vis-à-vis the Hague Convention, R. H. Mankiewicz astutely posits:

> In other words, the Convention applies to "domestic flights" outside the state of registration. Hence, it is rather difficult to understand why it is inapplicable to domestic flights within that state. In support of that exclusion it is argued that the unlawful seizure of an aircraft within the state of registration falls automatically under the state's jurisdiction and thus does not give rise to any international legal problem. This argument is weak, however, as it applies with equal force when the departure, hijacking and actual landing take place in the same state, if that state is not the one of registration. Moreover, the argument is illegal if one considers that the Convention does apply in such a case, even though the foreign registered aircraft, which has taken-off and actually landed within the same state, in fact is operated by an airline of that same state under a charter, lease or interchange agreement. Since such case of a purely "domestic" hijacking is treated as "international," it is surprising to discover that the sophisticated drafting of Article 3 results in preventing the application of the Convention when the places of take-off and actual landing, although situated within the state of registration, in fact are separated by the high seas or by a foreign state.

R. H. Mankiewicz, "The 1970 Hague Convention," Journal of Air Law and Commerce, Vol. 37, No. 2 (1971), 201-202.

[48]Several interesting problems manifest themselves by linking the scope of the Hague Convention to aircraft nationality. For example, what would happen in the case where a state is willing to exercise jurisdiction under the Convention provisions, but the involved aircraft is registered in a state not party to the Convention, and objects to such an application? Further, what would be the consequences if the aircraft were registered by a state which was party

empirical evidence[49] that would support this contention, crosstabulations were made on 352 recorded hijacking attempts[50] which occurred from January 1, 1960 to May 31, 1973. Three anticipated state enforcement responses--asylum, extradition, and prosecution--were treated as dependent

---

to the Convention, but is operated by an airline which is under the jurisdiction of another state which is not party to the Convention? See Mankiewicz, Ibid., p. 202. These questions have not gone unnoticed, as evidenced by Canadian and United States proposals advocating provision for sanctions against states defaulting their obligations under the Hague Convention. See Summary of the Work of the Legal Committee During its 18th Session, ICAO Doc. 8910; ICAO LC/SC CR WD/2.

[49]This digression into quantative analysis is expressly designed to determine: (1) the degree of enforcement reaction that has been forthcoming by the international community; (2) the likelihood of a certain enforcement response given various conditions (e.g., state status of termination, signatory or party to Tokyo or Hague Conventions, and national implications of aircraft registry); (3) general adherence to Convention provisions; (4) the feasibility of imposing Articles 3 and 7 of the Hague Convention; and (5) the evolutionary nature of international enforcement compliance during the last thirteen years. Theoretically, if greater compliance is evidenced, then the usefulness of international law-- through the convention process--would seem to be concomitantly strengthened.

[50]Preliminary data gathering revealed a total of 396 recorded illegal aircraft seizures occurring from 1930 to May 31, 1973. Of these, 25 took place prior to 1960, and were therefore eliminated. Of the remaining 371, insufficient information resulted in 19 more incidents being withdrawn from analysis, giving the present 352 cases. Dates for the eliminated post-1960 seizures are given below.

1. 7/19/60	6. 12/13/69	11. 2/4/71	16. 6/29/71
2. 3/17/62	7. 5/30/70	12. 5/8/71	17. 10/16/71
3. 6/4/69	8. 7/11/70	13. 5/13/71	18. 12/3/71
4. 8/12/69	9. 11/9/70	14. 5/18/71	19. 8/22/72
5. 11/30/69	10. 11/10/70	15. 6/12/71	

variables, and were statistically measured against several independent variables.[51]

TABLE 4

ENFORCEMENT RESPONSE BY STATE OF HIJACKING INITIATION

	Hijacking Terminated in Same State	Hijacking Terminated in Different State
Enforcement Response		
Asylum	0%	70%
Extradition	0%	10%
Prosecution	100%	20%
	100%	100%
	(N = 125)	(N = 227)

---

[51]The independent variables were: (1) Did the hijacking initiate in the state of termination?; (2) Was the aircraft registered in the state of termination?; (3) Was the "offender" a national of the termination state (or geographic region)?; (4) What was the motive of the hijacker? (This variable included six categories: refugee, desire of transportation, mentally unbalanced, political group, criminal, or profit); (5) Was the hijacking successful?; (6) Did extreme physical violence occur?; (7) Was external politics an issue?; (8) Did the state of aircraft termination become a signatory or party to the Tokyo Convention?; (9) Did the state of aircraft termination become signatory or party to the Hague Convention?; (10) Was the hijacker a national of the state where the incident began?; (11) Was the hijacker a national of the state where the incident terminated? Source data for variable verification included the following: New York _Times Index_ (1960-1973); Keesing's _Contemporary Archives_ (1960-1973); _Facts on File_ (1960-1973); F.A.A. _Chronology of Hijackings of U.S. Registered Aircraft_, updated February 1, 1973; references to incidents in all journals cited herein; and Congressional hearings and reports (see notes _supra_, 15, 25, and 38). Computations were done in accordance with "Subprogram Crosstabs," in Norman H. Nie,

Overall, the percentage of hijacking attempts which did not terminate in the same state where they were initiated account for nearly two-thirds (226) of the total sample. In the remaining cases (126) in which initiation and termination of the act were common to the same state, 100% of the offenders were prosecuted. Hence the overwhelming tendency is for states to prosecute offenders whose hijacking activities initiate and terminate within the same state. This constitutes a firmly established general principle of state practice,[52] lawfully sanctioned under the Hague international aviation agreement.[53]

Paragraph 3 of Article 3 asserts that the convention provisions apply ". . . only if the place of take-off or the place of actual landing of the aircraft on board which the offense is committed is situated outside the territory of the state of registration of the aircraft."[54] The resultant evidence from the findings indicates a similar pattern to that revealed in Table 4. Of 115 cases where the hijacked aircraft was registered in the terminating state, offenders

---

et al., Statistical Package for the Social Sciences (New York: McGraw-Hill Book Co., 1970), pp. 115-142. All calculations were run on CDC 6800 model computer.

[52]See Survey of International Law, prepared by the United Nations Secretariat. U.N. Doc. No. A/CN.4/Rev. 1, at 29-30 (1949).

[53]The Hague Convention, Article 4 (especially Paragraph 3), Article 6, and Article 7.

[54]*Ibid.*, Article 3, Paragraph 3.

were prosecuted in each instance; again, no cases resulted in either extradition or asylum for the hijackers. This complete percentage of prosecutions (100%) strongly supports the contention that nations whose registered aircraft were unlawfully seized, and the attempt is foiled while still within their territorial limits, will definitely prosecute the offenders under existing municipal laws. Table 5 has been constructed to reveal these findings:

TABLE 5

ENFORCEMENT RESPONSE BY HIJACKING INITIATION IN REGISTRATION STATE

	Hijacking Terminated in Registration State	Hijacking Terminated in Different State
Enforcement Response		
Asylum	0%	67%
Extradition	0%	10%
Prosecution	100%	23%
	100%	100%
	(N = 115)	(N = 237)

The Option to Prosecute or Extradite

Our findings conclusively demonstrate that states will prosecute offenders (in 100% of the attempts) under two conditions: (1) if the entire hijacking episode occurs in one state; (2) if the termination state is the same as the state of registry. The international significance of the Hague Convention is realized in these findings because it represents the evolutionary summit of designating legitimate international sanctions to municipal legal codes.[55]

Unlike the Tokyo Convention which failed to institute an international system to deter hijackers,[56] the Hague Convention obligates contracting parties to prosecute the offender if he is not extradited. Extradition is not specifically required, but Article 7 makes it clear that it is the only acceptable option to prosecution:

> The Contracting State in the territory of which the alleged offender is found shall, if it does not extradite him, be obliged, <u>without exception whatsoever</u> and whether or not the offence was committed in <u>its</u> territory, to submit the case to its competent authorities for the purpose of prosecution.
> Those authorities shall take their decision in the same manner as in the case of any ordinary offence of a serious nature under the law of that State.[57]

---

[55]International law remains a decentralized (or primitive) system of law, without a formal institution defining legal ramifications. Thus, it is primarily administered by the principle of self-help on the part of nation-states. This realization accents the Hague Convention's importance. That is, as a tool of international law (i.e., an international convention), the Hague Convention reveals the viable interaction and accommodation of international law vis-à-vis municipal legislation, and <u>vice</u> <u>versa</u>.

[56]See Raffat, "Control of Aircraft Hijacking," p. 147.

[57]The Hague Convention, Article 7. [Author's emphasis added.] The wording of Article 7 met with considerable controversy during the Diplomatic Conference (December 1-16, 1970). Australia and thirteen European countries contended that an absolute obligation to prosecute an "alleged offender" would be repugnant to several states wishing refrain from such action. A proposed alternative provision read: "shall . . . be obliged to submit the case to competent authorities for their decision whether to

To safeguard the individual rights of the accused offender, Article 6 establishes procedural guidelines to be followed by the jurisdictional state: Only "upon being satisfied that the circumstances so warrant" may the accused be taken into custody.[58] A factual investigation of the incident must be made and both the flag state and the alleged hijacker's nationality state must be notified of his detention.[59] Also, the state holding the offender may, ". . . if it considers it advisable, notify any other interested States of the fact that such person is in custody and of the circumstances which warrant the detention."[60]

It should not go unnoticed that the Tokyo Convention had similar requisite provisions to Article 6, but these were the only mandatory requirements set forth in the entire

---

prosecute him." Nonetheless, the proposal was rejected at the plenary meeting of the Conference by a twenty vote margin, with twenty-two states voting for passage, and eleven absentions.

The issue had formerly been pressed by the United States and the Soviet Union, who wished to add the phrase "irrespective of motivation," following "obliged." When opposition occurred, the Kenyan delegate proposed the wording, "without exception whatsoever," since these words were already in Resolution 2264 (XXV) of the United Nations' General Assembly. This was adopted by a sixty-one vote margin, with ten states in opposition, and eleven abstentions. Proposal Submitted to the Subcommittee on the Unlawful Seizure of Aircraft of the Legal Committee of ICAO, LG/SC. SA. WD 7 (May 5, 1969). See note 62, *infra*, p. 191.

[58]The Hague Convention, Article 6, Paragraph 1.

[59]*Ibid.*, Article 6, Paragraphs 2 and 3.

[60]*Ibid.*, Article 6, Paragraph 4.

convention.[61] The measured significance of the Hague's procedural principles regarding detention of the accused hijacker is heightened by the forceful provisions absent at Tokyo, i.e., Article 7, which requires prosecution ". . . without exception whatsoever,"[62] unless extradition arrangements have been made.[63]

In order to determine the extent of compliance with the punitive provisions laid down at the Hague in contrast to Tokyo, a comparative analysis was run by crosstabulating the termination states' enforcement responses against the question of formal convention participation. At the same time, it was hoped that these findings would compare the enforcement responses of "Convention" states vis-à-vis those of "non-Convention" states.

In response to the question, "Did the State in which the hijack episode terminated ever become a party or signatory

---

[61]See the Tokyo Convention, Articles 13-15, *infra*, pp. 288-89.

[62]The clause, "without exception whatsoever," found little unanimity among the delegates at the Conference. See Mankiewicz, "The 1970 Hague Convention," pp. 205-206; Guillaume, "La Convention de La Hague des 16 decembre 1970," *Annuaire Français de Droit International* (1970), 36; and Gillian M. E. White, "The Hague Convention for the Suppression of Unlawful Seizure of Aircraft," *Review of the International Commission of Jurists*, No. 6 (April - June, 1971), 42.

[63]Detailed provisions for extradition are found in Article 8. See discussion on extradition, *infra*, pp. 201-16.

to the Tokyo Convention?" the following data was obtained:

TABLE 6

ENFORCEMENT RESPONSE BY PARTICIPATION OF TERMINATING STATE IN THE TOKYO CONVENTION

	Hijacking Terminated in Tokyo Signatory or Party State	Hijacking Not Terminated in Tokyo Signatory or Party State
Enforcement Response		
Asylum	8%	69%
Extradition	5%	8%
Prosecution	87%	23%
	100%	100%
	(N = 138)	(N = 214)

Of the 138 cases where the landing state was a signatory or party to the Tokyo Convention, 87% of the offenders were prosecuted. In 11 incidents hijackers received asylum, and extradition was found in the remaining 7 attempts. Moreover, states which were neither signatories nor parties responded quite differently. Of the 214 incidents which terminated in a "non-Convention nation," asylum assumed the most frequent response and occurred in 147 (69%) of the hijackings; extradition resulted in 16 instances (8%); and prosecution in only 50 (23%) cases.

It is particularly interesting to note that when the aggregate hijacking enforcement response was subjected to regional analysis,[64] the majority of the offenders who received asylum (77%) terminated the aircraft sizure in

---

[64]Regional analysis evidenced these findings:

INFLUENCE OF REGIONAL ANALYSIS ON STATE ENFORCEMENT RESPONSE TO "HIJACKERS"

	Response by Region of Initiation			Response by Region of Termination		
Region	Asylum	Extradition	Prosecution	Asylum	Extradition	Prosecution
Latin America						
Number	63	13	30	124	18	41
Percent	40	13	18	78	79	24
North America						
Number	68	17	75	6	2	61
Percent	43	75	44	4	9	36
Western Europe						
Number	8	1	14	3	1	26
Percent	5	4	8	2	4	15
Eastern Europe						
Number	4	0	22	2	1	11
Percent	2	0	13	2	4	7
Middle East/ Arab Africa						
Number	3	1	8	14	1	12
Percent	2	4	5	9	4	7
All Others						
Number	13	1	21	10	0	19
Percent	8	4	12	6	0	11
Column Total	159	23	170	159	23	170

Latin American countries. The next most frequent area to grant asylum was the Middle East—Arab Africa region, accounting for nearly 9% of the relevant incidents.[65] These findings point up the weakness of an "incomplete convention," i.e., the success or failure of deterring unlawful activities in the international system depends upon the accession of reluctant states (in this case, viz., Cuba, Algeria, Syria, Lebanon, and Albania) that might harbor fugitives under the guise of "political crimes."[66] Even so, states which are parties and/or signatories to the Tokyo Convention do comply with the "spirit" of that agreement, as evidenced by the 92% prosecution—extradition rate found.

When the termination—state question was applied to the Hague Convention, a slight decrease in both total grants of asylum and prosecutions was realized. Using the

	Response by Region of Initiation			Response by Region of Termination		
Region	Asylum	Extradition	Prosecution	Asylum	Extradition	Prosecution
Column Percent	45	7	48	45	7	48

[65]See note 64, supra.

[66]See note 75, infra and accompanying text.

same sample of 352 hijacking attempts, the following results were tabulated:

TABLE 7

ENFORCEMENT RESPONSE BY PARTICIPATION OF TERMINATING STATE IN THE HAGUE CONVENTION

	Hijacking Terminated in Hague Signatory or Party State	Hijacking not Terminated in Hague Signatory or Party State
Enforcement Response		
Asylum	12%	74%
Extradition	4%	8%
Prosecution	84%	18%
	100%	100%
	(N = 164)	(N = 188)

On one hand, three-fourths (74%) of the hijacking attempts terminating in "non-Convention" states resulted in asylum for the offenders; extradition and prosecution enforcement responses only occurred in the remaining 49 incidents. Conversely, "Convention states" prosecuted or extradited accused hijackers in 88% of the instances. Unexpectedly, the total number of asylum grants to offenders was slightly higher in Hague terminal states than Tokyo states. While this may be explained by the greater number of states who have participated in the Hague Convention (88) relative to the Tokyo agreement (71), asylum still presents a perplexing issue that needs to be reckoned with. The Hague Convention embodies a mature legal evolution of international efforts to deter unlawful aircraft seizures. Even so, it is seriously disabilitated by the universally sanctioned municipal right of providing "safe-havens" for offenders under select circumstances. For this reason, it merits more detailed attention.

The extradite-or-prosecute obligation in the Hague Convention text is binding upon all contracting states, regardless of the location of the offense.[67] It is apparent that this provision (Article 7) is aimed at denying sanctuary to any alleged offenders, in every part of the global community. By so doing, the rewards and opportunities to escape punitive actions would be eliminated for potential hijackers, thereby discouraging future attempts. However, this has not fully materialized. Extradition has been grossly underused in jurisdictional settlements, whereas the legal antithesis--asylum--has been all too often the case. First, let us consider the basic implications of extradition.

Extradition involves denial of asylum and the surrender of an individual to a requesting state.[68] Customary international law provides no rule which imposes a duty

---

[67]The Hague Convention, Article 7.

[68]See Oppenheim, International Law, p. 696.

to extradite,[69] hence extradition becomes either a matter of comity or treaty between states.[70] In view of this, John McMahon frankly writes,

> No nation is a party to an extradition treaty with every other state, and the treaties which do exist fail to provide for the certainty of surrender which the hazards posed by air piracy demand. Thus, the present system of extradition does not make surrender or prosecution sufficiently certain to operate as an effective deterrent. This failure is evidenced by the two most common types of extradition treaties: (1) those that list the offenses for which extradition will be granted, and (2) those that grant extradition only for a crime punishable under both the requesting and granting states' laws. Only a few of the extradition treaties that list offenses for which extradition will be granted include the unlawful seizure of an aircraft.[71]

Despite the fact that "air piracy" has been largely omitted as an offense in "list" type extradition treaties, the Hague Convention contains a number of provisions which facilitate extradition for the offense between contracting

---

[69]See Harvard Research in International Law,"Draft Convention on Extradition and Comments," A.J.I.L., Vol. 29 (1935), 16-434.

[70]In Factor v. Laubenheimer, 290 U.S. 276, 287 (1933), it was stated that: "The principles of international law recognize no right to extradite apart from treaty. While a government may, if agreeable to its own constitution and laws, voluntarily exercise the power to surrender a fugitive from justice to the country from which he has fled, and it has been said that it is under a moral duty to do so, . . . the legal right to demand his extradition and the correlative duty to surrender him to the demanding country exist only when created by treaty." Quoted in Bishop, International Law, p. 471.

[71]John P. McMahon, "Air Hijacking: Extradition as a Deterrent," The Georgetown Law Journal, Vol. 58 (1970), 1137.

states. In full, Article 8 reads as follows:

> 1. The offence shall be deemed to be included as an extraditable offence in any extradition treaty existing between Contracting States, Contracting States undertake to include the offence as an extraditable offence in every extradition treaty to be concluded between them.
> 2. If a Contracting State which makes extradition conditional on the existence of a treaty receives a request for extradition from another Contracting State with which it has no extradition treaty, it may at its option consider this Convention as the legal basis for extradition in respect of the offence. Extradition shall be subject to the other conditions provided by the law of the requested State.
> 3. Contracting States which do not make extradition conditional on the existence of a treaty shall recognize the offence as an extraditable offence between themselves subject to the conditions provided by the law of the requested State.
> 4. The offence shall be treated, for the purpose of extradition between Contracting States, as if it had been committed not only in the place in which it occurred but also in the territories of the States required to establish their jurisdiction in accordance with Article 4, paragraph 1.[72]

From the above, it is easy to see that Article 8 ". . . serves the purpose of a multilateral extradition treaty between Contracting States. . . ."[73] in a threefold manner: first, the "offence" is included in all existing extradition treaties (Paragraph 1); second, there is provision for an option to allow states to utilize the Convention's definition of the offence ". . . as an extraditable offence between themselves." (Paragraph 3).

---

[72]The Hague Convention, Article 8.

[73]Jacobson, "From Piracy on the High Seas," p. 183. For a summary of rules governing extradition, see Kurt Von Schunschnigg, International Law (Milwaukee, Wisconsin: The Bruce Publishing Co., 1959), pp. 224-225.

Despite these laudatory facets of Article 8, there is an important omission which is usually included in bilateral treaties; i.e., the two non-extradition exceptions, nationals of the requested state[74] and "political offenders."[75] Herein the weakness of the Convention becomes manifest. Since Article 8 instructs states to exercise extradition as subject to the ". . . conditions provided by the law of the requested state,"[76] a nation may lawfully reject an extradition plea based upon the nationality or "political offender" exceptions should they appear in the extradition treaty with the requesting state. This realization exhumes the core of the

---

[74]Whiteman, Digest, Vol 6 (1968), pp. 800, 865. States relying on the nationality basis of jurisdiction are sometimes reluctant to extradite their own nationals and instead prefer to try them in domestic courts for offenses committed abroad. See Coumas v. Superior Court of San Joaquin Co., Supreme Court of California, 31 Cal. 2d 682 (1948) and Charlton v. Kelly, 229 U.S. 447 (1913).

[75]On the disputed issue of "political offence" as an extraditable crime, see Lora L. Deere, "Political Offenses in the Law and Practice of Extradition," A.J.I.L., Vol. 27 (1933), 247-270; Manuel R. Garcia-Mora, "Present Status of Political Offences in the Law of Extradition and Asylum," University of Pittsburg Law Review, Vol. 14 (1953), 371; Harvard Research in International Law, "Extradition," p. 15, 107; and Garcia-Mora, "The Nature of Political Offenses: A Knotty Problem of Extradition Law," Virginia Law Review, Vol. 48 (1962), 1229.

[76]The Hague Convention, Article 8, Paragraph 2.

extradite-or-prosecute dilemma as it become enmeshed in the time-honored[77] municipal right of states to grant asylum. Certainly, the decision to provide asylum is dependent upon an individual state's perceptions of the incident's ramifications.[78] That is to say, do the pertinent circumstances merit the consideration of safe haven for an offender as designated in the receiving state's municipal codes? If they do, asylum will be given, and the extradition request will be rejected. As seen in our data, the asylum phenomenon constitutes the most formidable obstacle hindering total prosecution of "alleged offenders," and thus reduces the international efficacy to suppress illegal aircraft seizure attempts. This brings us to the diplomatic nuances that earmark asylum.

---

[77]See Otto Kirchheimer, "Asylum," The American Political Science Review, Vol. 53 (December, 1959), 985-1016 and Manuel R. Garcia-Mora, International Law and Asylum as a Human Right (Washington: Public Affairs Press, 1956).

[78]This contention was realized in the heated debate over the wording in Article 7 during the Hague Convention proceedings. Gillian M. E. White well-stated the problem as he observed of Article 7:

> Those authorities must make their decision whether to prosecute or not in the same manner as in the case of any ordinary offence of a serious nature under the law of that State. These words were included because some South American States apparently take different factors into consideration in deciding whether to prosecute for a 'political' offence from those taken into account in deciding whether to prosecute for an 'ordinary' offence, with the result that a 'political' offender may be treated more leniently than an 'ordinary' offender. The Convention therefore requires that for the purpose of deciding whether to prosecute or not (though not for the

Asylum, Safe Haven, and the Political Crime

Article 14 of the United Nations Universal Declaration of Human Rights forcefully states, "Everyone has the right to seek and enjoy in other countries asylum from persecution."[79] A more recent General Assembly resolution[80] reaffirms this principle as it declares that the situation of persons invoking such a right is of concern to the international community, and such a person shall not be subject to expulsion or compulsory return to any state where he may be subject to persecution.[81]

Consequently, with regard to illegal aircraft seizures, an important question unfolds: are contracting states to the Hague Convention--which also support the 1948 Declaration of Human Rights and provide asylum for certain refugee hijackers--in violation of Article 7 which obligates prosecution or extradition "without exception whatsoever?" McMahon proposes some interesting considerations:

> purpose of deciding whether to extradite or not) hijacking must always be treated as an 'ordinary' (though serious) offence.

White, "The Hague Convention," p. 42.

[79]General Assembly Resolution 217, U.N. Doc. A/810, at 7 (1948), reprinted in A.J.I.L. Supp. Vol. 43 (1949), 129.

[80]General Assembly Resolution 2312, 22 U.N. GAOR Supp. 16, at 81, U.N. Doc. A/6716 (1967).

[81]*Ibid.*, Article 3.

> Hijacking . . . is inextricably interwined with the notion of political offenses and the concept of asylum. . . . Hence, if an international agreement requiring extradition or prosecution is to function in deterring the forcible diversion of aircraft, it must be a compromise between the preservation of the state's right to grant refuge to individuals who flee from prosecution and the need to discourage hijackers. The adoption of too liberal a provision on the issue of asylum will fail to solve the problem of hijacking, while too strict a requirement for extradition or prosecution will be unacceptable to many nations.[82]

The crux of the problem rests in the "political offences" category. Although the asylum exception for political offenses appears to be universal,[83] the term "political offense" remains largely undefined by treaty,[84] extradition laws,[85] or uniform states practices.[86] Therefore, nations practically have *carte blanche* in determining justification for asylum, especially in a non-listed

---

[82] McMahon, "Extradition as a Deterrent," p. 1150.

[83] Harvard Research on International Law. "Extradition," p. 108.

[84] See Alona Evans, "Reflections Upon the Political Offenses in International Practice," *A.J.I.L.*, Vol. 57 (1963), 8.

[85] Whiteman, *Digest*, Vol. 6, p. 800; Harvard Research on International Law, "Extradition," p. 113. A contrary proposition is put forth by Garcia-Mora, "The Nature of Political Offenses," p. 1229.

[86] Garcia-Mora, *Ibid.*, p. 1228.

extraditable offense such as hijacking.[87]

Since asylum proved to be such a significant enforcement response,[88] particularly when the terminal state had no other formal connection to the incident, an analysis was performed on asylum frequency as determined by hijacker motivation. Six motivation categories were then constructed and correlated to state enforcement responses.[89] Briefly,

---

[87]Even in the case of listed offences, the principle of "speciality" poses similar problems. For example, unlawful aircraft seizure involves elements of many crimes (robbery, kidnapping, assault, and larceny), but the hijacker can only be tried for the extraditable offense, often resulting "in a penalty less than that commensurate with the total offense." McMahon, "Extradition as a Deterrent," p. 1138. Also see Evans, "Reflections Upon the Political Offenses," p. 8.

[88]See Table 6, <u>supra</u>.

[89]The author wishes to acknowledge the five categories of motivation supplied by Lieutenant Colonel James S. G. Turner in "Piracy in the Air," pp. 89-93. The sixth category, "For the Purpose of Extortion," became a reality since his article was written (1969).

With regard to state enforcement responses, asylum figures were catalogued from incidents where the offender was given refuge without punitive action; extradition included persons returned through formal diplomatic extradition procedures, deportation, and voluntary return; prosecution figures reflect actual (municipal) trial efforts to adjudicate the guilt or innocence of an "offender." This encompassed not only prison convictions, but also juvenile detention and commitment to mental institutions.

It must be realized that the sources from which the hijackers' motivations were catalogued sometimes differed in their assessment of the motive. This was especially true in cases involving political groups committing extortions, and then using the aircraft as a vehicle of escape. These conflicting descriptions necessitated subjective discretion on the author's part to establish the chief motive, based on the consensus of reports. The sources used to determine the six motivation categories were:

1. The escaping political refugee. In this category were placed those persons who illegally seized aircraft to flee from "an oppressive political regime." The key phrase, "oppressive political regime" was defined as one which had restrictive exit regulations to the point where a person could not leave freely when he so desired.[90]

2. For purpose of transportation. Unlike political refugees, persons within this grouping were motivated by what Lissitzyn denotes as "travel purposes." The majority of cases involved Castro supporters in Colombia, Venezuela, and the United States. Since no regularly scheduled commercial air service operates between these countries and Cuba, the easiest means of transportation was to unlawfully divert an aircraft.[91]

3. The unbalanced person. Mentally disturbed individuals and "attention seekers" fell within this

---

motivation were: The New York Times Index (1960-1973); Keesing's Contemporary Archives (1960-1973); Facts on File (1960-1973); F.A.A., Chronology of Hijacking of U.S. Registered Aircraft, updated February 1, 1973; Hubbard, The Skyjacker: His Flights of Fantasy; all journal articles cited herein; and all Congressional reports and hearings cited herein.

[90]Admittedly, subjective discretion was used in this instance. Nations most often found in this category were: The Soviet Union, Poland, East Germany, Czechoslovakia, South Vietnam, and Cuba.

[91]As Turner reveals, "Cuba has scheduled commercial air service only to Mexico, Spain and various Soviet bloc nations." Turner, "Piracy in the Air," p. 112, at note 6.

classification. Characteristic of this type offender was what the ". ... Chief Surgeon of the Federal Aviation Administration has hypothesized to be a 'hijacker syndrome' in which the hijacker believes he can prove himself an effective human being by commandeering an airline. . . ."[92] In short, this describes the person who is plagued by mental, emotional, and social problems, and seeks media-wide publicity to compensate for personal failures in life.[93] Included also were offenders who used the hijacking experience as a rationalization for suicide.[94]

---

[92]Turner, Ibid., p. 92. See "What Can Be Done About Skyjacking?," Time, Vol. 96, No. 4 (January 31, 1969), pp. 19-20.

[93]Several interesting cases were discovered in this classification. D. L. Booth, a fourteen-year old Cincinnati youth, attempted to hijack a Delta airliner by holding an eighteen-year old girl at knifepoint, but was persuaded to surrender to authorities before the aircraft departed. His mother later attributed the boy's motive to avid interest in the Minichiello case (for details, see infra, p. 211), New York Times, November 11, 1969; 93: 4 and November 13, 1969; 16: 2. The most comprehensive study on the "hijacker's mentality" (with psychological case histories) is David G. Hubbard's The Skyjacker: His Flights of Fantasy. See especially pp. 97-101, 107-116, 130-148, 171-172, and 177-185. Also, Turner lists eight cases of mentally unbalanced persons, all linked by ". . . the idea in the hijacker's mind that he could start life anew in Cuba, gaining fame, glory, and recognition in the process." One hijacker even listed his name on the ticket as "El Pirata Cofrisi"--a famous 18th century Carribbean pirate. Turner, "Piracy in the Air," pp. 92-93.

[94]For commentary on the "suicide wish," see "Murder in the Sky: Eastern Airlines, DC-9," Newsweek, Vol. 75 (March 30, 1970), p. 23 and "Why Not Frisk," Nation, Vol. 210 (June 22, 1970), p. 741.

4. The political group. Antagonistic national ideologies have precipitated radical political groups who have used hijacking incidents for protest and propaganda purposes.[95] Perhaps the best known of these is the Palestine Liberation Front, but others not to be overlooked were the Black Panthers, the Eritean Liberation, and the "Red Army" students of Japan. Acts of terrorism[96] and plane sabotage[97] done to further a political movement were also included under this heading.

---

[95]Many "sensational" cases were found among these incidents: The El Al Case (July 23, 1968) in which Arab terrorists forcibly diverted an Israeli airliner to Algeria as "an act of war;" the Tshombe Case (June 30, 1967); the PFLP seizure and detention of two hundred passengers on board a TWA and Swiss Air Jet Liner in the Jordan desert for two weeks (September 8-30, 1970); the Galvao "supporters" who dropped political leaflets over Lisbon (November 10, 1961); and the recent seizure of a Colombian airliner by members of the National Liberation Army (ELN), a leftist organization. This was the record aircraft seizure, in time and distance--it lasted sixty hours, and covered eleven countries, with landings in five of them. (June 1-3, 1973. Excluded from statistical analysis because of the incident's late occurrence). Detailed information on the above incidents may be found on the respective dates in the New York Times.

[96]See "The Role of International Law in Combating Terrorism," Department of State Publication 8689, General Foreign Policy Series 270 (January, 1973), especially pp. 1, 2, and 5, and "Foreign Terrorism Spreading to U.S.?," U.S. News and World Report, Vol. 75, No. 3 (July 16, 1973), pp. 37-40.

[97]E.g., two Palestinian commandoes hijacked TWA Flight 840 (Rome to Athens) and landed in Damascus, Syria. A time bomb planted in the cockpit exploded, destroying the nose section, but no injuries were reported. See "This is Your Captain," Newsweek, Vol. 74, No. 10 (September 8, 1969), 37-38; "Arab Guerrillas Adopt Air Piracy as Tactic,"

5. The escaping criminal. Unlike the fleeing political refugee, this category comprised those persons with criminal backgrounds who used illegal aircraft diversion to escape trial or prosecution for some violation of a municipal code.[98] Counted also were criminals who, in the process of being transported from one confinement location to another, managed to escape current sentences by diverting the aircraft to another nation.[99]

6. For purpose of extortion. In recent years, hijacking attempts for "a profit motive" have become a common occurrence.[100] The robbery of individual passengers has been rare, but not so with "ransom" demands to ensure the the safety of the plane, the passengers, and the crew. It should be noted that this category was difficult to

---

Aviation Week and Space Technology (September 14, 1970), 33-38 and note 35, supra, p. 177 and accompanying text. Legal provisions to deter acts of sabotage are in the Montreal Convention, and are discussed infra, pp. 216-229.

[98]The most frequent destination of United States' criminals was Cuba, ". . . the inference being that these fugitives felt they would be safe from prosecution if they reached Cuba." Turner, "Piracy in the Air," p. 91.

[99]Only two incidents were found to be of this nature. Both involved United States aircraft, both were unsuccessful, and no injuries resulted. Dates for the incidents: May 30, 1969 and September 22, 1970. For discussion, see Turi, et al., Criminal Justice Monograph, pp. 156, 158.

[100]This category was omitted from Turner's analysis (1969) because no cases up to that time could be called "profit-motivated." Since then, forty-two incidents have occurred.

construct since often motives overlapped, especially those involving political undercurrents and a mentally unbalanced person.[101]

Since 1960, our findings revealed a total of 62 attempted aircraft seizures were perpetrated by "escaping political refugees." As expected, a large number (45%) were granted asylum in accordance with the Universal Declaration of Human Rights.[102] The high rate of prosecution (50%) can be accounted for by those attempts which failed, and those successful seizures which violated municipal laws where the aircraft landed.

Between January 1, 1960 and May 31, 1973, 148 aircraft seizure attempts were motivated for transportation from one nation to another. It may seem surprising to learn that 62% of these incidents resulted in asylum for the offenders, but this was largely explained by the 85 United States-to-Cuba flights, most of which were merely "for travel purposes."

Thirty-five offenders were found to be mentally unbalanced in their motivations. Only one person of this group was granted asylum, whereas 26 were prosecuted. Noteworthy also is the fact that the 23% extradition rate is the highest of any category.

---

[101]Extortion demands varied from a low of $50,000 (R. La Point, January 20, 1972 and D. B. Carre, June 30, 1972) to a high of $10,000,000 (H. Jackson, L. Cale, and M. Cale, November 10, 1972). For a comprehensive summation and listing of all extortion attempts, see""Domestic and Foreign Aircraft Hijackings," mimeograph publication of the Federal Aviation Administration Office of Air Transportation Security (December 1, 1972), especially pp. 34, ff.

[102]Article 14, Paragraph 2, General Assembly Resolution 217, U.N. Doc. A/810, at 7 (1948).

TABLE 8

ENFORCEMENT RESPONSE BY ALLEGED MOTIVATION OF HIJACKERS

	Transportation	Escaping Political Refugee	Political Group	Fleeing Criminal	Profit Motivation	Unbalanced Persons
Enforcement Response						
Asylum	62%	45%	50%	52%	12%	3%
Extradition	4%	5%	8%	7%	2%	23%
Prosecution	34%	50%	42%	41%	86%	74%
	100%	100%	100%	100%	100%	100%
	(N = 148)	(N = 62)	(N = 38)	(N = 27)	(N = 42)	(N = 35)

Nearly identical percentages were found in the "political group" and "fleeing criminal" motivational categories. Asylum was granted to members of politcal groups 50% of the time, to fleeing criminals 52% of the time; extradition was enacted at respective rates of 8% and 7%; and prosecution, 42% to 41%. It is interesting to observe that escaping criminals were greeted with asylum at a higher percentage than overt participants in an unlawful seizure motivated by political purposes.

The most highly prosecuted classification was the extortionists--in 86% of the incidents. The asylum rate was the lowest of any category (with the single exception of the lone mentally unbalanced recipient), and contrary to our expectations, only one extradition resulted from the profit—oriented "aerial piracy."

Several conclusions about enforcement response vis-à-vis motivation can be postulated from these findings. First, the offender's motivation is a prime factor in conditioning a state's perception of the hijacking incident. Second, where political undercurrents are present, asylum is a likely response. Formal legal reception of transportation—motivated offenders and fleeing criminals can be explained by the propaganda value of welcoming "oppressed fugitives from an imperialist power." Third, the mentally unstable person is a more likely candidate for extradition, and is almost certain to be prosecuted.[103] Fourth, the overt crime of extortion finds little sympathy among landing states. Fifth, although 45% of the entire sample received asylum, it should be remembered that conditions in the receiving state have often been inclement towards hijackers. This is especially true in Cuba where reports have revealed that offenders are confined to areas and oftentimes forced to labor in the fields.[104] Finally, prosecution and extradition accounted for more than half

---

[103]Prosecution in this instance is also inclusive of commitment to a mental institution. In the case of Corporal R. Minichiello, an AWOL Marine who hijacked a plane from Los Angeles to Rome, Italy, extradition pleas from the United States were rejected because "extradition need not be granted if penalties for the crime in the country requesting extradition are not permitted in the country that could grant it." Unlike the United States, Italy at that time (November, 1969) had no death penalty. New York Times, November 27, 1969; 11:5.

[104]A United States Congressional report declared:

> Again information is very limited respecting the fate that awaits the hijackers once they reach Cuba. Indications are that all undergo some period of detention immediately after their arrival and that many are subsequently released and given work, mostly hard labor in agriculture. The witness for the Department of State testified "our information is that the treatment there is not good, and that the hijackers are, in fact, mostly very unhappy with their lot."

U.S. Congress, House of Representatives, Aircraft Piracy. A Preliminary Report of the Committee on Interstate and Foreign Commerce, House Report No. 91-33, 91st Congress, 1st sess., 1969, p. 2. See also Frank E. Loy, "Some International Approaches to Dealing with Hijacking of Aircraft," International Lawyer, Vol. IV (1970), 446; Arthur I. Hirsch and David Fuller, "Aircraft Piracy and Extradition," New York Law Forum, Vol. 16 (Spring, 1970), 406-412; and U.S. Congress, Senate, Committee on Foreign Relations. Aircraft Hijacking Convention, Hearings before the Committee on Foreign Relations, on Executive A, 92nd Congress, 1st sess., 1971, pp. 22-29.

of the enforcement dispositions, designating aircraft seizure a violation of international law as provided by the Hague Convention.

The correlative import of motivation and enforcement response brought forth an intriguing thought: What variables hold the most predictive value in gauging state enforcement response? To explore this question, the "Multiple Response, Multi-Variate Probit Program"[105] was utilized, and produced the results in Table 9.

The "Probit" analysis shown in Table 9 produced four statistically significant variables of predictive capacity upon enforcement response: the nationality of the hijacker, the success of the seizure attempt, signature or ratification of the Hague Convention, and the motivation of the offender. Two other variables, viz., termination of the hijacking incident within a signatory and/or party state to the Tokyo Convention, and the diplomatic implications of "external" international politics in adjudicating the incident, registered significance at only the .10 level. Hence, though these latter two variables may influence the response of states towards offenders, the probability of chance or accident is too great to be of statistical significance.

---

[105]See Richard McKelvey and William Zavoina, "An IBM Fortran IV Program to Perform N-Chrotomous Multivariate Probit Analysis," Behavioral Science, Vol. 16, No. 2 (March, 1971), 186-87, and William Zavoina and Richard McKelvey, "A Statistical Model for the Analysis of Legislative Voting Behavior," (unpublished American Political Science Association Convention paper, 1969).

TABLE 9

IMPACT OF VARIABLES UPON PREDICTING STATE ENFORCEMENT RESPONSE TO "HIJACKERS"

Characteristics of Hijacking Incident	Maximum Likelihood Estimate (MLE)	Standard Error (SE)	MLE/SE	Significance Level
Hijacker's Nationality	-.711	.198	-3.595	.01
Success of Hijacking Attempt	-1.253	.282	-4.441	.01
Terminated within Signatory and/or Party State to the Hague Convention	.972	.256	3.797	.01
Alleged Motivation of Hijacker	.144	.064	2.256	.05
Terminated within Signatory and/or Party State to Tokyo Convention	.529	.275	1.924	.10
External International Politics Involved	.440	.245	1.799	.10
Excessive Violence Involved	.369	.256	1.441	n.s.
Hijacking Terminated in State of Aircraft Registry	-3.422	30.934	-.111	n.s.
Hijacking Begun and Terminated in Same State	5.134	30.933	.166	n.s.

These findings suggest that international conventions designed to suppress unlawful aircraft seizures must provide effective control responses for hijacker nationality, motivation of the offender, and success of the incident.[106] Moreover, "Probit" revealed the importance of the Hague Convention's impact upon state enforcement responses. The terminal state's decision to extradite, prosecute, or grant asylum to an offender was previously demonstrated to largely depend upon four factors: (1) the nationality of the offender; (2) the status of the incident as a "political offense;" (3) the motivation of the offender; (4) the success or failure of the seizure. Accordingly, "Probit" analysis verified the relative impact these variables had upon predicting state enforcement responses, and added another factor which must be considered, *viz.*, participation in the Hague Convention. In other words, the Hague Convention was shown to be a statistically significant variable in calculating what legal reactions nation-states will present when confronted with a hijacking episode within their territory.

---

[106]This is not to underestimate deterrent measures by municipal government and airport officials. These have been far-reaching and indeed effective. The sky marshal programs, electronic metal detection devices, television surveillance, rewards, and personal searches have been important factors in the noticeable decline of hijackings. A multiplicity of articles are available on these preparations but the following are particularly helpful: "Airport Security Searches and the Fourth Amendment," *Columbia Law Review*, Vol. 71

The Hague Convention is a hallmark in international cooperative efforts to suppress "skyjacking." The urgent need to free commercial air transport from the threat of seizure prompted nations to respond with a vigorous denunciation of the (un-named) "offence," and to provide more vehement punitive measures. Contracting states were now required to establish jurisdiction over the offender when apprehended, even if the offence did not occur within their territorial borders.[107] The fact that eighty-eight members of the international community have formally sanctioned the deterrent provisions condemning unlawful aircraft seizure has elevated this act to the status of an international crime.[108] Essentially, Artices 4 and 7 lay the groundwork

---

(June, 1971), 1039; "F.A.A. Outlines Actions Taken Against Crimes Aboard Aircraft," F.A.A. Information, Vol. 45 (May 12, 1964), 3; "Anti-Hijacking Plans Augmented," Aviation Week and Space Technology (November 9, 1970), 32; "New Traps for Skyjackers," U.S. News and World Report, Vol. 74, No. 3 (January 15, 1973), pp. 15-17; and McClintock, "Skyjacking," pp. 29-80.

[107]The Hague Convention, Article 7.

[108]Customary international law provides no institutionalized format or criteria to determine the presence of "an international crime." However, when an international action violates "human rights"--whether by a nation or an individual--it is subject to being termed "an international crime." Gerald J. Mangone enumerates three processes that aid in clarifying the status of an individual type of act in international law: (1) a declaration of common standards of human rights on which states can generally agree; (2) signing and ratification of a treaty in which the states undertake to provide basic human rights through their municipal laws; and (3) establishment of international judicial machinery to maintain both the rights of states

for exercising universal jurisdiction to apprehend and punish offenders, and by so doing, affixed the status of hijackers ". . . in the same category as sea pirates who may be prosecuted wherever they are found, regardless of where they commit offenses."[109]

The Montreal Convention

Another aspect of the international effort to secure safe civil air transport merits discussion at this time. Between June 16-30, 1970, an Extraordinary Session of the ICAO Assembly met in Montreal, Canada, to discuss further preventive hijacking measures.[110] This meeting was convened upon the request of eleven European states[111] to

---

against one another and the rights of individuals under the treaty. Respective to unlawful aircraft seizure, these processes were fulfilled by the Hague Convention, therefore making this act internationally sanctioned as a crime, subject to prosecution or extradition by municipal judicial procedures. Article 12 permits the parties to "refer the dispute (over application of the Convention) to the International Court of Justice by request in conformity with the Statute of the Court." Gerald J. Mangone, The Elements of International Law (Homewood, Illinois: The Dorsey Press, 1967), p. 255.

[109]U.S., President. Message from the President of the United States transmitting to the Senate the Convention for the Suppression of Unlawful Acts Against the Safety of Civil Aviation. Executive T, 92nd Cong., 2nd sess., 1972, p. 18.

[110]Boyle, "Aircraft Hijacking," p. 465.

[111]The formal request was made by Austria, Belgium, Denmark, Federal Republic of Germany, Finland, Netherlands, Norway, Spain, Sweden, Switzerland, and the United Kingdom. U.S., President. Message from the President of the United States transmitting to the Senate the Convention for the Suppression of Unlawful Acts Against the Safety of Civil Aviation. Executive T, 92nd Cong., 2nd sess., 1972, p. 7.

hammer out deterrent controls against acts of sabotage, such as those carried out against Austrian and Swiss airliners in February, 1970.[112]

First priority was given to negotiations to formulate a more comprehensive international agreement than provided in Article 1 of the Hague Convention. Preliminary documents submitted by the United States called for international condemnation of sabotage acts, terrorist attacks, and passenger use of firearms on board an aircraft.[113] Similar proposals advanced by other nations underscored this need for a "complementary" Hague Convention to encompass these unlawful operations.

In response to a draft resolution co-sponsored by the United States and eleven other nations, the Assembly unanimously adopted a series of related resolutions emphasizing the requisite immediacy of international action. During the course of the Conference, twenty-four resolutions, augmented by two appendices, were passed by the Assembly.[114]

---

[112]In one case, 47 persons died in the crash of a SWISSAIR plane on which an explosion occurred about nine minutes after its take-off at Zurich. In the other case, an Austrian Airlines plane which had taken off from Frankfurt experienced an explosion in the freight hold which blew a 2 by 3 foot hole in the fuselage. Fortunately, this aircraft landed safely with no casualties to the 33 passengers aboard. U.S., Congress, Senate, Aircraft Sabotage Convention, Executive Rept. No. 92-34, 92nd Cong., 2nd sess., 1972, p. 8.

[113]Message from the President of the United States, op cit., p. 7.

[114]ICAO Resolutions A17-1 to A17-24, Appendix A to Resolution A17-10 and Appendix B to Resolution A17-10. The

Of these, three deserve special mention for their posture towards civil aviation security. Resolution A17-1 (since termed "the Declaration of Montreal") vehemently denounced those ". . . acts of violence directed against international civil air transport and airports," and exhorted states ". . . not to have recourse, under any circumstances" to such acts.[115] To implement this resolution, the Assembly called upon nations (through Resolution A17-3) to attend the Diplomatic Conference scheduled for December, 1970, at the Hague.[116]

The third significant resolution (Resolution A17-20) directed the ICAO Legal Committee to convene no later than November, 1970, in order:

> . . . to prepare . . . a draft Convention on acts of unlawful interference against international aviation (other than those covered by the draft Convention on unlawful seizure of aircraft) with a view to adoption of the Convention at a diplomatic conference as soon as practicable and if possible not later than the summer of 1971 in the Northern Hemisphere. . . .[117]

In essence, this meant that plans were being laid to supercede the reaches of the Hague provisions, six months prior to their formal consideration by the community of nations. It is rare for international efforts to so overlap and to

---

full texts of the resolutions may be found in International Legal Materials, Vol. 9, No. 6 (November, 1970), 1274-1285.

[115] Ibid., p. 1275.

[116] Ibid., p. 1276.

[117] Ibid., p. 1280.

progress with such rapidity--an obvious signal that solutions could not be delayed. In fact, one diplomat has observed that the ". . . normal rules of procedure on study of draft convention were waived, and the Legal Committee met in late September 1970 in London to prepare the draft convention."[118] This became the Hague Convention's successor, the Montreal Sabotage Convention.

Thus, from September 29 to October 22, 1970, the Eighteenth Session of the ICAO Legal Committee convened in London to prepare the mandated draft convention. Ironically, the Committee used the yet unsanctioned Hague Convention as a directive model, which accounts for the many parallel provisions of the two documents. Even so, some aspects of the new agreement,[119] *viz*., definition of the offense,[120] the concepts of "aircraft in service" and "aircraft in flight,"[121] and jurisdictional provisions[122]

---

[118]Statement by Charles N. Brower, "Department Urges Senate Advice and Consent to Ratification of Montreal Convention on Aviation Sabotage," *Department of State Bulletin*, Vol. 67, No. 1738 (October 16, 1972), 445.

[119]Convention for the Suppression of Unlawful Acts Against the Safety of Civil Aviation, ICAO Doc. 8966. In *International Legal Materials*, Vol. 10, No. 1 (January, 1971), 133-36 and *Department of State Bulletin*, Vol. 64((1971), 53. (Hereinafter cited as the Montreal Convention.)

[120]The Montreal Convention, Article 1.

[121]*Ibid*., Article 2.

[122]*Ibid*., Article 5.

were greatly broadened in scope. These novel provisions exhausted the bulk of the twenty-six plenary meetings, the five meetings of a special Working Group, and the five meetings of a Drafting Group to prepare them.[123] Nonetheless, within less than one month, the Committee had adopted a final draft convention for international presentation.

In accordance with customary ICAO Committee procedures, the draft convention was then submitted to the ICAO Council. Without modification, the Council approved the Legal Committee's efforts, whereupon invitations for an International Conference on Air Law (to be held at ICAO headquarters in Montreal, September 8-23, 1971) were extended to all nations. It is appreciably remarkable that within a nine-month period (December, 1970 to September, 1971) the nations of the world had been requested to send delegates to attend two major international conventions on aviation safety, and most of them had complied.

The Montreal Convention for the Suppression of Unlawful Acts Against the Safety of Civil Aviation was specifically designed to deal with sabotage and terrorist incidents directed against aviation facilities. As previously indicated, this agreement greatly resembles the Hague Convention in all but five articles. Accordingly, the

---

[123]Gerald F. Fitzgerald, "The London Draft Convention on Acts of Unlawful Interference Against International Civil Aviation," in McWhinney, ed., Aerial Piracy, p. 42.

United States delegation reported that "the three most contentious issues before the Conference" were (1) Article 1 which defined the offenses covered by the Convention; (2) Article 4, Paragraph 3 which related to the Convention's applicability to unlawful incidents committed within one state; and (3) Article 5, Paragraph 2 which required states to establish jurisdiction to prosecute or extradite offenders found within their territory.[124] Of these, Article 1 evinces the greatest changes in both form and substance.

ARTICLE 1

1. Any person commits an offence if he unlawfully and intentionally:
   (a) Performs an act of violence against a person on board an aircraft in flight if that act is likely to endanger the safety of that aircraft; or
   (b) Destroys an aircraft in service or causes damage to such an aircraft which renders it incapable of flight or which is likely to endanger its safety in flight; or
   (c) Places or causes to be placed on an aircraft in service, by any means whatsoever, a device or substance which is likely to destroy that aircraft, or to cause damage to it which renders it incapable of flight, or cause damage to it which is likely to endanger its safety in flight; or
   (d) Destroys or damages air navigation facilities or interferes with their operation, if any such act is likely to endanger the safety of aircraft in flight; or
   (e) Communicates information which he knows to be false, thereby endangering the safety of an aircraft in flight.
2. Any person also commits an offence if he:
   (a) Attempts to commit any of the offences mentioned in paragraph 1 of this Article; or

---

[124] Message from the President of the United States, op. cit., p. 10.

(b) Is an accomplice of a person who commits or attempts to commit any such offence.[125]

Article 1 is novel because ". . . it describes a number of penal offences within the framework of multilateral convention which are . . . not always clearly defined--if at all--in national criminal codes. . . ."[126] For this reason, it will be useful to examine the provision in detail.

The introductory wording of Paragraph 1 makes clear that intention and unlawfulness must be present to constitute an "offense." Further, Paragraph 1(a) is reminiscent of Article 1 in the Hague Convention with its provision for "violence on board an aircraft in flight."[127] Hereafter, the uniqueness of this Article becomes apparent.

Paragraph 1, subparagraphs (b) through (e) relate to the paramount theme of the Montreal Convention, i.e., to deter acts of aviation sabotage. Subparagraph (b) deals with acts directed against the aircraft as distinct from the persons on board. This subparagraph includes bombing and discharge of weapons against an aircraft on the ground, as well as in the air.[128]

---

[126]Gerald F. FitzGerald, "Toward Legal Suppression of Acts Against Civil Aviation," International Conciliation, No. 585 (November, 1971), 67.

[127]Cf. The Hague Convention, Article 1, *infra*, p. 299.

[128]The concept of "aircraft in service" proved to be a troublesome problem for the delegates. As revealed by

Subparagraph (c) covers the placing of explosives on board an aircraft. The phrase, "by any means whatsoever" includes their being carried on board, sent on board by mail or in air cargo, or attached to the aircraft prior to departure.[129] Said Charles N. Brower, Deputy Legal Adviser for the United States State Department, "Subparagraph (c) of Article 1 is a symbolic provision referring specifically to bomb sabotage. As a matter of substance the acts described are covered in subparagraph (b) and the paragraph on attempts."[130] Essentially, this is correct, and was

---

FitzGerald:

> The expression "aircraft in service" found in subparagraphs (b) and (c) of Article 1(1) is important, since it serves to specify the physical position in which the aircraft must be if the acts covered by those subparagraphs are to come under the Convention. An extensive definition of the expression could encompass attacks against an aircraft while in a hanger or at a parking area. But the states at the Montreal Convention were not willing to go that far. This was because an extensive definition would mean that a state would, under another provision of the Convention (Article 7) be bound either to extradite the suspected author of such an attack or . . . submit the case to its competent authorities for the purpose of prosecution. . . .

FitzGerald, "Toward Legal Suppression of Acts Against Civil Aviation," p. 71. As ultimately defined, "An aircraft is considered to be 'in service' from the beginning of the preflight preparation of the aircraft by ground personnel or by the crew for a specific flight until twenty-four hours after any landing. . . ." The Montreal Convention, Article 2, Paragraph a.

[129]FitzGerald, "Towards Legal Suppression of Acts Against Civil Aviation," p. 68.

[130]Aircraft Sabotage Convention, op. cit., p. 13.

acceptable to most of the nations present. However, France vigorously opposed the implied extension of universal jurisdiction to cover bomb placement on board a civil aircraft, stemming from their reluctance to extradite French nationals.[131] Finally, subparagraph (c), in tandem with subparagraph (e) includes bomb hoaxes to be an offense, providing they endanger "the safety of an aircraft in flight."[132]

One of the most serious offenses banned by the Montreal Convention was destruction of air navigation facilities. Regrettably, any airport today which services international flights is vulnerable to acts of politically-motivated terrorism, disrupting communication equipment, radio services, meteorological services, runway lighting, or radar installations. Subparagraph (d) commits contracting states against such illegal acts to ensure the safety of airport personnel and passengers.

Lastly, Paragraph 2 holds special significance because it includes not only authors of the above acts as offenders, but also accomplices. Even so, "conspiracy to commit any of the offenses mentioned . . ." was omitted because "conspiracy" was not an offense under some municipal systems of penal law.[133]

---

[131] Ibid., p. 19.

[132] Ibid., p. 13.

[133] FitzGerald, "Towards Legal Suppression of Acts Against Civil Aviation," p. 70.

The "application" and "jurisdiction" provisions in the Montreal agreement closely resemble those in the Hague Convention. Article 4, (2) and (3) reaffirm the dominant right of the flag state to deal with offenders. Thus, the Convention applies in cases when:

> (a) The place of take-off or landing, actual or intended, of the aircraft is situated outside the territory of the State of registration of that aircraft; or
> (b) The offence is committed in the territory of a State other than the State of registration of the aircraft.[134]

In the case of air navigation facilities [subparagraph (d)] the Convention is applicable only if the facilities which are destroyed damaged, or interfered with are used in international air navigation.[135]

Article 5 evoked much controversy and debate in the course of the Montreal proceedings. This provision, like Article 4 of the Hague Convention, attempts to establish a form of universal jurisdiction over the alleged offender. Contracting states are obligated to take necessary measures to establish jurisdiction over offenses in these instances:

> (a) When the offence is committed in the territory of that State;
> (b) When the offence is committed against or on board an aircraft registered in that State;
> (c) When the aircraft on board which the offence is committed lands in its territory with the alleged offender still on board;

---

[134]The Montreal Convention, Article 4, Paragraphs a and b.

[135]*Ibid.*, Article 4, Paragraph 5.

(d) When the offence is committed against or on board an aircraft leased without crew to a lessee who has his principal place of business or, if the lessee has no such place of business, his permanent residence, in that State.[136]

However, these above provisions for establishing criminal jurisdiction, apply only to three of the five offences enumerated in Article 1(1). Subparagraphs (d) and (e) of Article 1(1) were excepted to allow the state whose facilities were damaged to prosecute alleged perpetrators according to its own criminal codes.[137]

The Montreal Convention reproduces the Hague provisions regarding assuming custody of alleged offenders; joint air transport operation organizations or international agencies subject to international registration; continuation of the journey by the passengers, crew, and aircraft; assistance between states to facilitate criminal proceedings; and, reports to the ICAO Council.[138]

Gerald F. FitzGerald has astutely posited some important observations on the latest efforts to suppress international hijacking of aircraft:

Thus the Montreal Convention breaks new ground--and goes beyond mere codification--in providing for international legal action to be taken by states in respect of many acts which, however, reprehensible they may be, previously have not been considered eligible for treatment in an international convention on

---

[136]<u>Ibid.</u>, Article 5.

[137]FitzGerald, "Towards Legal Suppression of Acts Against Civil Aviation," p. 74.

[138]<u>Ibid.</u>, p. 75.

criminal matters. Whether and to what extent states will be prepared to implement such a Convention is difficult to determine. With the larger aircraft now coming into service and the greater prospects of high loss of life in the case of sabotage, to say nothing of astronomical possibilities of property damage, few states will dismiss lightly a convention aimed at preserving safety even if its principles are somewhat novel.[139]

International response to this latest effort to suppress threats to civil aviation safety was well demonstrated, as it was adopted by a vote of 50 in favor to none against, with 8 abstentions. The Montreal Convention entered into force on January 26, 1973.

Despite this revolutionary development in international law, there still remains the problem of asylum versus mandatory extradition. As a decentralized legislative process,[140] the viable effectiveness of international legal agreements certainly depends upon adherence to those compliance norms set up by the participating states.[141]

---

[139] Ibid.

[140] See Hans Kelsen, General Theory of Law and State (Cambridge: Harvard University Press, 1945), pp. 325-340, and also Kelsen, "Centralization and Decentralization," in Authority and the Individual (Cambridge: Harvard University Press, 1937), pp. 211-239.

[141] See generally, James L. Brierly, The Basis of Obligation in International Law (Oxford: The Clarendon Press, 1958); Christopher C. Joyner, "Obligation and Authority vis-à-viz International Law in Hans Kelsen's 'Pure Theory:' A Critical Interpretation," (unpublished manuscript, Florida State University, 1972); and Hans Kelsen, Principles of International Law (New York: Rinehart and Co., 1952), pp. 92-100, 408-418.

Nonetheless, when basic prerogatives of national sovereignty, such as asylum, come into play, the law of nations may fall prey to the caprice of international politics.[142] This is unfortunate, and points up the basic need for greater discretion in deciding the jurisdictional status of an alleged offender.

States are obligated under the age old principle of pacta sunt servanda[143] to respect international agreements as inviolable promises of good faith. One nation's breach of an agreement does not signal the total abrogation by all other nations. The paucity of aircraft seizures thus far in 1973--only six--testifies to the Hague and Montreal Conventions' effectiveness in promoting universal deterrence measures under the auspices of international law. Only through continuing such concerted action can the safety of world-wide civil air transport be maintained.

The crimes enumerated in the Montreal Convention scarcely resemble traditional sea piracy as indiscriminate plunder on the high seas. Yet, several of the characteristics and legal deterrents attributed to both criminal activities are amazingly similar. The concluding analysis

---

[142] L. C. Green, "Hijacking and the Right of Asylum," in McWhinney, ed., Aerial Piracy, p. 144.

[143] Pacta sunt servanda is critically analyzed as a force in international law by Josef L. Kunz, "The Meaning and Range of the Term Pacta Sunt Servanda," A.J.I.L., Vol. 39 (April, 1945), 180-97.

reveals those common transitional elements, as well as the concomitant distinctions, which have evolved from customary piracy *jure gentium* to the international crime of unlawful aircraft seizure.

CHAPTER 5

THE EVOLUTION OF PIRACY IN INTERNATIONAL LAW

The international legal conceptualization of piracy has undergone three fundamental transformations since the sixteenth century: (1) the "traditional" maritime concept, defined by customary international law; (2) the "contemporary" twentieth-century maritime concept, necessitated by technological advances in oceanic transportation; (3) and the "conventional" concept, implemented to rapidly secure the safety of international civil air services. These definitional transformations have been so great as to make the crime of piracy on the high seas legally distinct from piracy in the high skies. The following assessment explains why.

Traditional Piracy

Throughout the ages international law has demonstrated a remarkable ability to adapt to changing times and circumstances. Early in its development, the law of nations evidenced strong cooperation by maritime states to suppress piratical acts. Even before the recognition of the nation-state system through the Treaty of Westphalia (1648), governments combated piratical attacks with the most powerful legal weapon available--universal jurisdiction, the common and equal right to seize and try alleged offenders.

Universal jurisdiction is a pivotal concept in international maritime law. States generally claim exclusive jurisdiction over those vessels which fly their flag. In essence, then, public vessels become movable pieces of territory over which national criminal jurisdiction applies. However, through customarily adopting the legal principle of universal jurisdiction, the absolute sovereign right to rule by the "law of the flag" was compromised ". . . to punish crimes of a heinous nature which threaten the international community as a whole (e.g., piracy). . . ."[1]

Thus, if the crime were not detrimental to nations' interests "as a whole," other established legal principles were available to punish crimes by nationals wherever they occurred. Jurisdiction may be exercised on the basis of "territoriality," where nationals or foreigners are punished for crimes committed within a state's territory.[2] Also, there is "active nationality," which involves punishment of a state's nationals regardless of the location of the offence.[3] A third principle in point is that of "passive

---

[1]D. H. N. Johnson, Rights in Air Space, p. 76.

[2]See Harvard Research, "Jurisdiction in Respect to Crime," A.J.I.L. Supp. 29 (1935), 480-519.

[3]Ibid., p. 519-42. Also see Blackmer v. United States, 284 U.S. 421 (1932).

personality," under which the nationality of the person injured by the offence can be the basis for assuming jurisdiction by his state.[4] Finally, there is the "protective principle," invoked when an act was initiated outside the national territory, but its effect takes place in that territory.[5]

Indeed, with the sweeping alternatives provided in the above jurisdictional principles, it would be difficult to find any piracy cases which might escape jurisdiction of one kind or another. Nonetheless, universal jurisdiction is paramount. The common denominator binding nations to forfeit their exclusive jurisdiction over piracy was the intrinsic abridgement of traditional freedom of the high seas. By violating this sacred principle guaranteeing free passage for seafaring trade, the pirate became *hostis humani generis*--an enemy of the human race, subject to punishment by all nations.[6]

Yet all pirates were not held to be violators of international law. In his Annual Message delivered on December 6, 1886, President Cleveland stated: "By the law

---

[4]"Jurisdiction with Respect to Crime," *A.J.I.L. Supp.* 29, pp. 563-92.

[5]*Ibid*., pp. 543-63. Also see The Cutting Case, Mexico, Bravos District Court, 1886, found in Moore, *Digest*, Vol. 2, pp. 228-42.

[6]See John Bassett Moore, in the Steamship *Lotus*, P.I.C.J., Series A, No. 10 (1927), pp. 70-71 and Brierly, *The Law of Nations*, p. 154.

of nations, no punishment can be inflicted by a sovereign on citizens of other countries unless in conformity with those sanctions of justice which all civilized nations have in common."[7] In other words, those rules of conduct agreed upon by the international community to suppress piracy jure gentium must be made distinct from the elements which constitute solely a municipal offence. However, this is complicated by the fact that international and municipal laws against piracy contained certain common elements (which have remained even in the evolution of unlawful aircraft seizure as an international crime). To visually portray this linkage, Fig. 2, "Evolution of the Crime of Piracy in International Law," was constructed.

Undoubtedly, all piratical acts impinge upon the safety of international ocean transportation, and consequently the law of nations permits any state to assume jurisdiction over such acts. Once apprehended, a pirate may be tried and prosecuted under the municipal criminal codes of the capturing state.[8] Since the lack of uniformity in municipal definitions of piracy may cause conflicting judgments among nations, the question becomes: what are the characteristics of piracy under international law vis-à-vis statutory piracy, both of which are enforced through municipal courts?

---

[7]Moore, Digest, Vol. 2, p. 229.

[8]Wheaton, International Law, pp. 163-164.

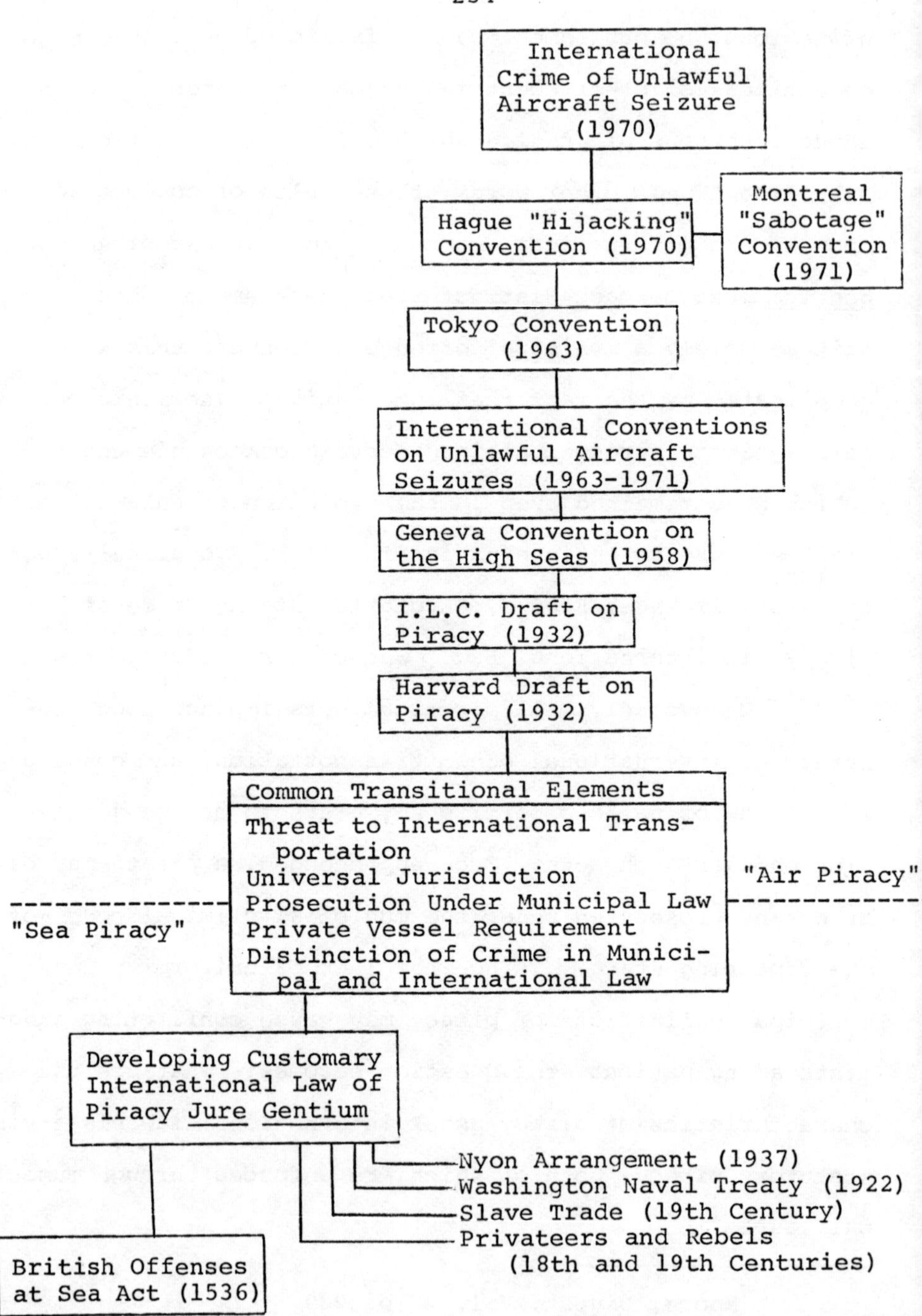

Fig. 2.--Evolution of the crime of piracy in international law (1536-1973).

It is this fact, i.e., that penal measures against pirates are dispensed by municipal courts, that contributes greatly to the confusion between piracy _jure gentium_ and statute piracy. Accordingly, judicial authorities must be able to distinguish what constitutes a violation of either one or both laws. The core of the controversy lies in the location of the offense and the descriptive analysis of those acts committed during the course of the offense.

To constitute piracy _jure gentium_, an act must be "adequate in degree, . . . for instance, robbery, destruction by fire, or other injury to persons or property. . . ."[9] It must be committed on the high seas, as opposed to similar acts committed within some state's territorial jurisdiction.[10] Finally, ". . . the offenders, at the time of the commission of the act, should be, in fact free from lawful authority . . . in the predicament of _outlaws_."[11]

Pirates not claiming allegiance to any sovereign, nor flying a foreign flag, pose no difficulty for the extension of universal jurisdiction over their crime _jure gentium_. This is qualified only in the knowledge that a private pirate vessel may have possessed ". . . a national character before it was engaged in piracy."[12] That

---

[9] _Ibid_.

[10] _Ibid_.

[11] _Ibid_.

[12] Whiteman, _Digest_, Vol. 2, p. 650.

state from which the pirate claimed previous allegiance may intercede diplomatically to exercise ordinary jurisdictional grounds over their nationals or flag vessels. Moreover, that state may insist upon the right to try such pirates in its municipal courts even though this right is not paramount to the claim of universal jurisdiction.[13]

Thus, the international crime of piracy _jure gentium_ is predicated upon indiscriminate plunder by a private (i.e., pirate) vessel against commercial vessels on the high seas. The most prevalent phrase used to describe traditional piracy is "robbery on the high seas," and was well expressed by Justice Story in United States v. Smith:

> Whatever may be the diversity of definitions, in other respects, all writers concur in holding, that robbery, or forcible depredations upon the sea, _animo furandi_, is piracy.[14]

Nonetheless, while municipal law definitions contain some common elements cited in traditional piracy _jure gentium_, novel modifications applicable to particular states have been added. For example, the British "Offenses at Sea Act of 1536" considered as piracy ". . . all treasons, felonies, robberies, murders, and confederacies hereafter to be committed in or upon the sea."[15] It is conceivable that the

---

[13]See Hackworth, _International Law_, Vol. 2, p. 681.

[14]United States v. Smith (1820), cited in Lenoir, "Piracy Cases in the Supreme Court," p. 532.

[15]Fairman, "Re Piracy _Jure Gentium_," p. 509.

commission of some or all of these illegal acts on the high seas may constitute international piracy. Yet the murder of one subject on the high seas by another, not involving a pirate ship against another vessel, would hardly brand the murderer as a pirate *jure gentium*. Whatever the crimes locus, such an incident is punishable as a felony under English statutes, but is not a violation of customary piracy in international law.

Other legal statutory modifications include the capture of rebels, insurgents, or privateers who traverse territorial waters or the high seas.[16] Such "political" piratical acts are usually confined to depredations against the ships of one state. It remains a political, not a legal, question whether rebellious acts may also be adjudged as violations of the law of nations. Internal governmental policies are capricious, particularly during periods of war. Hence, rebels, insurgents, or privateers may be captured and held as prisoners of war or tried for treason, murder, or piracy, depending upon the whims of executive officials. Vacillating municipal statute interpretations add little except confusion to the legal concept of piracy in international law.

---

[16]E.g., the 1777 Act of Parliament directed against the activities of American armies and navies, and President Lincoln's Proclamation of April 19, 1861, branding those United States citizens sailing under confederate authority as pirates. See Wheaton, *International Law*, pp. 164-167, and Quincy Wright, "The American Civil War, 1861-65," in Falk, ed., *The International Law of Civil War*, pp. 52-53.

Later modifications of traditional high seas piracy through multi-state agreements made slave trading an act of piracy, and were prevalent in the nineteenth century. Yet traditional piracy as an international crime did not include transportation of slaves on the high seas. Opposition to the practice, as supported by the multilateral treaties, was only effected between contracting states. Thus, ". . . when in 1858, before the abolition of slavery in America, British men-of-war molested American vessels, suspected of carrying slaves, the United States rightfully complained.[17] Indeed, slave-trading has been periodically added to the roster of criminal acts associated with piracy, but it is to the professional pirate who indiscriminately preyed upon international ocean commerce that universal jurisdiction appropriately applies.

The vindictive penalties vented against genuine sea pirates by municipal courts were often well deserved. Criminal courts generally levied the more severe penalties, usually capital punishment, upon offenders (when sufficient evidence was available to prove guilt).[18]

However, municipal legal proceedings were sometimes hampered because of the expeditious manner in which pirates

---

[17] Lauterpaucht, Oppenheim's International Law, Vol. 1, pp. 608-9.

[18] See Philip Gosse, The History of Piracy (London: Longmans and Green and Co., 1932) and A. T. Whatley, "Historical Sketch of Piracy," Law Magazine and Review (1874), 536-618.

treated their victims. Lenoir concludes:

> Although this older type of pirate disappeared with the development of large national navies, it was he who brought into existence the national laws against piracy and aided in the development of a rule of customary law condemning the practice. It is he who is the obsolete factor in piracy, and not the law of states or the rules developed among nations to suppress his activities.[19]

Contemporary Piracy

Lenoir's contention is correct in that many of the common elements of traditional piracy were carried over into the twentieth century. The customary, unwritten laws by which nations abided still served as viable forces to deter piracy on the high seas should the nefarious characters to which the laws were directed reappear. Concomitant with the demise of traditional sea piracy came a revolution in travel modes, i.e., sailing ships, to steam vessels, to modern ocean liners, to heavier than air flights. Advances, culminating in wireless communication and radar equipment, heightened state ability to apprehend fugitive pirates. Therefore, these great technological developments required a corresponding expansion in the law of nations.

Accordingly, the evolution of piracy as a crime in international law ". . . shows a gradual widening of the earlier definition of piracy to bring it from time to time more in consonance with situations either not thought of or

---

[19]Lenoir, "Piracy Cases," pp. 536-37.

not in existence when the older jurisconsults were expressing their opinions."[20]

The first multi-state attempt to deal with piracy in the twentieth century occurred shortly after World War I. Vivid memories of the destruction of merchant vessels through submarine warfare tactics led five nations--the United States, Great Britain, France, Japan, and Italy--to condemn such future attacks as acts of piracy, subsequently codified in the Washington Naval Treaty of 1922.[21] Admittedly, submarine attacks posed a serious threat to merchant shipping and endangered the lives of hundreds of seamen not officially associated with the war effort. But the common grounds of international piracy dictated that the attack be made from a private vessel, not a public warship. The inhumanity of acts performed by submarine commanders under superior orders fell under the aegis of the rules of warfare, not the international law of piracy. The attempt to equate submarine warfare with acts of piracy in both the Washington Naval Treaty of 1922 and the later Nyon Arrangement of 1937[22] failed to gain wide approval in the international community and went largely unenforced.

---

[20]Fairman, "In Re Piracy *Jure Gentium*," p. 509.

[21]Carnegie Endowment for International Peace, *Yearbook, 1922*, p. 142.

[22]See "The Nyon Arrangements," p. 200.

When the League of Nations shelved it as a topic for legal codification, the task of assembling and updating customary piracy laws was performed by Harvard Research on International Law. Recognized for their wide expertise and ". . . unhampered by claims of geographical representation,"[23] the drafters of the Harvard Research on Piracy presented an ". . . exhaustive account of existing practice, and at the same time indicated what, in the absence of an agreed or satisfactory practice, ought to be the law of the future."[24]

As they focused upon piracy's significance in international law, Harvard Research scholars attempted to modernize existing customary law to meet the challenge of technological developments in commerce and travel. This was realized when the final draft conceded the first reference to attacks from aircraft as potential, logical extensions of piracy from the high seas to the high skies.[25]

It was of primary import to the authors of the Harvard Research on Piracy that a general workable meaning

---

[23]Hersch Lauterpacht, "Codification and Development of International Law, in Leo Gross, ed., International Law in the Twentieth Century (New York: Appleton-Century-Crofts, 1969), p. 65.

[24]Ibid.

[25]Harvard Draft Research, Article 3, Section 1.

of international law piracy be promulgated. In order to do so, certain precepts were cited as basic guidelines for the project. First, the Draft Convention was based on the premise that piracy does not constitute an international crime.[26] Phrases formerly associated with traditional piracy, especially piracy *jure gentium* and *hostis humani generis*, were omitted in favor of a clear, concise definition of the crime. Second, emphasis was placed on defining the extraordinary jurisdiction of states to seize, prosecute, and punish high seas pirates, *viz.*, the reaffirmation of the universal jurisdiction principle.[27] And third, no attempt was made to synchronize diverse state statutes on piracy. Rather, the Harvard Draft deferred to states the right to define and punish crimes of piracy, noting that significant differences are often evident between municipal law (statute piracy), occurring within state territorial limits, and piracy under international law, which necessarily takes place outside the territorial jurisdiction of any state.[28]

The Harvard Draft defined piracy more comprehensively than the traditional concept of piracy as high seas banditry. Article 3 provides that:

> Piracy is any of the following acts, committed in a place not within the territorial jurisdiction of any state:

---

[26]"Comments," *A.J.I.L. Supp.* 26, p. 749.

[27]Jacobson, "From Piracy on the High Seas," p. 166.

[28]*Ibid.* Also see "Comments," *A.J.I.L. Supp*. 26, p. 749.

> Any act of violence or of depredation committed with intent to rob, rape, wound, enslave, imprison or kill a person or with intent to steal or destroy property, for private ends and without bona fide purpose of asserting a claim of right, provided that the act is connected with an attack on or from the sea or in or from the air. If the act is connected with an attack which starts from on board ship, either that ship or another ship which is involved must be a pirate ship or a ship without national character.[29]

Many of the common, traditional elements associated both with sea piracy and air piracy stem from this definition, yet some specific points show variations from the traditional concept of piracy. Indeed, any of these enumerated acts performed on the high seas pose a genuine threat to international commerce. Subsequent articles re-state the right of universal jurisdiction over offenders and confirm that ". . . the law of the state which exercises such jurisdiction defines the crime, governs the procedure and prescribes the penalty."[30]

The Harvard Draft definition of piracy omits reference to indiscriminate plunder on the high seas, but insists that the act be motivated for "private ends."[31] Thus, piracy attempts with "political overtones" (i.e., with ". . . bona fide purpose of asserting a claim of right") are systematically excluded from the auspices of the Draft. In addition, one ship involved in the attack ". . . must be a pirate ship or a ship without national character."

---

[29]Harvard Draft Research, Article 3.

[30]*Ibid.*, Article 14, Section 2.

[31]*Ibid.*, Article 3, Section 1.

There are dramatic implications involved in imposing these qualifications to potential acts of "air piracy." Significant legal differences arise when comparing sea piracy to "air piracy" according to the criteria set in the Harvard Draft Research. Aircraft seizures usually involve the take-over of an aircraft by a person on board, and subsequent deviation in the established flight plan. Such acts do not involve more than one aircraft, nor do they occur entirely within international airspace. The locus of take-off and descent of a plane falls within the territory of a state, thus superceding the very essence of the international claim for universal jurisdiction (viz., that the act occur outside state territorial jurisdiction).

Though authoritative, the Harvard Draft on Piracy was not proffered as an international treaty agreement. Rather, it stands as a prominent example of creativity in the codification efforts of a private research organization. Since it represents the opinions of distinguished scholars of international law, the Harvard Draft has been cited in the judicial proceedings of Re Piracy *Jure Gentium*,[32] and was later used as a guideline for the codification of piracy rules by the U.N. International Law Commission.[33] After

---

[32]See Fairman, "Re Piracy *Jure Gentium*," pp. 508-511.

[33]See International Law Commission Report, 10 U.N. GOAR, Supp. 9. U.N. Doc. A/2934 (1955).

seven years of study, the I.L.C. Draft on Piracy was submitted in 1956 for inclusion in the proposed Geneva Convention on the High Seas.[34]

The definition of piracy formulated by the Commission was thereafter adopted as Article 15, Section 1 of the 1958 Geneva Convention on the High Seas. While the Geneva definition of piracy is broader in scope than the Harvard Draft, it contains a parallel reference to aircraft as vehicles for piratical activities. Article 15(1)(a) defines piracy as:

> [A]ny illegal acts of violence, detention or any act of depredation, committed for private ends by the crew or the passengers of a private ship or a private aircraft, and directed on the high seas, against another ship or aircraft or against persons or property on board ship or aircraft.[35]

According to this definition, piracy need not be confined to robbery or pillage at sea. As long as an act of violence takes place on the high seas or outside the jurisdiction of any state, is committed for private reasons, and is performed on a private ship or aircraft against another aircraft, the criteria for international law piracy are met. The perpetrator of such an act becomes subject to universal jurisdiction by any state which seizes him.

---

[34] International Law Commission Report, 11 U.N. GOAR, Supp. 9. U.N. Doc. A/3159 (1956).

[35] The Convention on the High Seas, Article 15, Paragraph 1(a) U.N. Doc. A/Conf. 13/38.

There is no doubt that the crime of "air piracy" was defined and accepted into the body of international law when the Geneva Convention came into force in 1962.[36] Although it is argumentative whether the Convention applies to violent acts associated with what is commonly referred to as "hijacking" or "skyjacking," significant legal and conceptual difficulties do exist between "piracy in the air" and contemporary aircraft hijackings. The Geneva definition of piracy clearly does not describe the act of "aircraft hijacking." Its fallacies lie in the fact that (1) hijacking involves only one aircraft; (2) the act of hijacking an aircraft takes place wholly or partially within the territorial airspace or territory of a state; and (3) the act must be committed for private ends. When any of these three fundamental requirements are absent, the crime cannot be considered air piracy under international law.

As rudimentary attempts to extend customary piracy law to piracy in the air, the Harvard, I.L.C., and Geneva Convention definitions greatly stifled international efforts to suppress the rising tide of aircraft seizures. An ironic dilemma was obvious: sea piracy was well defined in international law, but had only anachronistic case references; "air piracy" was ill-defined, but was replete with current incidents. This problem necessitated a

---

[36]See Jacobson, "From Piracy on the High Seas," pp. 174-175.

revolutionary approach in international law, one which replaced the gradual evolution of custom with the immediacy of specific conventions.

Over twenty years ago, John Fenston suggested:

> The civilized world condemns piracy as a crime against mankind, and the jurisdiction to try a pirate is vested equally in all nations. Would it be such an unbearable shock to our innate sense of justice to consider--for the purpose of jurisdiction--an offence committed on board aircraft in flight, a crime against mankind? . . . Let the world accept the proposition that a crime de droit commun committed on board aircraft in flight, anywhere, is an international crime, and that each civilized nation is charged with the duty and responsbility to suppress and punish the same.[37]

Yet, as early as 1932, Lord McNair had warned that ". . . from a juristic point of view, the analogy between a ship and an aircraft is fundamentally wrong and misleading . . . and any attempt to invest the aircraft, as such and wherever it may be, with the characteristic legal panoply which belongs to a ship will be disastrous."[38]

What was vitally needed to reconcile both of these viewpoints was to distinctly recognize the novel crime of aircraft seizure, and at the same time, realize that its serious impact upon international air transport necessitated continuation of the international legal tools formerly used to suppress sea piracy. In order to avoid doctrinal

---

[37] John Fenston and Hamilton de Saussure, "Crimes on Board Aircraft," McGill Law Journal, 56 91952), pp. 81, 83.

[38] Lord McNair, The Law of the Air (London: Stevens, 1932), p. 91.

controversies of the past, it was imperative that a new title with international significance be attached to the crime.

Conventional Law of "Air Piracy"

The Geneva Convention on the High Seas (1958) which placed "air piracy" and "sea piracy" in the same definitional category was obsolete by the time it came into force in 1962. One year later, nations joined together under the invitation of the ICAO to discuss a convention on recommendations originally made in 1959,[39] relating to offenses committed on board aircraft. Consequently,

> . . . major factors contributing to this decision were the disparity of national laws relating to offenses on board aircraft, the need to provide for a jurisdiction in which the person alleged to have committed such an offense could be tried, and the need to empower the aircraft commander to take measures to check any acts on board endangering the safety of flight and to preserve order on board."[40]

The Plenary approved, in total, the ideas embodied in the suggested ICAO legal framework. To the smaller states not greatly affected by aircraft siezures, the provisions appeared quite adequate to enable a safe, expeditious continuation of the diverted aircraft's voyage. In addition, Article 11 of the resultant Tokyo Convention

---

[39]FitzGerald, "Toward Legal Suppression of Acts AGainst Civil Aviation," p. 45; for a summary of the various jurisdictional claims by ICAO members in 1959, see ICAO Doc. 8111-LC/146-2 at 160-165 (1959).

[40]Ibid.

of 1963 specified that in the case of an anticipated or actual unlawful, forcible seizure of an aircraft in flight, contracting states were obliged to take all appropriate measures to restore control of the plane to its lawful commander. Here, humanitarian concern for the safety of unsuspecting passengers and crew becomes apparent. But a universal obligation to expedite safe passage for transients aboard the vessel left unanswered the question of what to do with the hijacker.

The Convention's foremost objective was to ensure that offenses, wherever committed, should not go unpunished. Articles 3 and 4 provided for concurrent jurisdiction among states directly affected by the seizure, but the thrust of the provisions affirmed the competence of the flag state to exercise jurisdiction.[41] Though certain procedures were required to be followed when a hijacker had been placed in custody,[42] the receiving state was virtually free to do as it wished with the offender. No legalities in the Tokyo Convention were violated if the offender received only a minimal sentence or was not prosecuted at all.

The Tokyo Convention tested how far states were willing to go in conceding jurisdictional claims over crimes

---

[41]See McKeithen, "Prospects for the Prevention," p. 64, and generally, Mendelsohn,"In-Flight Crime," pp. 513-14.

[42]The Tokyo Convention, Articles 9, 10, 11, 12, 13, 14, and 15.

aboard aircraft. In 1963, securing international cooperation to quickly return an aircraft to its normal commercial flight plan took precedence over prosecution of the diverters. However, by the time the Tokyo agreement came into force (1969), nations showed great willingness to deal with the entire hijacking menace.[43] Incidents occurring at an average of over seven per month necessitated tougher international controls than those provided in the Tokyo Convention. The time was ripe to effectuate a Convention solely for the purpose of deterring hijackers.

Proponents of the Hague Convention for the Suppression of Unlawful Seizure of Aircraft sought to fill the void in the legal system created by the Tokyo Convention. Emphasis was placed on the punishment of the hijacker, as can be seen in the chronology of articles to the Convention; Articles 1 and 2 define the offense and obligate contracting states to punish offenders by severe penalties; Article 4 provides that states having the strongest incentive to prosecute "skyjackers," viz., states directly affected by the incident, will be granted priority to exercise jurisdiction over them; Article 6 makes provision for the offender's arrest, while Article 7 calls for referral of the case to local authorities for

---

[43]Butler, "The Path to International Legislation Against Hijacking," pp. 27-30, and Horlick, "Aircraft Hijacking," pp. 145-147.

prosecution, if the receiving state does not extradite the offender. Finally, Article 8 requires contracting states to treat hijacking as an extraditable offense.[44]

The Hague "Hijacking" Convention is considered ". . . a milestone both in the general development of an international criminal air law and in the fight against aerial hijacking specifically."[45] Its provisions that any state where the hijacker is found may take jurisdiction over him[46] gives the unlawful seizure of aircraft the status of an international crime. Even if the offender is granted asylum in the receiving state, the risk of prosecution by other states serves as a forceful incentive for his remaining in the asylum state.

Nation-states' eagerness to gain wide acceptance of the Hague Convention was evidenced in its procedural characteristics. After December 31, 1970, the United States, Great Britain, and the Soviet Union accepted deposits of state ratifications.[47] Though ICAO authorized Conventions are usually drafted in three working languages, the Hague Convention was drawn up in four authentic texts,

---

[44]See John B. Rhinelander, "The International Law of Aerial Piracy. New Proposals for the New Decision," in McWhinney, ed. Aerial Piracy, pp. 59-71.

[45]Mankiewiez, "The 1970 Hague Convention," p. 195.

[46]These provisions are found in Articles 4, 5, 7, and 8 of the Hague Convention.

[47]FitzGerald, "Toward Legal Suppression of Acts Against Civil Aviation," p. 65.

viz., English, French, Spanish, and Russian.[48] In addition, the Convention would come into effect with the ratifications of only ten states.[49] As seen in the statistical data on aggregate state participation in response to the Tokyo Convention, nations more readily accede to a Convention after it has come into force.[50] The experience learned from the Tokyo Convention was put to wise use in the Hague Agreement.

The precedent set in the procedural and substantive arrangements for the Hague Convention was repeated in the Montreal agreement. With exception of the original signatories deposited at Montreal, the same three depository states and four working languages were agreed upon.[51] The Montreal "Sabotage" Convention greatly parallels its "sister" agreement, the Hague Convention, but extends to acts of unlawful interference against international civil aviation not covered in the latter.

Within the ten-year period 1963-1973, three major international agreements concerned with the safety of international civil air transport and the elimination of "skyjacking" were put into effect. The heightened support for the convention trilogy and the implementation of hijacker

---

48 White, "The Hague Convention," p. 44.

49 This is qualified in that the ten ratifying states must have participated in the Diplomatic Conference held at the Hague. See The Hague Convention, Article 13, Paragraph 3.

50 See Fig. 1 and accompanying text, *supra*, pp. 161 *et seq*.

51 FitzGerald, "Toward Legal Suppression of Acts Against Civil Aviation," p. 75.

detection devices at local airports have contributed to the sharp decline in hijacking attempts. In order to ascertain the degree of individual state participation in each Convention, the "Index of International Cooperation to Suppress 'Skyjacking'" was devised.

The cumulative number of state participants to the Tokyo, the Hague, and the Montreal Conventions is depicted in Tables 10-11. Participation was weighted according to (1) the number of conventions a state participated in (one point; (2) becoming a signatory to each convention (one point); (3) depositing ratifications to each convention (two points).

For example, Brazil (Table 10, Section A) received one point for each convention in which it participated (three points); one point for the signing of each convention (three points); and two points for each convention it became a party to (six points), for a total weighted score of twelve. Conversely, Nicaragua and Yemen (Table 12, Section C) only signed the Montreal Convention, registering a score of two points, respectively.

Three categories emerged which reveal each state's degree of participation in any or all of the conventions, and are ranked from highest to lowest degree according to the weighted score. States with equal scores are enumerated alphabetically in Sections A, B, C, D, etc., followed by the respective section score. Thus, Table 10, Section A,

TABLE 10

INDEX OF INTERNATIONAL COOPERATION TO SUPPRESS "SKYJACKING:" DEGREE OF STATE PARTICIPATION IN THREE CONVENTIONS (SEPTEMBER 14, 1963-JUNE 11, 1973)

State	Tokyo Convention		Hague Convention		Montreal Convention	
	Signatory	Party	Signatory	Party	Signatory	Party
Section A (12 pts.)						
Brazil	x	xx	x	xx	x	xx
Canada	x	xx	x	xx	x	xx
Republic of China	x	xx	x	xx	x	xx
Denmark	x	xx	x	xx	x	xx
Israel	x	xx	x	xx	x	xx
Niger	x	xx	x	xx	x	xx
Panama	x	xx	x	xx	x	xx
Phillipines	x	xx	x	xx	x	xx
Portugal	x	xx	x	xx	x	xx
Spain	x	xx	x	xx	x	xx
United States	x	xx	x	xx	x	xx
Yugoslavia	x	xx	x	xx	x	xx
Section B (11 pts.)						
Chad	-	xx	x	xx	x	xx
Gaben	-	xx	x	xx	x	xx
Hungary	-	xx	x	xx	x	xx
South Africa	-	xx	x	xx	x	xx
Trinidad and Tobago	-	xx	x	xx	x	xx
Section C (10 pts.)						
Mexico	x	xx	x	xx	x	-
Switzerland	x	xx	x	xx	x	-
United Kingdom	x	xx	x	xx	x	-

State	Tokyo Convention		Hague Convention		Montreal Convention	
	Signatory	Party	Signatory	Party	Signatory	Party
Section D (9 pts.)						
Argentina	-	xx	x	xx	x	-
Australia	-	xx	x	xx	x	-
Costa Rica	-	xx	x	xx	x	-
Fiji	-	xx	x	xx	x	-
Ivory Coast	-	xx	-	xx	-	x
Malawi	-	xx	-	xx	-	x
Mali	-	xx	-	xx	-	x
Paraguay	-	xx	x	xx	x	-
Poland	-	xx	x	xx	x	-
Section E (8 pts.)						
Barbados	x	xx	x	-	x	-
Belgium	x	xx	x	-	x	-
Federal Republic of Germany	x	xx	x	-	x	-
Greece	x	xx	x	-	x	-
Guatemala	x	xx	x	-	x	-
Italy	x	xx	x	-	x	-
Netherlands	x	xx	x	-	x	-
Senegal	x	xx	x	-	x	-
Section F (7 pts.)						
Cyprus	-	xx	-	xx	x	-
Dominican Republic	-	xx	x	-	x	-
Laos	-	xx	x	-	x	-
Luxembourg	-	xx	x	-	x	-
Rwanda	-	xx	x	-	x	-
Singapore	-	xx	x	-	x	-

Table 10--Continued

State	Tokyo Convention		Hague Convention		Montreal Convention	
	Signatory	Party	Signatory	Party	Signatory	Party
Section G (6 pts.)						
Venezuela	x	-	x	-	x	-

TABLE 11

INDEX OF INTERNATIONAL COOPERATION TO SUPPRESS "SKYJACKING:"
DEGREE OF STATE PARTICIPATION IN TWO CONVENTIONS
(SEPTEMBER 14, 1963-JUNE 11, 1973)

State	Tokyo Convention		Hague Convention		Montreal Convention	
	Signatory	Party	Signatory	Party	Signatory	Party
Section A (8 pts.)						
Bulgaria	-	-	x	xx	x	xx
Byelerussian, S.S.R. S.S.R.	-	-	x	xx	x	xx
Ecuador	x	xx	x	xx	-	-
Finland	x	xx	x	xx	-	-
France	x	xx	x	xx	-	-
Democratic Republic of Germany	-	-	x	xx	x	xx
Japan	x	xx	x	xx	-	-
Jordan	-	-	x	xx	x	xx
Mongolia	-	-	x	xx	x	xx
Norway	x	xx	x	xx	-	-
Sweden	x	xx	x	xx	-	-
Ukrainian, S.S.R.	-	-	x	xx	x	xx
U.S.S.R.	-	-	x	xx	x	xx
Section B (7 pts.)						
Republic of Korea	x	xx	-	xx	-	-
Section C (6 pts.)						
Burundi	-	xx	x	-	x	-
Czechslovakia	-	-	x	xx	x	-
Guyana	-	-	-	xx	-	xx
Romania	-	-	x	xx	x	-

Table 11--Continued

State	Tokyo Convention		Hague Convention		Montreal Convention	
	Signatory	Party	Signatory	Party	Signatory	Party
Section D (5 pts.)						
Lesotho	-	xx	x	-	-	-
Sierra Leone	-	xx	x	-	-	-
Thailand	-	xx	x	-	-	-
Section E (4 pts.)						
Austria	-	-	x	-	x	-
Columbia	x	-	x	-	-	-
Congo (Brazzaville)	x	-	-	-	x	-
Ethiopia	-	-	x	-	x	-
India	-	-	x	-	x	-
Indonesia	x	-	x	-	-	-
Jamaica	-	-	x	-	x	-
New Zealand	-	-	x	-	x	-
Pakistan	x	-	x	-	-	-
Turkey	-	-	x	-	x	-

TABLE 12

INDEX OF INTERNATIONAL COOPERATION TO SUPPRESS "SKYJACKING:"
DEGREE OF STATE PARTICIPATION IN ONE CONVENTION
(SEPTEMBER 14, 1963-JUNE 11, 1973)

State	Tokyo Convention		Hague Convention		Montreal Convention	
	Signatory	Party	Signatory	Party	Signatory	Party
Section A (4 pts.)						
Chile	-	-	x	xx	-	-
Dahomey	-	-	z	xx	-	-
El Salvador	-	-	x	xx	-	-
Iran	-	-	x	xx	-	-
Iraq	-	-	x	xx	-	-
Malagasy Republic	x	x	-	-	-	-
Nigeria	x	xx	-	-	-	-
Saudi Arabia	x	xx	-	-	-	-
Upper Volta	x	xx	-	-	-	-
Section B (3 pts.)						
Iceland	-	xx	-	-	-	-
Kenya	-	xx	-	-	-	-
Libya	-	xx	-	-	-	-
Togo	-	xx	-	-	-	-
Uganda	-	-	-	xx	-	-
Zambia	-	xx	-	-	-	-
Section C (2 pts.)						
Afghanistan	-	-	x	-	-	-
Botswana	-	-	-	-	x	-
Egypt	-	-	-	-	x	-
Equatorial Guinea	-	-	x	-	-	-

Table 12--Continued

State	Tokyo Convention		Hague Convention		Montreal Convention	
	Signatory	Party	Signatory	Party	Signatory	Party
Section C--cont'd						
Gambia	-	-	x	-	-	-
Ghana	-	-	x	-	-	-
Haiti	-	-	-	-	x	-
Holy See	x	-	-	-	-	-
Ireland	x	-	-	-	-	-
Khmer Republic (formerly Cambodia)	-	-	x	-	-	-
Kuwait	-	-	x	-	-	-
Liberia	x	-	-	-	-	-
Liechtenstein	-	-	x	-	-	-
Malaysia	-	-	x	-	-	-
Nicaraqua	-	-	-	-	x	-
Yemen (Arab Republic)	-	-	-	-	x	-

lists those nations which have given total support to all the conventions. On the other hand, Section G reveals that Venezuela has signed all three conventions, but never chose to ratify any of them.

The resistance of some nations to join the "anti-hijacking" movement did not dissuade 107 states from participating in one, or all of the agreements. Nor did remnants of the Cold War split between the Eastern and Western bloc nations fail to unite efforts against skyjacking. While the Soviet Union and satellite countries refused participation in the Tokyo Convention, provisions in the Hague and Montreal Conventions allowed all states (including non-members to the United Nations) to accede. Table 11, Section A places Bulgaria, Byelorussian, S.S.R., the Democratic Republic of Germany, Ukrainian, S.S.R., and the U.S.S.R., in the highest category of participation in two conventions. It is still early to tell whether other Soviet satellite states, viz., Czechoslovakia and Romania (Section C) will become parties to the Montreal Convention.

The significance of the trilogy of hijacking conventions rests in the fact that they (1) compound and build upon the foundation laid by one another; (2) elevate the crime of "unlawful seizure of aircraft" to the status of an international crime; (3) provide universal jurisdiction among contracting states to apprehend the offender wherever he is found; (4) provide a forceful deterrent to the free travel of hijackers who receive asylum in a non-participating state; and (5) continue the common customary law deterrents associated with piracy _jure gentium_ without officially attempting to give the same name (piracy) to the offense. The sobriquet, "Air Piracy," continues to be used by the news media and in municipal statutes to describe the "offense," which is the Conventions' designation of the crime. But the evolution of the crime of piracy in international law reveals a common linkage only to certain transitional elements (as indicated in Fig. 2). The actual definitive qualifications of the offense show obvious growing pains from four centuries of development and expansion both in international commerce and in international law.

A Concluding Assessment

Several important conclusions can be drawn from this study. First, the traditional concept of piracy as applied on the high seas is not wholly analogous to the relatively novel crime of unlawful aircraft seizure. In the words of Haro F. VanPanhuys, "The scope of the traditional concept of piracy is rather limited and that any automatic or mechanical application to air piracy of the existing rules of international law with regard to sea piracy would not lead to a satisfactory result."[51]

[52]VanPanhuys, "Aircraft Hijacking and International Law," p. 11.

Admittedly, common elements exist between these two concepts of piracy, i.e., both are threats to international transportation, both possess universal jurisdiction as a sanctioning force, both use municipal legal systems to enforce prosecution of offenders, both require private vessels for the crime's commission, and both call for legal definitional distinctions in municipal and international law. Yet, the crimes are not the same.

By definition, an act of sea piracy must be committed on the high seas, external to any state's territorial jurisdiction. Unlawful aircraft seizure is always perpetrated entirely or partially within the territorial airspace, or territory, of some state. Even if it is committed outside national airspace, the plane must land in some nation's territory. Secondly, sea piracy requires one private vessel indiscriminately plundering a flag ship of some nation. Unlawful aircraft seizure occurs only aboard one aircraft and is usually perpetrated by a passenger. Thirdly, traditional piracy as defined was done for "private ends." Aircraft hijacking involves other motives, often with political overtones.

A second conclusion revolves around the applied nomenclature. Terms such as "air piracy," "aerial piracy," and "aircraft piracy" are continually used by the media to describe the crime in question. Though merely labels, these descriptions contribute to the confusion between the disparate legal characteristics of traditional piracy and aircraft seizures. Even the terms "hijacking" and "sky-jacking" are inappropriate because of their reflections upon the Prohibition Era.[53] It is certainly unfortunate that no sound designation (other than the "offense") has been forthcoming by the international community. It is this author's contention that the most suitable designation for this crime is "unlawful aircraft seizures," with implied definitional extensions to include those offenses enumerated in Article 1 of the Montreal Convention.

A third conclusion emanates from the flexibility of international law. In the short span of ten years, the international community recognized the existence of a threat to global air safety, organized and executed three multilateral agreements, and implemented forceful municipal legislation. Moreover, the technological revolution in transportation modes necessitated an expeditious transformation of attitudes and international legal procedure.

The gradual evolution of customary usage proved too slow and burdensome for global security needs. Thus, the tool used to effect this legislative process was the international convention--the primary source of internat-ional law.

A fourth conclusion is couched in the political implications of unlawful aircraft seizures. There still

---

[53]Evans, "Aircraft Hijacking," p. 696.

exists the need for internationally legitimized provisions guaranteeing genuine asylum from political persecution (as enumerated in the Universal Declaration of Human Rights), but one which also ensures mandatory extradition or prosecution for all other offenders. The solution is to be found by changing capricious municipal legal perceptions, not in rectifying the mores of international law.

A fifth conclusion can be drawn from the signing of the Cuban-U.S. "Memorandum of Understanding on Hijacking of Aircraft and Vessels and other Offenses." Since the conclusion of this communique on February 15, 1973, no incidents have occurred to date (July, 1973) involving U.S.-Cuban or Cuban-U.S. flights. The validity of the agreement remains to be tested. However, the fact that hijackers have chosen other destinations in the first half of 1973 may be viewed as a positive sign of deterrence. Should the untried agreement be invoked in the future, ". . . on the bases of equality and strict reciprocity,"[54] the desirability of "skyjacking" aircraft from the United States to Cuba, and vice-versa, may be greatly decreased.

The final conclusion rests in the international legal system itself. International law has sometimes been accused of decrepitude or even non-existence;[55] yet, the

---

[54]For text of agreement, see Appendix I, <u>infra</u>, pp. 317-19.

[55]See Karl Deutsch and Stanley Hoffmann, ed., <u>The Relevance of International Law</u> (New York: Anchor Books, 1971), especially John H. E. Freid, "International Law--Neither Orphan nor Harlot, Neither Jailer nor Never-Never Land," pp. 124-76.

reaction to unlawful aircraft seizures by the international community makes unmistakably clear its import as a tool to suppress crimes impinging upon people everwhere. The international convention is patent testimony to world-wide concern of an immediate problem, and in the case of unlawful aircraft seizures, the action was strikingly swift and forceful. Even so, only the future can reveal the ultimate impact international law will have in halting threats to civil aviation. But one thing is certain. The concerted action taken by the global community to suppress these crimes amply demonstrates a willingness to cooperate under the husbandry of an historically sanctioned international legal order. It is only through continuation of such cooperative efforts that man will be able to travel in peace and security--both in the air and through history.

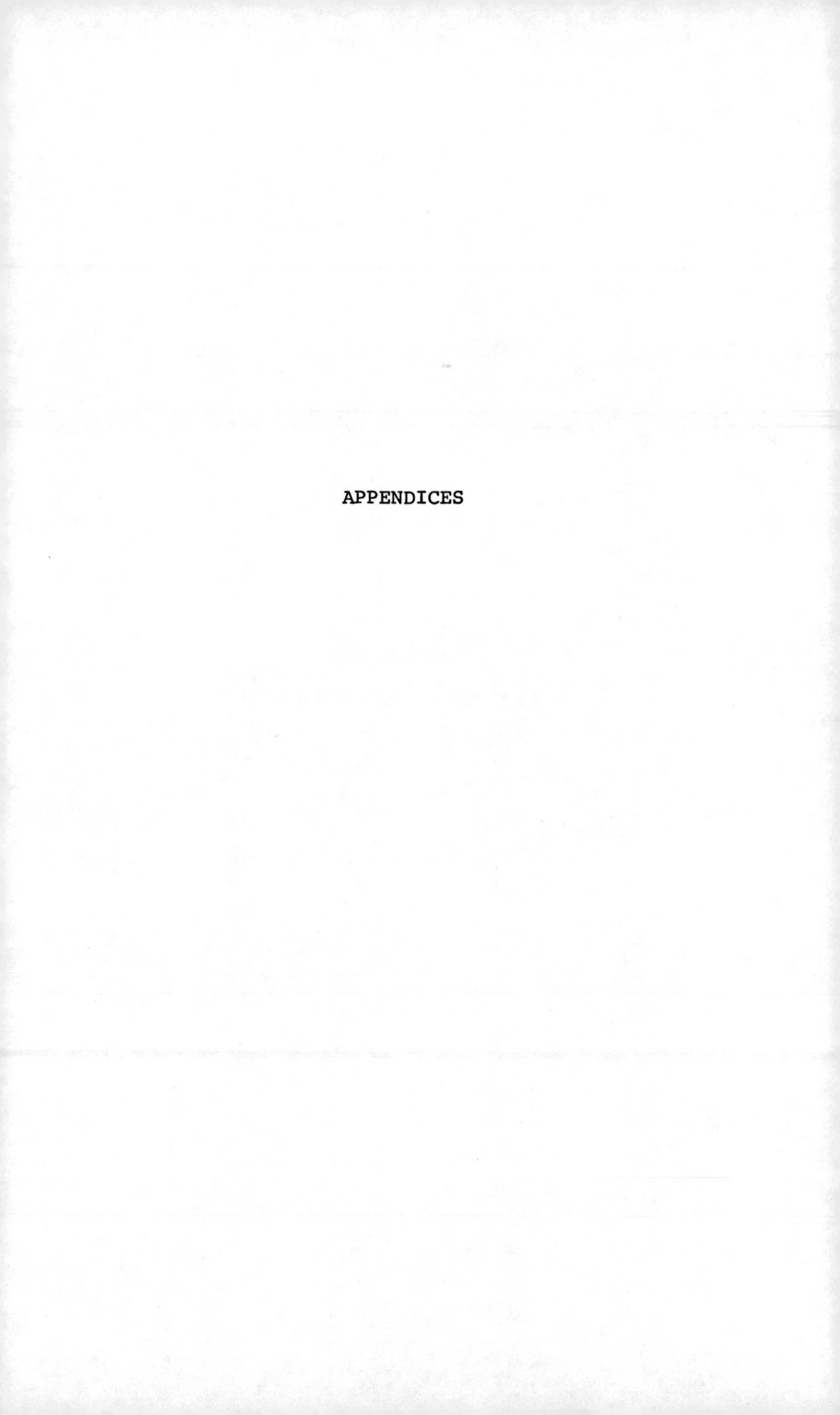

APPENDICES

APPENDIX A

THE OFFENCES AT SEA ACT, 1536

The Offences at Sea Act, 1536

An Acte for punnysshement of Pyrotes and Robbers of the See

WHERE traitours pirotes theves robbers murtherers and confederatours uppon the see, many tymes escape unpunysshed because the triall of their offences hath heretofore ben ordered judged and detmyned before the admyrall or his lyeutenante or comissary, after the course of the civile lawes, the nature wherof is that before any judgement of death canne be yeven ayenst the offendours, either they must playnly confesse their offences (which they will never doo without torture or paynes) or els their offences be so playnly and directly pved by witness indifferente, suche as sawe their offences comytted, which cannot be gotten but by chaunce at fewe tymes by cause such offendours comytt their offences uppon the see, and at many tymes murder and kill such psons being in the shipp or bote where they comytt their offences which shulde sytnes ayenst them in that behalfe, and also suche as shulde bere witnes be comonly maryners and shipment, which by cause of their often viages and passages in the sees departe without long tarying and ptraction of tyme to the great coste and charges as well of the Kynges Highnes as suche as wolde pursue such offendours: For reformacion wherof be it enacted by the auctoritie of this psent Parliament, that all treasons felonyes robberies murders and confederacies, herafter to be comytted in or uppon the see, or in any other haven ryve creke or place where the admyrall or admyralls have or ptende to have power auctoritie or jurisdiction, shall be enquired tried harde detmyned and judged in such shires and places in the realme as shall be lymytted by the Kynges comission or comissions to be directed for the same, in like fourme and condicion as if any such offence or offences hadd ben comytted or done in or uppon the lande; and such comissions shall be hadd under the Kinges greate seale directed to the admyrall or admyrals, or to his or their lieutenaunt deputie or deputies, and to iij or iiij such other substanciall psons as shall be named or appoynted by the lorde chauncellor of Englande for the tyme being from tyme to tyme and as often as nede shall require, to here and detymne suche offences after the comon course of the lawes of this lande, used for tresons felonies robberies murders & confederacies of the same done and comytted upon the lande within this realme.

2. AND . . . that such psonnes to whom such commission or comissions shall be directed, or iiij of them at the leaste, shall have full power and auctoritie to enquire of suche

offences and of evy of them by the othes of twelve good and laufull inhitaunte in the shire lymytted in their comission, in suche like mane and fourme as if suche offences hadd ben comytted uppon the lande, within the same shire; and that evy inditement founde and psented before such comissioners, of any treasons felonies robberies murders manslaughters or such other offences comytted or done in or uppon the sees, or done in or uppon any other haven river or creake, shall be good and effectuall in the lawe; and if eny pson or psons happen to be indited for eny such offence done or herafter to be done upon the sees, or in any other places above lymytted, that then suche order pcesse judgement and execucion shall be used hadd done and made, to and agaynst evy such pson and psons so being indited, as agaynst traytours felons and murderers for treason felony robbery murder or other such offences done uppon the lande, as by the lawes of the realme is accustomed: and that the triall of such offence or offences, if it be denyed by the offendour or offendours, shall be had by xij laufull men inhabited in the shere lymytted within such comission which shall be directed as is aforsaid, . . .

APPENDIX B

HARVARD DRAFT

PIRACY

ARTICLE 1

As the terms are used in this convention:

1. The term "jurisdiction" means the jurisdiction of a state under international law as distinguished from municipal law.

2. The term "territorial jurisdiction" means the jurisdiction of a state under international law over its land, its territorial waters and the air above its land and territorial waters. The term does not include the jurisdiction of a state over its ships outside its territory.

3. The term "territorial sea" means that part of the sea which is included in the territorial waters of a state.

4. The term "high sea" means that part of the sea which is not included in the territorial waters of any state.

5. The term "ship" means any water craft or air craft of whatever size.

ARTICLE 2

Every state has jurisdiction to prevent piracy and to seize and punish persons and to seize and dispose of property because of piracy. This jurisdiction is defined and limited by this convention.

ARTICLE 3

Piracy is any of the following acts, committed in a place not within the territorial jurisdiction of any state:

1. Any act of violence or of depredation committed with intent to rob, rape, wound, enslave, imprison or kill a person or with intent to steal or destroy property, for private ends without bona fide purpose of asserting a claim of right, provided that the act is connected with an attack on or from the sea or in or from the air. If the act is connected with an attack which starts from on board ship, either that ship or another ship which is involved must be a pirate ship or a ship without national character.

2. Any act of voluntary participation in the operation of a ship with knowledge of facts which make it a pirate ship.

3. Any act of instigation or of intentional facilitation of an act described in paragraph 1 or paragraph 2 of this article.

ARTICLE 4

1. A ship is a pirate ship when it is devoted by the persons in dominant control to the purpose of committing an act described in the first sentence of paragraph 1 of Article 3, or to the purpose of committing any similar act within the territory of a state by descent from the high sea, provided in either case that the purposes of the persons in dominant control are not definitely limited to committing such acts against ships or territory subject to the jurisdiction of the state to which the ship belongs.

2. A ship does not cease to be a pirate ship after the commission of an act described in paragraph 1 of Article 3, or after the commission of any similar act within the territory of a state by descent from the high sea, as long as it continues under the same control.

ARTICLE 5

A ship may retain its national character although it has become a pirate ship. The retention or loss of national character is determined by the law of the state from which it was derived.

ARTICLE 6

In a place not within the territorial jurisdiction of another state, a state may seize a pirate ship or a ship taken by piracy and possessed by pirates, and things or persons on board.

ARTICLE 7

1. In a place within the territorial jurisdiction of another state, a state may not pursue or seize a pirate ship or a ship taken by piracy and possessed by pirates; except that if pursuit of such a ship is commenced by a state within its own territorial jurisdiction or in a place not within the territorial jurisdiction of any state, the

pursuit may be continued into or over the territorial sea of another state and seizure may be made there, unless prohibited by the other state.

2. If a seizure is made within the territorial jurisdiction of another state in accordance with the provisions of paragraph 1 of this article, the state making the seizure shall give prompt notice to the other state, and shall tender possession of the ship and other things seized and the custody of persons seized.

3. If the tender provided for in paragraph 2 of this article is not accepted, the state making the seizure may proceed as if the seizure had been made on the high sea.

ARTICLE 8

If a pursuit is continued or a seizure is made within the territorial jurisdiction of another state in accordance with the provisions of paragraph 1 of Article 7, the state continuing the pursuit or making the seizure is liable to the other state for any damage done by the pursuing ship, other than damage done to the pirate ship or the ship possessed by pirates, or to persons and things on board.

ARTICLE 9

If a seizure because of piracy is made by a state in violation of the jurisdiction of another state, the state making the seizure shall, upon the demand of the other state, surrender or release the ship, things and persons seized, and shall make appropriate reparation.

ARTICLE 10

If a ship seized on suspicion of piracy outside the territorial jurisdiction of the state making the seizure, is neither a pirate ship nor a ship taken by piracy and possessed by pirates, and if the ship is not subject to seizure on other grounds, the state making the seizure shall be liable to the state to which the ship belongs for any damage caused by the seizure.

ARTICLE 11

1. In a place not within the territorial jurisdication of any state, a foreign ship may be approached and on reasonable suspicion that it is a pirate ship or a ship taken by piracy and possessed by pirates, it may be stopped and questioned to ascertain its character.

2. If the ship is neither a pirate ship nor a ship taken by piracy and possessed by pirates, and if it is not subject to such interference on other grounds, the state making the interference shall be liable to the state to which the ship belongs for any damage caused by the interference.

ARTICLE 12

A seizure because of piracy may be made only on behalf of a state, and only by a person who has been authorized to act on its behalf.

ARTICLE 13

1. A state, in accordance with its law, may dispose of ships and other property lawfully seized because of piracy.
2. The law of the state must conform to the following principles:
(a) The interests of innocent persons are not affected by the piratical possession or use of property, nor by seizure because of such possession or use.
(b) Claimants of any interest in the property are entitled to a reasonable opportunity to prove their claims.
(c) A claimant who establishes the validity of his claim is entitled to receive the property or compensation therefor, subject to a fair charge for salvage and expenses of administration.

ARTICLE 14

1. A state which has lawful custody of a person suspected of piracy may prosecute and punish that person.
2. Subject to the provisions of this convention, the law of the state which exercises such jurisdiction defines the crime, governs the procedure and prescribes the penalty.
3. The law of the state must, however, assure protection to accused aliens as follows:
(a) The accused person must be given a fair trial before an impartial tribunal without unreasonable delay.
(b) The accused person must be given humane treatment during his confinement pending trial.
(c) No cruel and unusual punishment may be inflicted.
(d) No discrimination may be made against the nationals of any state.
4. A state may intercede diplomatically to assure this protection to one of its nationals who is accused in another state.

ARTICLE 15

A state may not prosecute an alien for an act of piracy for which he has been charged and convicted or acquitted in a prosecution in another state.

ARTICLE 16

The provisions of this convention do not diminish a state's right under international law to take measures for the protection of its nationals, its ships and its commerce against interference on or over the high sea, when such measures are not based upon jurisdiction over piracy.

ARTICLE 17

1. The provisions of this convention shall supersede any inconsistent provisions relating to piracy in treaties in force among parties to this convention, except that such inconsistent provisions shall not be superseded in so far as they affect only the interests of the parties to such treaties inter se.

2. The provisions of this convention shall not prevent a party from entering into an agreement concerning piracy containing provisions inconsistent with this convention which affect only the interests of the parties to that agreement inter se.

ARTICLE 18

The parties to this convention agree to make every expedient use of their powers to prevent piracy, separately and in cooperation.

ARTICLE 19

1. If there should arise between the High Contracting Parties a dispute of any kind relating to the interpretation or application of the present convention, and if such dispute cannot be satisfactorily settled by diplomacy, it shall be settled in accordance with any applicable agreements in force between the parties to the dispute providing for the settlement of international disputes.

2. In case there is no such agreement in force between the parties to the dispute, the dispute shall be referred to arbitration or judicial settlement. In the absence of agreement on the choice of another tribunal, the dispute

shall, at the request of any one of the parties to the dispute, be referred to the Permanent Court of International Justice, if all the parties to the dispute are parties to the Protocol of December 16, 1920, relating to the Statute of that Court; and if any of the parties to the dispute is not a party to the Protocol of December 16, 1920, to an arbitral tribunal constituted in accordance with the provisions of the Convention for the Pacific Settlement of International Disputes, signed at The Hague, October 18, 1907.

APPENDIX C

GENEVA CONVENTION, 1958

CONVENTION ON THE HIGH SEAS

(GENEVA, 1958)*

ARTICLE 14

All States shall cooperate to the fullest possible extent in the repression of piracy on the high seas or in any other place outside the jurisdiction of any State.

ARTICLE 15

Piracy consists of any of the following acts:

1. Any illegal acts of violence, detention or any act of depredation, committed for private ends by the crew or the passengers of a private ship or a private aircraft, and directed:

    (a) On the high seas, against another ship or aircraft, or against persons or property on board such ship or aircraft;

    (b) Against a ship, aircraft, persons or property in a place outside the jurisdiction of any State;

2. Any act of voluntary participation in the operation of a ship or of an aircraft with knowledge of facts making it a pirate ship or aircraft;

3. Any act of inciting or of intentionally facilitating an act described in sub-paragraph 1 or sub-paragraph 2 of this article.

ARTICLE 16

The acts of piracy, as defined in article 15, committed by a warship, government ship or government aircraft whose crew has mutinied and taken control of the ship or aircraft are assimilated to acts committed by a private ship.

ARTICLE 17

A ship or aircraft is considered a pirate ship or aircraft if it is intended by the persons in dominant control to be used for the purpose of committing one of the acts referred to in Article 15. The same applies if the ship or aircraft has

---

*Done at Geneva, April 29, 1958. Entered into force September 30, 1962.

been used to commit any such act, so long as it remains under the control of the persons guilty of that act.

ARTICLE 18

A ship or aircraft may retain its nationality although it has become a pirate ship or aircraft. The retention or loss of nationality is determined by the law of the State from which such nationality was originally derived.

ARTICLE 19

On the high seas, or in any other place outside the jurisdiction of any State, every State may seize a pirate ship or aircraft, or a ship taken by piracy and under the control of pirates, and arrest the persons and seize the property on board. The courts of the State which carried out the seizure may decide upon the penalties to be imposed, and may also determine the action to be taken with regard to the ships, aircraft or property, subject to the rights of third parties acting in good faith.

ARTICLE 20

Where the seizure of a ship or aircraft on suspicion or piracy has been effected without adequate grounds, the State making the seizure shall be liable to the State the nationality of which is possessed by the ship or aircraft, for any loss or damage caused by the seizure.

ARTICLE 21

A seizure on account of piracy may only be carried out by warships or military aircraft, or other ships or aircraft on government service authorized to that effect.

ARTICLE 22

1. Except where acts of interference derive from powers conferred by treaty, a warship which encounters a foreign merchant ship on the high seas is not justified in boarding her unless there is reasonable ground for suspecting:

(a) That the ship is engaged in piracy; or

(b) That the ship is engaged in the slave trade; or

(c) That, though flying a foreign flag or refusing to show its flag, the ship is, in reality, of the same nationality as the warship.

2. In the cases provided for in sub-paragraphs (a), (b) and (c) above, the warship may proceed to verify the ship's right to fly its flag. To this end, it may send a boat under the command of an officer to the suspected ship. If suspicion remains after the documents have been checked, it may proceed to a further examination on board the ship, which must be carried out with all possible consideration.

3. If the suspicions prove to be unfounded, and provided that the ship boarded has not committed any act justifying them, it shall be compensated for any loss or damage that may have been sustained.

APPENDIX D

TOKYO CONVENTION 1963

THE CONVENTION ON OFFENSES AND CERTAIN OTHER ACTS COMMITTED ON BOARD AIRCRAFT*

Tokyo, 14 September 1963
The States Parties to this Convention
Have agreed as follows:

CHAPTER I

SCOPE OF THE CONVENTION

ARTICLE 1

1. This Convention shall apply in respect of:

(a) offences against penal law;

(b) acts which, whether or not they are offences, may or do jeopardize the safety of the aircraft or of persons or property therein or which jeopardize good order and discipline on board.

2. Except as provided in Chapter III, this Convention shall apply in respect of offences committed or acts done by a person on board any aircraft registered in a Contracting State, while that aircraft is in flight or on the surface of the high seas or of any other area outside the territory of any State.

3. For the purposes of this Convention, an aircraft is considered to be in flight from a moment when power is applied for the purpose of take-off until the moment when the landing run ends.

4. This Convention shall not apply to aircraft used in military, customs, or police services.

ARTICLE 2

Without prejudice to the provisions of Article 4 and except when the safety of the aircraft or of persons or property on board so requires, no provision of this Convention shall be interpreted as authorising or requiring any action in respect of offences against penal laws of a political nature or those based on racial or religious discrimination.

---

*DONE at Tokyo September 14, 1963. Entered into force December 4, 1969, TIAS 6768.

CHAPTER II

JURISDICTION

ARTICLE 3

1. The State of registration of the aircraft is competent to exercise jurisdication over offences and acts committed on board.

2. Each Contracting State shall take such measures as may be necessary to establish its jurisdiction as the State of registration over offences committed on board aircraft registered in such State.

3. This Convention does not exclude any criminal jurisdiction exercised in accordance with national law.

ARTICLE 4

A Contracting State which is not the State of registration may not interfere with an aircraft in flight in order to exercise its criminal jurisdiction over an offence committed on board except in the following cases:

(a) the offence has effect on the territory of such State:

(b) the offence has been committed by or against a national or permanent resident of such State;

(c) the offence is against the security of such State;

(d) the offence consists of a breach of any rules or regulations relating to the flight or manoeuvre of aircraft in force in such State;

(e) The exercise or jurisdiction is necessary to ensure the observance of any obligation of such State under a multilateral international agreement.

CHAPTER III

POWERS OF THE AIRCRAFT COMMANDER

ARTICLE 5

1. The provisions of this Chapter shall not apply to offences and acts committed or about to be committed by a person on board an aircraft in flight in the airspace of the State of registration or over the high seas or any other area outside the territory of any State unless the last point of takeoff or the next point of intended landing is situated in a State other than that of registration, or the aircraft subsequently flies in the airspace of a State other than that of registration with such person still on board.

2. Notwithstanding the provisions of Article 1, paragraph 3, an aircraft shall for the purposes of this Chapter, be considered to be in flight at any time from the moment when all its external doors are closed following embarkation until the moment when any such door is opened for disembarkation. In the case of a forced landing, the provisions of this Chapter shall continue to apply with respect to offences and acts committed on board until competent authorities of a State take over the responsibility for the aircraft and for the persons and property on board.

ARTICLE 6

1. The aircraft commander may, when he has reasonable grounds to believe that a person has committed, or is about to commit, on board the aircraft, an offence or act contemplated in Article 1, paragraph 1, impose upon such person reasonable measures including restraint which are necessary:

(a) to protect the safety of the aircraft, or of persons or property therein; or

(b) to maintain good order and discipline on board; or

(c) to enable him to deliver such person to competent authorities or to disembark him in accordance with the provisions of this Chapter

2. The aircraft commander may require or authorise the assistance of other crew members and may request or authorise, but not require, the assistance of passengers to restrain any person whom he is entitled to restrain. Any crew member

or passenger may also take reasonable preventive measures without such authorisation when he has reasonable grounds to believe that such action is immediately necessary to protect the safety of the aircraft, or of persons or property therein.

ARTICLE 7

1. Measures of restraint imposed upon a person in accordance with Article 6 shall not be continued beyond any point at which the aircraft lands unless:

(a) such point is in the territory of non-Contracting State and its authorities refuse to permit disembarkation of that person or those measures have been imposed in accordance with Article 6 paragraph 1 (c) in order to enable his delivery to competent authorities;

(b) the aircraft makes a forced landing and the aircraft commander is unable to deliver that person to competent authorities; or

(c) that person agrees to onward carriage under restraint.

2. The aircraft commander shall as soon as practicable, and if possible before landing in the territory of a State with a person on board who has been placed under restraint in accordance with the provisions of Article 6, notify the authorities of such State of the fact that a person on board is under restraint and of the reasons for such restraint.

ARTICLE 8

1. The aircraft commander may, in so far as it is necessary for the purpose of subparagraph (a) or (b) of paragraph 1 of Article 6, disembark in the territory of any State in which the aircraft lands any person who he has reasonable grounds to believe has committed, or is about to commit, on board the aircraft an act contemplated in Article 1, paragraph 1 (b).

2. The aircraft commander shall report to the authorities of the State in which he disembarks any person pursuant to this Article, the fact of, and the reasons for, such disembarkation.

ARTICLE 9

1. The aircraft commander may deliver to the competent authorities of any Contracting State in the territory of which the aircraft lands any person who he has reasonable grounds to believe has committed on board the aircraft an act which, in his opinion, is a serious offence according to the penal law of the State of registration of the aircraft.

2. The aircraft commander shall as soon as practicable and if possible before landing in the territory of a Contracing State with a person on board whom the aircraft commander intends to deliver in accordance with the preceding paragraph, notify the authorities of such State of his intention to deliver such person and the reasons therefor.

3. The aircraft commander shall furnish the authorities to whom any suspected offender is delivered in accordance with the provisions of this Article with evidence and information which, under the law of the State of registration of the aircraft, are lawfully in his possession.

ARTICLE 10

For actions taken in accordance with this Convention, neither the aircraft commander, any other member of the crew, any passenger, the owner or operator of the aircraft, nor the person on whose behalf the flight was performed shall be held responsible in any proceeding on account of the treatment undergone by the person against whom the actions were taken.

CHAPTER IV

UNLAWFUL SEIZURE OF AIRCRAFT

ARTICLE 11

1. When a person on board has unlawfully committed by force or threat thereof an act of interference, seizure, or other wrongful exercise of control of an aircraft in flight or when such an act is about to be committed, Contracting States shall take all appropriate measures to restore control of the aircraft to its lawful commander or to preserve his control of the aircraft.

CHAPTER V

POWERS AND DUTIES OF STATES

ARTICLE 12

Any Contracting State shall allow the commander of an aircraft registered in another Contracting State to disembark any person pursuant to Article 8, paragraph 1.

ARTICLE 13

1. Any Contracting State shall take delivery of any person whom the aircraft commander delivers pursuant to Article 9, paragraph 1.

2. Upon being satisfied that the circumstances so warrant, any Contracting State shall take custody or other measures to ensure the presence of any person suspected of an act contemplated in Article 11, paragraph 1, and of any person of whom it has taken delivery. The custody and other measures shall be as provided in the law of that State but may only be continued for such time as is reasonably necessary to enable any criminal or extradition proceedings to be instituted.

3. Any person in custody pursuant to the previous paragraph shall be assisted in communicating immediately with the nearest appropriate representative of the State of which he is a national.

4. Any Contracting State, to which a person is delivered pursuant to Article 9, paragraph 1, or in whose territory an aircraft lands following the commission of an act contemplated in Article 11, paragraph 1, shall immediately make a preliminary enquiry into the facts.

5. When a State, pursuant to this Article, has taken a person into custody, it shall immediately notify the State of registration of the aircraft and the State of nationality of the detained person and, if it considers it advisable, any other interested State of the fact that such person is in custody and of the circumstances which warrant his detention. The State which makes the preliminary enquiry contemplated in paragraph 4 of this Article shall promptly report its findings to the said States and shall indicate whether it intends to exercise jurisdiction.

ARTICLE 14

1. When any person has been disembarked in accordance with Article 8, paragraph 1, or delivered in accordance with Article 9, paragraph 1, or has disembarked after committing an act contemplated in Article 11, paragraph 1, and when such person cannot or does not desire to continue his journey and the State of landing refuses to admit him, that State may, if the person in question is not a national or permanent resident of that State, return him to the territory of the State of which he is a national or permanent resident or to the territory of the State in which he began his journey by air.

2. Neither disembarkation, nor delivery, nor the taking of custody or other measures contemplated in Article 13, paragraph 2, nor return of the person concerned, shall be considered as admission to the territory of the Contracting State concerned for the purpose of its law relating to entry or admission of persons and nothing in this Convention shall affect the law of a Contracting State relating to the expulsion of persons from its territory.

ARTICLE 15

1. Without prejudice to Article 14, any person who has been disembarked in accordance with Article 8, paragraph 1, or delivered in accordance with Article 9, paragraph 1, or has disembarked after committing an act contemplated in Article 11, paragraph 1, and who desires to continue his journey shall be at liberty as soon as practicable to proceed to any destination of his choice unless his presence is required by the law of the State of landing for the purpose of extradition or criminal proceedings.

2. Without prejudice to its law as to entry and admission to, and extradition and expulsion from its territory, a Contracting State in whose territory a person has been disembarked in accordance with Article 8, paragraph 1, or delivered in accordance with Article 9, paragraph 1, or has disembarked and is suspected of having committed an act contemplated in Article 11, paragraph 1, shall accord to such person treatment which is no less favourable for his protection and security than that accorded to nationals of such Contracting State in like circumstances.

CHAPTER VI

OTHER PROVISIONS

ARTICLE 16

1. Offences committed on aircraft registered in a Contracting State shall be treated, for the purpose of extradition, as if they had been committed not only in the place in which they have occurred but also in the territory of the State of registration of the aircraft.

2. Without prejudice to the provisions of the preceding paragraph, nothing in this Convention shall be deemed to create an obligation to grant extradition.

ARTICLE 17

In taking any measures for investigation or arrest or otherwise exercising jurisdiction in connection with any offence committed on board an aircraft the Contracting States shall pay due regard to the safety and other interests of air navigation and shall so act as to avoid unnecessary delay of the aircraft, passengers, crew or cargo.

ARTICLE 18

If Contracting States establish joint air transport operating organisations or international operating agencies, which operate aircraft not registered in any one State those States shall, according to the circumstances of the case, designate the State among them which, for the purposes of this Convention, shall be considered as the State of registration and shall give notice thereof to the International Civil Aviation Organisation which shall communicate the notice to all States Parties to this Convention.

CHAPTER VII

FINAL CLAUSES

ARTICLE 19

Until the date on which this Convention comes into force in accordance with the provisions of Article 21, it shall remain open for signature on behalf of any State which at that date is a Member of the United Nations or any of the Specialised Agencies.

ARTICLE 20

1. This Convention shall be subject to ratification by the signatory States in accordance with their constitutional procedures.

2. The instruments of ratification shall be deposited with the International Civil Aviation Organisation.

ARTICLE 21

1. As soon as twelve of the signatory States have deposited their instruments of ratification of this Convention, it shall come into force between them on the ninetieth day after the date of the deposit of the twelfth instrument of ratification. It shall come into force for each State ratifying thereafter on the ninetieth day after the deposit of its instrument of ratification.

2. As soon as this Convention comes into force, it shall be registered with the Secretary-General of the United Nations by the International Civil Aviation Organisation.

ARTICLE 22

1. This Convention shall, after it has come into force, be open for accession by any State Member of the United Nations or of any of the Specialised Agencies.

2. The accession of a State shall be effected by the deposit of an instrument of accession with the International Civil Aviation Organisation and shall take effect on the ninetieth day after the date of such deposit.

ARTICLE 23

1. Any Contracting State may denounce this Convention by notification addressed to the International Civil Aviation Organisation.

2. Denunciation shall take effect six months after the date of receipt by the International Civil Aviation Organisation of the notification of denunciation.

ARTICLE 24

1. Any dispute between two or more Contracting States concerning the interpretation or application of this Convention which cannot be settled through negotiation, shall, at the request of one of them, be submitted to arbitration. If within six months from the date of the request for arbitration the Parties are unable to agree on the organisation of the arbitration, any one of those Parties may refer the dispute to the International Court of Justice by request in conformity with the Statute of the Court.

2. Each State may at the time of signature or ratification of this Convention or accession thereto, declare that it does not consider itself bound by the preceding paragraph. The other Contracting States shall not be bound by the preceding paragraph with respect to any Contracting State having made such a reservation.

3. Any Contracting State having made a reservation in accordance with the preceding paragraph may at any time withdraw this reservation by notification to the International Civil Aviation Organisation.

ARTICLE 25

Except as provided in Article 24 no reservation may be made to this Convention.

ARTICLE 26

The International Civil Aviation Organisation shall give notice to all States Members of the United Nations or of any of the Specialised Agencies:

(a) of any signature of this Convention and the date thereof;

(b) of the deposit of any instrument of ratification or accession and the date thereof;

(c) of the date on which this Convention comes into force in accordance with Article 21, paragraph 1;

(d) of the receipt of any notification of denunciation and the date thereof; and

(e) of the receipt of any declaration or notification made under Article 24 and the date thereof.

IN WITNESS whereof the undersigned Plenipotentiaries, having been duly authorised, have signed this Convention.

DONE at Tokyo on the fourteenth day of September One Thousand Nine Hundred and Sixty-three in three authentic texts drawn up in the English, French and Spanish languages.

This Convention shall be deposited with the International Civil Aviation Organisation with which, in accordance with Article 19, it shall remain open for signature and the said Organization shall send certified copies thereof to all States Members of the United Nations or of any Specialised Agency.

APPENDIX E

INTERNATIONAL CIVIL AVIATION ORGANIZATION

RESOLUTION A16-37

The Assembly of the International Civil Aviation Organization (ICAO) of Buenos-Aires, September 1968

Resolution A16-37

This Assembly noting that unlawful seizure of civil aircraft had a serious adverse effect on safety, efficiency and regularity of air navigation, passed the following resolution:

"The Assembly

" - noting that Article 11 of the Tokyo Convention on Offences and certain other acts committed on Board Aircraft provides certain remedies for the situation evisaged;

- being of the opinion, however, that this article does not provide a complete remedy,

(1) URGES all States to become parties as soon as possible to the Tokyo Convention on Offences and certain other Acts Committed on Board Aircraft;

(2) INVITES States, even before ratification of, or adherence to, the Tokyo Convention, to give effect to the principles of Article 11 of that Convention; and

(3) REQUESTS the Council, at the earliest possible date to institute a study of other measures to cope with the problem of unlawful seizure."

This resolution was transmitted to contracting States by state letter dated 31 October 1968, recalling to States the provisions of Article 11 of the Tokyo Convention.

APPENDIX F

UNITED NATIONS GENERAL ASSEMBLY

RESOLUTION 2551

UNITED NATIONS GENERAL ASSEMBLY

Resolution on forcible diversion of civil Aircraft in flight
[Resolution 2551 (XXIV), December 12, 1969]

RESOLUTION ADOPTED BY THE GENERAL ASSEMBLY
(on the report of the Sixth Committee A/7845)

2551 (XXIV). Forcible diversion of civil aircraft in flight

THE GENERAL ASSEMBLY,

DEEPLY CONCERNED over acts of unlawful interference with international civil aviation,

CONSIDERING it necessary to recommend effective measures against hijacking in all its forms, or any other unlawful seizure or exercise of control of aircraft,

MINDFUL that such acts may endanger the life and health of passengers and crew in disregard of commonly accepted humanitarian considerations,

AWARE that international civil aviation can only function properly in conditions guaranteeing the safety of its operations and the due exercise of the freedom of air travel,

1. CALLS UPON States to take every appropriate measure to ensure that their respective national legislations provide an adequate framework for effective legal measures against all kinds of acts of unlawful interference with seizure of, or other wrongful exercise of control by force or threat thereof over, civil aircraft in flight;
2. URGES States in particular to ensure that persons on board who perpetrate such acts are prosecuted;
3. URGES full support for the efforts of the International Civil Aviation Organization directed towards the speedy preparation and implementation of a convention providing for appropriate measures, inter alia, with respect to making the unlawful seizure of civil aircraft a punishable offence and to the prosecution of persons who commit that offence;
4. INVITES States to ratify or accede to the Convention on Offences and Certain Other Acts Committed on Board Aircraft, signed at Tokyo on 14 September 1963, in conformity with the Convention.

1831st plenary meeting,
12 December 1969

APPENDIX G

THE HAGUE CONVENTION, 1970

THE HAGUE CONVENTION, 1970

Convention for the Suppression of Unlawful Seizure of Aircraft*

(The Hague, December 16, 1970)

PREAMBLE

THE STATES PARTIES TO THIS CONVENTION

CONSIDERING THAT unlawful acts of seizure or exercise of control of aircraft in flight jeopardize the safety of persons and property, seriously affect the operation of air services, and undermine the confidence of the peoples of the world in the safety of civil aviation;

CONSIDERING that the occurrence of such acts is a matter of grave concern;

CONSIDERING that, for the purpose of deterring such acts, there is an urgent need to provide appropriate measures for punishment of offenders;

HAVE AGREED AS FOLLOWS:

ARTICLE 1

Any person who on board an aircraft in flight:

(a) unlawfully, by force or threat thereof, or by any other form of intimidation, seizes, or exercises control of, that aircraft, or attempts to perform any such act, or

(b) is an accomplice of a person who performs or attempts to perform any such act commits an offence (hereinafter referred to as "the offence").

ARTICLE 2

Each Contracting State undertakes to make the offence punishable by severe penalties.

ARTICLE 3

1. For the purposes of this Convention, an aircraft is considered to be in flight at any time from the moment

---

*Done at the Hague December 16, 1970. Entered into force October 14, 1971, TIAS 7192.

when all its external doors are closed following embarkation until the moment when any such door is opened for disembarkation. In the case of a forced landing, the flight shall be deemed to continue until the competent authorities take over the responsibility for the aircraft and for persons and property on board.

2. This Convention shall not apply to aircraft used in military, customs or police services.

3. This Convention shall apply only if the place of take-off or the place of actual landing of the aircraft on board which the offence is committed is situated outside the territory of the State of registration of that aircraft; it shall be immaterial whether the aircraft is engaged in an international or domestic flight.

4. In the cases mentioned in Article 5, this Convention shall not apply if the place of take-off and the place of actual landing of the aircraft on board which the offence is committed are situated within the territory of the same State where that State is one of those referred to in that Article.

5. Notwithstanding paragraphs 3 and 4 of this Article, Articles 6, 7, 8 and 10 shall apply whatever the place of take-off or the place of actual landing of the aircraft, if the offender or the alleged offender is found in the territory of a State other than the State of registration of that aircraft.

ARTICLE 4

1. Each Contracting State shall take such measures as may be necessary to establish its jurisdiction over the offence and any other act of violence against passengers or crew committed by the alleged offender in connection with the offence, in the following cases:

(a) when the offence is committed on board an aircraft registered in that State;

(b) when the aircraft on board which the offence is committed lands in its territory with the alleged offender still on board;

(c) when the offence is committed on board an aircraft leased without crew to a lessee who has his principal place of business or, if the lessee has no such place of business, his permanent residence, in that State.

2. Each Contracting State shall likewise take such measures as may be necessary to establish its jurisdiction over the offence in the case where the alleged offender is present in its territory and it does not extradite him pursuant to Article 8 to any of the States mentioned in paragraph 1 of this Article.

3. This Convention does not exclude any criminal jurisdiction exercised in accordance with national law.

ARTICLE 5

The Contracting States which establish joint air transport operating organizations or international operating agencies, which operate aircraft which are subject to joint or international registration shall, by appropriate means, designate for each aircraft the State among them which shall exercise the jurisdiction and have the attributes of the State of registration for the purpose of this Convention and shall give notice thereof to the International Civil Aviation Organization which shall communicate the notice to all States Parties to this Convention.

ARTICLE 6

1. Upon being satisfied that the circumstances so warrant, any Contracting State in the territory of which the offender or the alleged offender is present, shall take him into custody or take other measures to ensure his presence. The custody and other measures shall be as provided in the law of that State but may only be continued for such time as is necessary to enable any criminal or extradition proceedings to be instituted.

2. Such State shall immediately make a preliminary enquiry into the facts.

3. Any person in custody pursuant to paragraph 1 of this Article shall be assisted in communicating immediately with the nearest appropriate representative of the State of which he is a national.

4. When a State, pursuant to this Article, has taken a person into custody, it shall immediately notify the State of registration of the aircraft, the State mentioned in Article 4, paragraph 1 (c), the State of nationality of the detained person and, if it considers it advisable, any other interested States of the fact that such person is in

custody and of the circumstances which warrant his detention. The State which makes the preliminary enquiry contemplated in paragraph 2 of this Article shall promptly report its findings to the said States and shall indicate whether it intends to exercise jurisdiction.

ARTICLE 7

The Contracting State in the territory of which the alleged offender is found shall, if it does not extradite him, be obliged, without exception whatsoever and whether or not the offence was committed in its territory, to submit the case to its competent authorities for the purpose of prosecution.

Those authorities shall take their decision in the same manner as in the case of any ordinary offence of a serious nature under the law of that State.

ARTICLE 8

1. The offence shall be deemed to be included as an extraditable offence in any extradition treaty existing between Contracting States. Contracting States undertake to include the offence as an extraditable offence in every extradition treaty to be concluded between them.

2. If a Contracting State which makes extradition conditional on the existence of a treaty receives a request for extradition from another Contracting State with which it has no extradition treaty, it may at its option consider this Convention as the legal basis for extradition in respect of the offence. Extradition shall be subject to the other conditions provided by the law of the requested State.

3. Contracting States which do not make extradition conditional on the existence of a treaty shall recognize the offence as an extraditable offence between themselves subject to the conditions provided by the law of the requested State.

4. The offence shall be treated, for the purpose of extradition between Contracting States, as if it had been committed not only in the place in which it occurred but also in the territories of the States required to establish their jurisdiction in accordance with Article 4, paragraph 1.

ARTICLE 9

1. When any of the acts mentioned in Article 1 (a) has occurred or is about to occur, Contracting States shall take all appropriate measures to restore control of the aircraft to its lawful commander or to preserve his control of the aircraft.

2. In the cases contemplated by the preceding paragraph, any Contracting State in which the aircraft or its passengers or crew are present shall facilitate the continuation of the journey of the passengers and crew as soon as practicable, and shall without delay return the aircraft and its cargo to the persons lawfully entitled to possession.

ARTICLE 10

1. Contracting States shall afford one another the greatest measure of assistance in connection with criminal proceedings brought in respect of the offence and other acts mentioned in Article 4. The law of the State requested shall apply in all cases.

2. The provisions of paragraph 1 of this Article shall not affect obligations under any other treaty, bilateral or multilateral, which governs or will govern, in whole or in part, mutual assistance in criminal matters.

ARTICLE 11

Each Contracting State shall in accordance with its national law report to the Council of the International Civil Aviation Organization as promptly as possible any relevant information in its possession concerning:

(a) the circumstances of the offence;

(b) the action taken pursuant to Article 9;

(c) the measures taken in relation to the offender or the alleged offender, and, in particular, the results of any extradition proceedings or other legal proceedings.

ARTICLE 12

1. Any dispute between two or more Contracting States concerning the interpretation or application of this Convention which cannot be settled through negotiation, shall, at the request of one of them, be submitted to arbitration. If within six months from the date of the request for arbitration the Parties are unable to agree on the organization of the arbitration, any one of those Parties may refer the dispute to the International Court of Justice by request in conformity with the Statute of the Court.

2. Each State may at the time of signature or ratification of this Convention or accession thereto, declare that it does not consider itself bound by the preceding paragraph. The other Contracting States shall not be bound by the preceding paragraph with respect to any Contracting State having made such a reservation.

3. Any Contracting State having made a reservation in accordance with the preceding paragraph may at any time withdraw this reservation by notification to the Depositary Governments.

ARTICLE 13

1. This Convention shall be open for signature at the Hague on 16 December 1970, by States participating in the International Conference on Air Law held at the Hague from 1 to 16 December 1970 (hereinafter referred to as The Hague Convention). After 31 December 1970, the Convention shall be open to all States for signature in Moscow, London and Washington. Any State which does not sign this Convention before its entry into force in accordance with paragraph 3 of this Article may accede to it at any time.

2. This Convention shall be subject to ratification by the signatory States. Instruments of ratification and instruments of accession shall be deposited with the Governments of the Union of Soviet Socialist Republics, the United Kingdom of Great Britain and Northern Ireland, and the United States of America, which are hereby designated the Depositary Governments.

3. This Convention shall enter into force thirty days following the date of the deposit of instruments of ratification by ten States signatory to this Convention which participated in The Hague Conference.

4. For other States, this Convention shall enter into force on the date of entry into force of this Convention in accordance with paragraph 3 of this Article, or thirty days following the date of deposit of their instruments of ratification or accession, whichever is later.

5. The Depositary Governments shall promptly inform all signatory and acceding States of the date of each signature, the date of deposit of each instrument of ratification or accession, the date of entry into force of this Convention, and other notices.

6. As soon as this Convention comes into force, it shall be registered by the Depositary Governments pursuant to Article 102 of the Charter of the United Nations and pursuant to Article 83 of the Convention on International Civil Aviation (Chicago, 1944).

ARTICLE 14

1. Any Contracting State may denounce this Convention by written notification to the Depositary Governments.

2. Denunciation shall take effect six months following the date on which notification is received by the Depositary Governments.

In witness whereof the undersigned Plenipotentiaries, being duly authorised thereto by their Governments, have signed this Convention

Done at The Hague, this sixteenth day of December, one thousand nine hundred and seventy, in three originals, each being drawn up in four authentic texts in the English, French, Russian and Spanish languages.

APPENDIX H

THE MONTREAL CONVENTION

C O N V E N T I O N

FOR THE SUPPRESSION OF UNLAWFUL ACTS AGAINST THE SAFETY OF CIVIL AVIATION*

THE STATES PARTIES TO THIS CONVENTION

CONSIDERING that unlawful acts against the safety of of civil aviation jeopardize the safety of person and property, seriously affect the operation of air services, and undermine the confidence of the peoples of the world in the safety of civil aviation;

CONSIDERING that the occurrence of such acts is a matter of grave concern;

CONSIDERING that, for the purpose of deterring such acts, there is an urgent need to provide appropriate measures for punishment of offenders:

HAVE AGREED AS FOLLOWS:

ARTICLE 1

1. Any person commits an offense if he unlawfully and intentionally:

(a) performs an act of violence against a person on board an aircraft in flight if that act is likely to endanger the safety of that aircraft; or

(b) destroys an aircraft in service or causes damage to such an aircraft which renders it incapable of flight or which is likely to endanger its safety in flight; or

(c) places or causes to be placed on an aircraft in service, by any means whatsoever, a device or substance which is likely to destroy that aircraft, or to cause damage to it which is likely to endanger its safety in flight; or

(d) destroys or damages air navigation facilities or interferes with their operation, if any

---

*Done at Montreal September 23, 1971. Entered into force, January 26, 1973. TIAS 7570.

such act is likely to endanger the safety of aircraft in flight; or

(e) communicates information which he knows to be false, thereby endangering the safety of an aircraft in flight.

2. Any person also commits an offense if he:

(a) attempts to commit any of the offenses mentioned in paragraph 1 of this Article; or

(b) is an accomplice of a person who commits or attempts to commit any such offense.

ARTICLE 2

For the purpose of this Convention:

(a) an aircraft is considered to be in flight at any time from the moment when all its external doors are closed following embarkation until the moment when any such door is opened for disembarkation; in the case of a forced landing; the flight shall be deemed to continue until the competent authorities take over the responsibility for the aircraft and for persons and property on board;

(b) an aircraft is considered to be in service from the beginning of the preflight preparation of the aircraft by ground personnel or by the crew for a specific flight until twenty-four hours after any landing; the period of service shall, in any event, extend for the entire period during which the aircraft is in flight as defined in paragraph (a) of this Article.

ARTICLE 3

Each Contracting State undertakes to make the offenses mentioned in Article 1 punishable by severe penalties.

ARTICLE 4

1. This Convention shall not apply to aircraft used in military, customs or police services.

2. In the cases contemplated in subparagraphs (a), (b), (c) and (e) of paragraph 1 of Article 1, this Convention shall apply, irrespective of whether the aircraft is engaged in an international or domestic flight, only if:

(a) the place of take-off or landing, actual or intended, of the aircraft is situated outside the territory of the State of registration of that aircraft; or

(b) the offense is committed in the territory of a State other than the State of registration of the aircraft.

3. Notwithstanding paragraph 2 of this Article, in the cases contemplated in subparagraphs (a), (b), (c) and (e) of paragraph 1 of Article 1, this Convention shall also apply if the offender or the alleged offender is found in the territory of a State other than the State of registration of the aircraft.

4. With respect to the States mentioned in Article 9 and in the cases mentioned in subparagraphs (a), (b), (c) and (e) of paragraph 1 of Article 1, this Convention shall not apply if the places referred to in subparagraph (a) of paragraph 2 of this Article are situated within the territory of the same State where that State is one of those referred to in Article 9, unless the offense is committed or the offender or alleged offender is found in the territory of a State other than that State.

5. In the cases contemplated in subparagraph (d) of paragraph 1 of Article 1, this Convention shall apply only if the air navigation facilities are used in international air navigation.

6. The provisions of paragraphs 2, 3, 4 and 5 of this Article shall also apply in the cases contemplated in paragraph 2 of Article 1.

ARTICLE 5

1. Each Contracting State shall take such measures as may be necessary to establish its jurisdiction over the offenses in the following cases:

(a) when the offense is committed in the territory of that State;

(b) when the offense is committed against or on board an aircraft registered in that State;

(c) when the aircraft on board which the offense is committed lands in its territory with the alleged offender still on board;

(d) when the offense is committed against or on board an aircraft leased without crew to a lessee who has his principal place of business or, if the lessee has no such place of business, his permanent residence, in that State.

2. Each Contracting State shall likewise take such measures as may be necessary to establish its jurisdiction over the offenses mentioned in Article 1, paragraph 1 (a), (b) and (c), and in Article 1, paragraph 2, in so far as that paragraph relates to those offenses, in the case where the alleged offender is present in its territory and it does not extradite him pursuant to Article 8 to any of the States mentioned in paragraph 1 of this Article.

3. This Convention does not exclude any criminal jurisdiction exercised in accordance with national law.

ARTICLE 6

1. Upon being satisfied that the circumstances so warrant, any Contracting State in the territory of which the offender or the alleged offender is present, shall take him into custody or take other measures to ensure his presence. The custody and other measures shall be as provided in the law of that State but may only be continued for such time as is necessary to enable any criminal or extradition proceedings to be instituted.

2. Such State shall immediately make a preliminary enquiry into the facts.

3. Any person in custody pursuant to paragraph 1 of this Article shall be assisted in communicating immediately with the nearest appropriate representative of the State of which he is a national.

4. When a State, pursuant to this Article, has taken a person into custody, it shall immediately notify the States mentioned in Article 5, paragraph 1, the State of nationality of the detained person and, if it considers it advisable, any other interested States of the fact that such person is in custody and of the circumstances which warrant his detention. The State which makes the preliminary enquiry contemplated in paragraph 2 of this Article shall promptly report its findings to the said States and shall indicate whether it intends to exercise jurisdiction.

ARTICLE 7

The Contracting State in the territory of which the alleged offender is found shall, if it does not extradite him, be obliged, without exception whatsoever and whether or not the offense was committed in its territory, to submit the case to its competent authorities for the purpose of prosecution. Those authorities shall take their decision in the same manner as in the case of any ordinary offense of a serious nature under the law of that State.

ARTICLE 8

1. The offenses shall be deemed to be included as extraditable offenses in any extradition treaty existing between Contracting States. Contracting States undertake to include the offenses as extraditable offenses in every extradition treaty to be concluded between them.

2. If a Contracting State which makes extradition conditional on the existence of a treaty receives a request for extradition from another Contracting State with which it has no extradition treaty, it may at its option consider this Convention as the legal basis for extradition in respect of the offenses. Extradition shall be subject to the other conditions provided by the law of the requested State.

3. Contracting States which do not make extradition conditional on the existence of a treaty shall recognize the offenses as extraditable offenses between themselves subject to the conditions provided by the law of the requested State.

4. Each of the offenses shall be treated, for the purpose of extradition between Contracting States, as if it had been committed not only in the place in which it occurred but also in the territories of the States required to establish their jurisdiction in accordance with Article 5, paragraph 1 (b), (c) and (d).

ARTICLE 9

The Contracting States which establish joint air transport operating organizations or international operating agencies, which operate aircraft which are subject to joint or international registration shall, by appropriate means, designate for each aircraft the State among them which shall exercise the jurisdiction and have the attributes of the State of registration for the purpose of this Convention and shall give notice thereof to the International Civil Aviation Organization which shall communicate the notice to all States Parties to this Convention.

ARTICLE 10

1. Contracting States shall, in accordance with international and national law, endeavour to take all practicable measures for the purpose of preventing the offenses mentioned in Article 1.

2. When, due to the commission of one of the offenses mentioned in Article 1, a flight has been delayed or interrupted, any Contracting State in whose territory the aircraft or passengers or crew are present shall facilitate the continuation of the journey of the passengers and crew as soon as practicable, and shall without delay return the aircraft and its cargo to the persons lawfully entitled to possession.

ARTICLE 11

1. Contracting States shall afford one another the greatest measure of assistance in connection with criminal proceedings brought in respect of the offenses. The law of the State requested shall apply in all cases.

2. The provisions of paragraph 1 of this Article shall not affect obligations under any other treaty, bilateral or multilateral, which governs or will govern, in whole or in part, mutual assistance in criminal matters.

ARTICLE 12

Any Contracting State having reason to believe that one of the offenses mentioned in Article 1 will be committed shall, in accordance with its national law, furnish any relevant information in its possession to those States which it believes would be the States mentions in Article 5, Paragraph 1.

ARTICLE 13

Each Contracting State shall in accordance with its national law report to the Council of the International Civil Aviation Organization as promptly as possible any relevant information in its possession concerning:

(a) the circumstances of the offense;

(b) the action taken pursuant to Article 10, paragraph 2;

(c) the measures taken in relation to the offender or the alleged offender and, in particular, the results of any extradition proceedings or other legal proceedings.

ARTICLE 14

1. Any dispute between two or more Contracting States concerning the interpretation or application of this Convention which cannot be settled through negotiation, shall, at the request of one of them, be submitted to arbitration. If within six months from the date of the request for arbitration the Parties are unable to agree on the organization of the arbitration, any one of those Parties may refer the dispute to the International Court of Justice by request in conformity with the Statute of the Court.

2. Each State may at the time of signature or ratification of this Convention or accession thereto, declare that it does not consider itself bound by the preceding paragraph. The other Contracting States shall not be bound by the preceding paragraph with respect to any Contracting State having made such a reservation.

3. Any Contracting State having made a reservation in accordance with the preceding paragraph may at any time withdraw this reservation by notification to the Depositary Governments.

ARTICLE 15

1. This Convention shall be open for signature at Montreal on 23 September 1971, by States participating in the International Conference on Air Law held at Montreal from 8 to 23 September 1971 (hereinafter referred to as the Montreal Conference). After 10 October 1971, the Convention shall be open to all States for signature in Moscow, London and Washington. Any State which does not sign this Convention before its entry into force in accordance with paragraph 3 of this Article may accede to it at any time.

2. This Convention shall be subject to ratification by the signatory States. Instruments of ratification and instruments of accession shall be deposited with the Governments of the Union of Soviet Socialist Republics, the United Kingdom of Great Britain and Northern Ireland, and the United States of America, which are hereby designated the Depositary Governments.

3. This Convention shall enter into force thirty days following the date of the deposit of instruments of ratification by ten States signatory to this Convention which participated in the Montreal Conference.

4. For other States, this Convention shall enter into force on the date of entry into force of this Convention in accordance with paragraph 3 of this Article, or thirty days following the date of deposit of their instruments of ratification or accession, whichever is later.

5. The Depositary Governments shall promptly inform all signatory and acceding States of the date of each signature, the date of deposit of each instrument of ratification or accession, the date of entry into force of this Convention, and other notices.

6. As soon as this Convention comes into force, it shall be registered by the Depositary Governments pursuant to Article 102 of the Charter of the United Nations and pursuant to Article 83 of the Convention on International Civil Aviation (Chicago, 1944).

ARTICLE 16

1. Any Contracting State may denounce this Convention by written notification to the Depositary Governments.

2. Denunciation shall take effect six months following the date on which notification is received by the Depositary Governments.

IN WITNESS WHEREOF the undersigned Plenipotentiaries, being duly authorized thereto by their Governments, have signed this Convention.

DONE at Montreal, this twenty-third day of September, one thousand nine hundred and seventy-one, in three originals, each being drawn up in four authentic texts in the English, French, Russian and Spanish languages.

APPENDIX I

TEXT OF NOTE SIGNED TODAY BY SECRETARY OF STATE WILLIAM P. ROGERS CONTAINING AGREEMENT WITH CUBA ON HIJACKING

EMBARGOED FOR RELEASE AT 11:45 a.m. EST THURSDAY, FEBRUARY 15, 1973. NOT TO BE PREVIOUSLY PUBLISHED, QUOTED FROM OR USED IN ANY WAY.

Sir:

I refer to the Memorandum of Understanding on the hijacking of aircraft and vessels and other offenses which has resulted from conversations which have taken place between the Embassy of Switzerland, representative of the interests of the United States of America in Cuba, and representatives of the Government of the Republic of Cuba, the text of which is as follows:

MEMORANDUM OF UNDERSTANDING ON HIJACKING OF AIRCRAFT AND VESSELS AND OTHER OFFENSES

The Government of the United States of America and the Government of the Republic of Cuba, on the bases of equality and strict reciprocity, agree:

FIRST: Any person who hereafter seizes, removes, appropriates or diverts from its normal route or activities an aircraft or vessel registered under the laws of one of the parties and brings it to the territory of the other party shall be considered to have committed an offense and therefore shall either be returned to the party of registry of the aircraft or vessel to be tried by the courts of that party in conformity with its laws or be brought before the courts of the party whose territory he reached for trial in conformity with its laws for the offense punishable by the most severe penalty according to the circumstances and the seriousness of the acts to which this Article refers. In addition, the party whose territory is reached by the aircraft or vessel shall take all necessary steps to facilitate without delay the continuation of the journey of the passengers and crew innocent of the hijacking of the aircraft or vessel in question, with their belongings, as well as the journey of the aircraft or vessel itself with all goods carried with it, including any funds obtained by extortion or other illegal means, or the return of the foregoing to the territory of the first party; likewise, it shall take all steps to protect the physical integrity of the aircraft or vessel and all goods, carried with it, including any funds obtained by extortion or other illegal means, and the physical integrity of the passengers and crew innocent of the hijacking, and their belongings, while they are in its territory as a consequence of or in connection with the acts to which this Article refers.

In the event that the offenses referred to above are not punishable under the laws existing in the country to which the persons committing them arrived, the party in question shall be obligated, except in the case of minor offenses, to return the persons who have committed such acts, in accordance with the applicable legal procedures, to the territory of the other party to be tried by its courts in conformity with its laws.

SECOND: Each party shall try with a view to severe punishment in accordance with its laws any person who, within its territory, hereafter conspires to promote, or promotes, or prepares, or directs, or forms part of an expedition which from its territory or any other place carries out acts of violence or depredation against aircraft or vessels of any kind or registration coming from or going to the territory of the other party or who, within its territory, hereafter conspires to promote, or promotes, or prepares, or directs, or forms part of an expedition which from its territory or any other place carries out such acts or other similar unlawful acts in the territory of the other party.

THIRD: Each party shall apply strictly its own laws to any national of the other party who, coming from the territory of the other party, enters its territory, violating its laws as well as national and international requirements pertaining to immigration, health, customs and the like.

FOURTH: The party in whose territory the perpetrators of the acts described in Article FIRST arrive may take into consideration any extenuating or mitigating circumstances in those cases in which the persons responsible for the acts were being sought for strictly political reasons and were in real and imminent danger of death without a viable alternative for leaving the country, provided there was no financial extortion or physical injury to the members of the crew, passengers, or other persons in connection with the hijacking.

FINAL PROVISIONS:

This Agreement may be amended or expanded by decision of the parties.

This Agreement shall be in force for five years and may be renewed for an equal term by express decision of the parties.

Either party may inform the other of its decision to terminate this Agreement at any time while it is in force by written denunciation submitted six months in advance.

This Agreement shall enter into force on the date agreed by the parties.

Done in English and Spanish texts which are equally authentic.

In compliance with the express instructions of my Government, I wish to convey its acceptance of the Memorandum of Understanding transcribed above, as well as its agreement that the simultaneous exchange of notes taking place in Washington between the Department of State and the Embassy of the Czechoslovak Socialist Republic, representative of the interests of the Republic of Cuba in the United States of America, and in Havana between the Embassy of Switzerland, representative of the interests of the United States of America in Cuba, and the Ministry of Foreign Relations, shall constitute the agreement on the hijacking of aircraft and vessels and other offenses between the Government of the United States of America and the Government of the Republic of Cuba, which shall take effect on the date of this note.

Accept, Sir, the renewed assurances of my high consideration.

BIBLIOGRAPHY

BIBLIOGRAPHY

Books

Arey, James A. The Sky Pirates. New York: Scribner, 1972

Baldwin, Hanson W. The Great Arms Race. New York: Praeger Press, 1958.

Bishop, William W., Jr. International Law: Cases and Materials. Boston: Little, Brown, and Company, 1962.

Bowett, D. W. The Law of International Institutions. New York: Frederick A. Praeger, Publisher, 1963.

Brierly, James L. The Basis of Obligation in International Law. Oxford: The Clarendon Press, 1958.

__________. The Law of Nations. Oxford: Clarendon Press, 1928.

__________. The Law of Nations. 4th ed. Oxford: Clarendon Press, 1949.

Buergenthal, Thomas. Law-Making in the International Civil Aviation Organization. New York: Syracuse University Press, 1969.

Coplin, William D. The Functions of International Law: An Introduction to the Role of International Law in the Contemporary World. Chicago: Rand McNally and Company, 1966.

Corbett, Percy E. Law and Society in the Relations of States. New York: Harcourt, Brace and World, Inc., 1951.

Deutsch, Karl and Hoffmann, Stanley, ed. The Relevance of International Law. New York: Anchor Books, 1971.

Erickson, Richard. International Law and the Revolutionary State. Dobbs Ferry, New York: Oceana Publications, Inc., 1972.

Falk, Richard A., ed. The International Law of Civil War. Baltimore: John Hopkins Press, 1971.

Fenwick, Charles G. International Law. 3rd ed. New York: Appleton-Century-Crofts, Inc., 1948.

Fleming, Denna F. The United States and World Organization: 1920-1933. New York: AMS Press, Inc., 1966.

Friedmann, Wolfgang. The Changing Structure of International Law. New York: Columbia University Press, 1964.

Garcia-Mora, Manuel R. International Law and Asylum as a Human Right. Washington, D.C.: Public Affairs Press, 1956.

Gosse, Philip. The History of Pirates. London: Longmanns, Green and Company, 1932.

__________. The Pirates' Who's Who. London: Dulau and Company, Ltd., 1924.

Gross, Leo, ed. International Law in the Twentieth Century. New York: Appleton-Century-Crofts, 1969.

Grotius, Hugo. De Jure Belli ac Pacis Libri Tres. Translated by Francis W. Kelsey. Indianapolis: The Bobbs-Merrill Company, Inc., 1923.

__________. The Freedom of the Seas. Translated by Ralph Magoffin. New York: Oxford University Press, 1916.

Hackworth, Green Haywood. Digest of International Law. Washington, D.C.: Government Printing Office, 1940-1944.

Hall, William E. A Treatise on International Law. Oxford: Clarendon Press, 1924.

Halleck, Henry W. International Law. Vol. I, 3rd ed., Philadelphia: G. S. Appleton, 1866.

Hill, Norman L. The Public International Conference. Stanford: Stanford University Press, 1929.

Hubbard, David G. The Skyjacker: His Flights of Fantasy. New York: MacMillan Company, 1971.

Hurren, B. J. Airports of the World. London: Wolfe Publishing Ltd., 1970.

Jessup, Philip. A Modern Law of Nations. New York: Macmillan, 1950.

Johnson, D. H. N. Rights in Air Space. Dobbs Ferry, New York: Oceana Publications, Inc., 1965.

Kelsen, Hans. Authority and the Individual. Cambridge: Harvard University Press, 1937.

__________. General Theory of Law and State. Cambridge: Harvard University Press, 1945.

__________. Principles of International Law. New York: Rinehart and Company, Inc., 1952.

Kim, Young Hum. Twenty Years of Crises: The Cold War Era. Englewood Cliffs, N.J.: Prentice Hall, Inc., 1968.

Korovin, Y. A., et al. International Law. Translated by Dennis Ogden. Moscow: Foreign Languages Publishing House, n.d.

Lauterpacht, Hersch. International Law and Human Rights. New York: Praeger, 1950.

__________. Oppenheim's International Law. 8th ed. London: Longmanns, Green, and Company, 1955.

__________. Recognition in International Law. Cambridge: Cambridge University Press, 1947.

Lawrence, Thomas J. The Principles of International Law. New York: D.C. Heath and Company, 1910.

Leopold, Richard W. The Growth of American Foreign Policy. New York: Alfred A. Knopf, Inc., 1962.

McDougal, Myres S., and Burke, William T. The Public Order of the Oceans. New Haven: Yale University Press, 1962.

McNair, Arnold D. The Law of the Air. London: Stevens, Inc., 1932.

McNair, Arnold D. The Law of Treaties. New York: Columbia University Press, 1938.

McWhinney, Edward, ed. Aerial Piracy and International Law. Dobbs Ferry, New York: Oceana Publications, Inc., 1971.

Mangone, Gerald J. The Elements of International Law. Homewood, Illinois: The Dorsey Press, 1967.

Matte, Nicholas M. Aerospace Law. London: Sweet and Maxwell, Ltd., 1969.

Moore, John Bassett. Digest of International Law. Washington, D.C.: Government Printing Office, 1906.

Mueller, Gerhard O. W., and LePoole-Griffiths, Fre. Comparative Criminal Procedure. New York: University Press, 1969.

__________, and Wise, Edward M., ed. International Criminal Law. South Hackensack, N.J.: Fred B. Rothman and Company, 1965.

Nie, Norman H., et al. Statistical Package for the Social Sciences. New York: McGraw-Hill Book Company, 1970.

Oglesby, Roscoe R. Internal War and the Search for Normative Order. The Hague: Martinus Nijhoff, 1971.

Oppenheim, Lassa F. L. International Law. London: Longmanns and Company, 1905.

__________. International Law, A Treatise, ed. Hersh Lauterpacht. London: Longmanns, Green, and Company, 1947.

Poulantzas, Nicholas M. The Right of Hot Pursuit in International Law. Leyden: A. W. Sijthoff, 1969.

Rienow, Robert. The Test of the Nationality of a Merchant Vessel. New York: Columbia University Press, 1937.

Riensenfeld, Stefan A. Protection of Coastal Fisheries Under International Law. Washington, D.C.: Carnegie Endowment for International Peace, 1942.

Robinson, William M., Jr. The Confederate Privateers. New Haven: Yale University Press, 1928.

Schunschnigg, Kurt von. International Law. Milwaukee, Wisconsin: The Bruce Publishing Co., 1959.

Schwarzenberger, Georg. International Criminal Law. Edited by Gerhard O. W. Mueller and Edward M. Wise. South Hackensack, N.J.: Fred B. Rothman and Co., 1965.

Scott, James B. The Project of a Permanent Court of International Justice and Resolutions of the Advisory Committee of Jurists. Report and Commentary Pamphlet No. 35 of the Division of International Law. Washington: Carnegie Endowment for International Peace, 1920.

__________. ed. The Reports to the Hague Conference of 1899 and 1907. Oxford: Clarendon Press, 1917.

Smith, Herbert A. The Law and Custom of the Sea. London: Stevens Publishers, 1959.

Stephen, James F. A Digest of the Criminal Law. London: Macmillan and Company, 1877.

Stiel, Paul. Der Talbestand der Piratorie. Leipzig: Duncker and Humblet Publishers, 1905.

Stimson, Henry L. The Far Eastern Crisis. New York: Harper and Bros., 1936.

Tung, William L. International Organization Under the United Nations System. New York: Thomas Y. Crowell Co., 1969.

Turi, Robert T.; Friel, Charles M.; Sheldon, Robert B.; and Matthews, John P. Criminal Justice Monograph. "Descriptive Study of Aircraft Hijacking." Sam Houston State University: Institute of Contemporary Corrections and the Behavioral Sciences, 1972.

Weis, Paul. Nationality and Statelessness in International Law. London: Stevens and Sons, 1956.

Wheaton, Henry. Elements of International Law. Edited by George G. Wilson. Oxford: Oxford University, 1936.

Whiteman, Marjorie M. Digest of International Law. Washington, D.C.: Department of State, 1965.

Woetzel, Robert K. The Nuremburg Trials in International Law. London: Stevens and Sons, 1960.

Weelsey, Theodore D. International Law. New York: Charles Scribner's Sons, 1892.

Zawodny, J. K. Guide to the Study of International Relations. San Francisco, Calif.: Chandler Publishing Co., 1966.

Articles and Periodicals

Aggarwala, Narinder. "Political Aspects of Hijacking." International Conciliation, No. 585 (November, 1971), 7-27.

"Airport Security Searches and the Fourth Amendment." Columbia Law Review, 71 (June, 1971), 1039-1058.

"Anti-Hijacking Plans Augmented." Aviation Week and Space Technology, November 9, 1970, p. 32.

"Anti-Hijacking Proposals Proliferate." Aviation Week and Space Technology, 93, No. 12, September 21, 1970, p. 27.

"Arab Guerrillas Adopt Air Piracy as a Tactic." Aviation Week and Space Technology, September 14, 1970, pp. 33-38.

Boyle, Robert P. "International Action to Combat Aircraft Hijacking." Lawyer of the Americas, 4 (October, 1972), 460-473.

__________., and Pulsifer, Roy. "The Tokyo Convention on Offenses and Certain Other Acts Committed on Board Aircraft." Journal of Air Law and Commerce, 30 (1964), 305-345.

Cheng, Bin. "Crimes on Board Aircraft." Current Legal Problems, 12 (1959), 177-207.

Deen, Arthur H. "The Geneva Convention on the Law of the Sea: What was Accomplished." American Journal of International Law, 58 (1958), 608-28.

Deere, Lora L. "Political Offenses in the Law and Practice of Extradition." American Journal of International Law, 27 (1933), 247-270.

Denaro, Jacob M. "Inflight Crimes, The Tokyo Convention and Federal Judicial Jurisdiction." Journal of Air Law and Commerce, 35 (Spring, 1969), 171-203.

Dody, Lawrence. "Anti-Hijacking Drive Gains Impetus." Aviation Week and Space Technology, 93, No. 16, October 19, 1970, p. 27.

Evans, Alona E. "Aircraft Hijacking: Its Causes and Cure." American Journal of International Law, 63 (October, 1969), 695-710.

__________. "Reflections Upon the Political Offenses in International Practice." American Journal of International Law, 57 (1963), 1-24.

"F.A.A. Outlines Actions Taken Against Crimes Aboard Aircraft." F.A.A. Information, 45, May 12, 1964, p. 3.

Fairman, Charles. "A Note on Re Piracy Jure Gentium." American Journal of International Law, 29 (July, 1935), 508-512.

Fenston, John, and de Saussure, Hamilton. "Conflict in the Competence and Jurisdiction of Courts of Different States to Deal with Crimes Committed on Board Aircraft and Persons Involved Therein." McGill Law Journal, 56 (1952), 66-83.

Fenwick, Charles. "Piracy in the Caribbean." American Journal of International Law, 55 (1961), 410-426.

Fick, Ronald L.; Gordon, Jon I.; and Patterson, John C. "Aircraft Hijacking: Criminal and Civil Aspects." University of Florida Law Review, 22 (Summer, 1969), 72-100.

Finch, G. A. "Nuremburg Trials and International Law." American Journal of International Law, 41 (1947), 770-794.

__________. "Piracy in the Mediterranean." American Journal of International Law, 31 (1937), 659-65.

FitzGerald, Gerald F. "Towards Legal Suppression of Acts Against Civil Aviation." International Conciliation, No. 585 (November, 1971), 42-78.

"Fly Me to Pyongyang: Japan Airlines 727." Newsweek, 75, April 13, 1970, p. 40.

"Foreign Terrorism Spreading to U.S.?" U.S. News and World Report, 75, July 16, 1973, pp. 37-40.

Garcia-Mora, Manuel R. "Present Status of Political Offences in the Law of Extradition and Asylum." University of Pittsburg Law Review, 14 (1953), 371-96.

__________. "The Nature of Political Offenses: A Knotty Problem of Extradition Law." Virginia Law Review, 48 (1962), 122-57.

Harvard Research in International Law. "Draft Convention on Extradition and Comments." American Journal of International Law, 29 (1935), 16-434.

__________. "Draft Convention on Piracy with Comments." American Journal of International Law, Supplement, 26 (1932), 739-885.

__________. "Draft Convention on Territorial Waters." American Journal of International Law Spec. Supplement, 23 (1929), 241-380.

__________. "Jurisdiction in Respect to Crime." American Journal of International Law, Supplement, 29 (1935), 445-592

Hirsch, Arthur I., and Fuller, David. "Aircraft Piracy and Extradition." New York Law Forum, 16 (Spring 1970), 392-419.

Horlick, Gary. "The Developing Law of Air Hijacking." Harvard International Law Journal, 12 (Winter, 1971), 33-70.

__________. "The Public and Private International Response to Aircraft Hijacking." Vanderbilt Journal of Transnational Law, 6 (1972), 144-185.

Hotz, R. "More on Hijacking." Aviation Week and Space Technology, 91, No. 19, November 10, 1969, p. 11.

"IFALPA Mounts Anti-Hijack Drive." Aviation Week and Space Technology, 91, No. 10, September 8, 1969.

Jacobson, Peter M. "From Piracy on the High Seas to Piracy in the High Skies: A Study of Aircraft Hijacking." Cornell International Law Journal, 5 (1972), 161-87.

Johnson, D. H. N. "Piracy in Modern International Law." Transactions of the Grotius Society, 43 (1957), 63-85.

Kelsen, Hans. "Will the Judgements in the Nuremburg Trial Constitute a Precedent in International Law?." International Law Quarterly, 1 (Summer, 1947), 153-71.

Kirchheimer, Otto. "Asylum." American Political Science Review, 53 (December, 1959), 985-1016.

Kunz, Josef L. "The Meaning and Range of the Term Pacta Sunt Servanda." American Journal of International Law, 39 (April, 1945), 180-197.

Lauterpacht, Hersch. "Positions of Individuals in International Law." Transactions of the Grotius Society, 29 (1944), 1-33.

Lenoir, James J. "Piracy Cases in the Supreme Court." Journal of Criminal Law, Criminology and Political Science, 25 (1934), 532-553.

Lissitzyn, Oliver J. "International Control of Aerial Hijacking: The Role of Values and Interests." American Journal of International Law, 65 (September, 1971), 80-86.

Loy, Frank E. "Some International Approaches to Dealing with Hijacking of Aircraft." The International Lawyer, 4 (1970), 444-452.

"Luftpiraterie als rechtsproblem." Zeitschrift fur Luftricht und Weltraumrichtsfragen, 18 (April 1, 1969), 77-80.

Lynn, Robert H. "Air Hijacking as a Political Crime--Who Should Judge?." California Western International Law Journal, 2 (1971), p2-108.

McClintock, Michael C. "Skyjacking: It's Domestic Civil and Criminal Ramifications." Journal of Air Law and Commerce, 39 (January, 1973), 29-80.

McKeithen, R. L. Smith. "Prospects for the Prevention of Aircraft Hijacking Through Law." Columbia Journal of Transnational Law, 9 (Spring, 1970), 60-80.

McKelvey, Richard, and Zavoina, William. "An IBM Fortran IV Program to Perform N-Chrotomous Multivariate Probit Analysis." Behavioral Science, 16 (March, 1971), 186-187.

McMahon, John P. "Air Hijacking: Extradition as a Deterrent." The Georgetown Law Journal, 58 (1970), 1135-1152.

McWhinney, Edward. "New Developments in the Law of International Aviation: The Control of Aerial Hijacking." American Journal of International Law, 55 (1971), 71-75.

Malmborg, K. E. "Malmborg Sees Advance in Hijack Conventions." Virginia Law Weekley, DICTA, 24, No. 17, 1972, p. 1.

Mankiewicz, R. H. "The 1970 Hague Convention." Journal of Air Law and Commerce, 37 (1971), 195-210.

Martin, Peter. "The Unlawful Seizure of Aircraft." The Law Society's Gazette, 66 (July, 1969), 714-716.

Mendelsohn, A. I. "In-Flight Crime: The International and Domestic Picture Under the Tokyo Convention." Virginia Law Review, 53 (April, 1967), 509-63.

Montgomery, de J. E. G. "The Barbary States in the Law of Nations." Transactions of the Grotius Society, 4 (1918), 87-94.

Morrison, Stanley. "A Collection of Piracy Laws of Various Countries." American Journal of International Law Supplement, 26 (1932), 887-1013.

"Murder in the Sky: Eastern Airlines, DC-9." Newsweek, 75, March 30, 1970, p. 23.

"New Traps for Skyjackers." U.S. News and World Report, 74, November 9, 1970, pp. 15-17.

"Panel: New Developments in the Law of International Civil Aviation: The Control of Aerial Hijacking." Proceedings of the American Society of International Law, 65 (September, 1971), 71-96.

Partridge, Eric. "History of Pirates." Quarterly Review, 262 (1934), 142-153.

"Pirates in the Sky." Time, Vol. 96, September 21, 1970, p. 12.

Poulantzas, Nicholas M. "Hijacking or Air Piracy?." Nederlands Juristenblad, 566, No. 20 (1970).

Rafat, Amir. "Control of Aircraft Hijacking: The Law of International Civil Aviation." World Affairs, 134 (Fall, 1971), 143-156.

Revue Generale de l'Air et de L'Espace. Vol. 32 (1969), 249-358.

Ruppenthal, Karl M. "World Law and the Hijackers." The Nation, 208, No. 5, February 3, 1969, p. 144.

Schwarzenberger, Georg. "Title to Territory: Response to a Challenge." American Journal of International Law, 51 (1957), 308-24.

"Seeking a Definition for Piracy in the Air." ITA Bulletin, 13 (March 30, 1970), pp. 321-24.

Shepard, Ira M. "Air Piracy: The Role of the International Federation of Airline Pilots Associations." Cornell International Law Journal, 3 (1970), 79-91.

Smith, Chester Lee. "The Probable Necessity of an International Prison in Solving Aircraft Hijacking." The International Lawyer, 5 (April, 1971), 269-278.

Steep, Thomas. "Warriors and Pirates of Modern China." Travel, 59 (June, 1932), 45-46.

Stephen, John E. "Going South--Air Piracy and Unlawful Interference with Air Commerce." International Lawyer, 4 (1970), 433-443.

"This is Your Captain." Newsweek, 74, September 8, 1969, pp. 37-38.

Turner, James S. G. "Piracy in the Air." Naval War College Review, 22 (1969), 86-116.

Van Panhuys, Haro F. "Aircraft Hijacking and International Law." Columbia Journal of Transnational Law, 9 (Spring, 1970), 1-22.

Volpe, John A. and Steward, John T. "Aircraft Hijacking: Some Domestic and International Responses." Kentucky Law Journal, 59 (Winter, 1970), 273-318.

Whang, Paul K. "Anti-Piracy Measures." The China Weekly Review, 66 (September 2, 1933), 24.

"What Can be Done about Skyjacking?." Time, 93, January 31, 1969, pp. 19-20.

Whatley, A.T. "Historical Sketch of Piracy." Law Magazine and Review (1874), 536-618.

White, Gillian M. E. "The Hague Convention for the Suppression of Unlawful Seizure of Aircraft." Review of the International Commission of Jurists, 6 (April-June, 1971), 39-45.

"Why Not Frisk?." Nation, 210, June 22, 1970, p. 741.

Wurfel, Seymour W. "Aircraft Piracy--Crime or Fun?." William and Mary Law Review, 70 (Spring, 1969), 820-873.

Yearbooks

Beckett, W. E. "The Exercise of Criminal Jurisdiction over Foreigners." British Yearbook of International Law, 1925. New York: Oxford University Press, 1926.

Carnegie Endowment for International Peace. Yearbook, 1922. Washington: Carnegie Endowment for International Peace, 1922.

Carnegie Endowment for International Peace. Yearbook, 1927. Washington: Carnegie Endowment for International Peace, 1927.

Carnegie Endowment for International Peace. Yearbook, 1932. Washington: Carnegie Endowment for International Peace, 1932.

Corbett, Percy E. "The Consent of States and the Sources of the Law of Nations." British Yearbook of International Law, 1925. New York: Oxford University Press, 1926.

Facts on File. New York: Facts on File, Inc., January 1, 1960-June 30, 1973.

FitzGerald, Gerald F. "The Development of International Rules Concerning Offenses and Certain Other Acts Committed on Board Aircraft." Canadian Yearbook of International Law, 1963. Vancouver: University of British Columbia, 1963.

Guillaume, Gilbert. "La Convention de La Hague des 16 des decembre 1970." Annuaire Francais de Droit International. 1970.

"International Civil Aviation Organization." Yearbook of International Organizations, 1971. Brussels: Union of International Organizations, 1972.

Keesing's Contemporary Archives. London: Keesing's Publications, Ltd., January 1, 1960 - June 30, 1973.

"The Nyon Arrangements." British Yearbook of International Law. New York: Oxford University Press, 1938.

Paxton, John, ed. The Statesman's Yearbook, 1972-1973. London: The Macmillan Press, Ltd., 1972.

Samuels, Alec. "Crimes Committed on Board Aircraft: Tokyo Convention Act, 1967." British Yearbook of International Law, 1967. New York: Oxford University Press, 1967.

Shubber, Sami. "Is Hijacking of Aircraft Piracy in International Law?." British Yearbook of International Law, 1968-1969. New York: Oxford University Press, 1969.

Watt, D. C. Survey of International Affairs, 1961. New York: Oxford University Press, 1965.

Public Documents

International Civil Airport Association. Hijacking. Doc. 7111 - GEN/15, December, 1971.

International Legal Materials. Washington, D.C.: American Society of International Law, 1960-1973.

League of Nations. Official Journal. Records of the Fifth Assembly, Plenary Meetings (1924).

League of Nations. Official Journal. Records of the Eighth Ordinary Session of the Assembly. Meetings of the First Committee (Constitutional and Legal Questions), Special Supplement #55 (1927).

__________. Official Journal. "The Nyon Arrangement and the Agreement Supplementary to the Nyon Arrangement. Communication from the Minister for Foreign Affairs of France, President of the Mediterranean Conference of Nyon." (C. 409. M. 273. 1937. VII). (Ser. L.O.N.P., 1937, VII, 2).

__________. Publications of the Permanent Court of International Justice. "The Lotus Case." Series A. No. 10 (1927).

__________. "Report of the Sub-Committee of the League of Nations Committee of Experts for the Progressive Codification of International Law." Doc. 196. M. 70.V (1927).

United Nations. Conference on the Law of the Sea. Official Records. Geneva, 1958. A/Conf. 13/.

__________. General Assembly, 24th Session, December 12, 1969, Forcible Diversion of Civil Aircraft in Flight, A/Res/2551.

__________. General Assembly Resolution 2312, 22 U.N. GAOR, Supplement 16. U.N. Doc. A/6716 (1967).

__________. General Assembly. Universal Declaration of Human Rights. Res. 217, A/10 (1948).

__________. International Civil Aviation Organization. Documents of the Legal Committee. Fourteenth Session, Doc. 8302, LC 150-1, 1963.

__________. International Civil Aviation Organization. International Conference on Air Law. Tokyo, August-September, 1963. Doc. 8565-LC/152-2.

__________. International Civil Aviation Organization. Minutes of the Legal Committee. Fourteenth Session, 1963. ICAO Doc. 8302, LC/150-1.

__________. International Civil Aviation Organization. Proposals Submitted to the Subcommittee on the Unlawful Seizure of Aircraft of the Legal Committee. LG/SC. SA. WD 7, May 5, 1969.

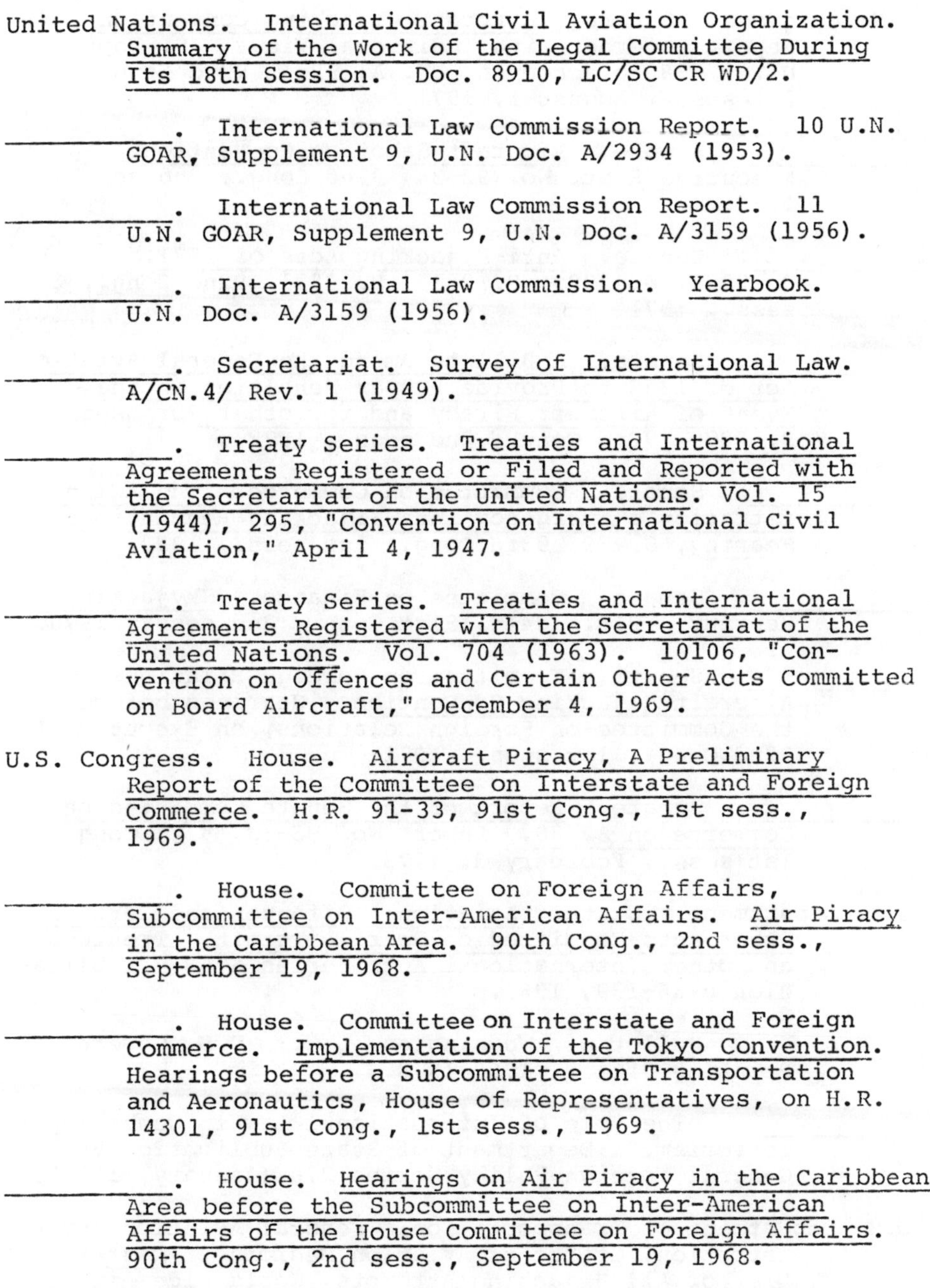

United Nations. International Civil Aviation Organization. Summary of the Work of the Legal Committee During Its 18th Session. Doc. 8910, LC/SC CR WD/2.

__________. International Law Commission Report. 10 U.N. GOAR, Supplement 9, U.N. Doc. A/2934 (1953).

__________. International Law Commission Report. 11 U.N. GOAR, Supplement 9, U.N. Doc. A/3159 (1956).

__________. International Law Commission. Yearbook. U.N. Doc. A/3159 (1956).

__________. Secretariat. Survey of International Law. A/CN.4/ Rev. 1 (1949).

__________. Treaty Series. Treaties and International Agreements Registered or Filed and Reported with the Secretariat of the United Nations. Vol. 15 (1944), 295, "Convention on International Civil Aviation," April 4, 1947.

__________. Treaty Series. Treaties and International Agreements Registered with the Secretariat of the United Nations. Vol. 704 (1963). 10106, "Convention on Offences and Certain Other Acts Committed on Board Aircraft," December 4, 1969.

U.S. Congress. House. Aircraft Piracy, A Preliminary Report of the Committee on Interstate and Foreign Commerce. H.R. 91-33, 91st Cong., 1st sess., 1969.

__________. House. Committee on Foreign Affairs, Subcommittee on Inter-American Affairs. Air Piracy in the Caribbean Area. 90th Cong., 2nd sess., September 19, 1968.

__________. House. Committee on Interstate and Foreign Commerce. Implementation of the Tokyo Convention. Hearings before a Subcommittee on Transportation and Aeronautics, House of Representatives, on H.R. 14301, 91st Cong., 1st sess., 1969.

__________. House. Hearings on Air Piracy in the Caribbean Area before the Subcommittee on Inter-American Affairs of the House Committee on Foreign Affairs. 90th Cong., 2nd sess., September 19, 1968.

U.S. Congress. Senate. Aircraft Hijacking Convention Report together with Individual Views. S. Rept. No. 92-98 to accompany EX. A, 92-1, 92nd Cong., 1st sess., August 5, 1971.

__________. Senate. Aircraft Sabotage Convention. Executive Rept. No. 92-34, 92nd Cong., 2nd sess., 1972.

__________. Senate. Anti-Hijacking Acts of 1971. S. 2280, S. 2299, S. 2815, S. 3871, 92nd Cong., 2nd sess., 1971.

__________. Senate. A Bill to Amend the Federal Aviation Act of 1958 to Provide Proper Penalties in the Event of Aircraft Piracy and for other Purposes. S. 2299, 92nd Cong., 2nd sess., 1972.

__________. Senate. Committee on Commerce. The Administration's Emergency Anti-Hijacking Regulations, Hearing, S. 39, 93rd Cong., 1st sess., 1973.

__________. Senate. Committee on Finance. Skyjacking Hearing. H.R. 19444, 91st Cong., 2nd sess., 1970.

__________. Senate. Committee on Foreign Relations. Aircraft Hijacking Convention. Hearings before the Committee on Foreign Relations, on Executive A, 92nd.Cong., 1st sess., 1971.

__________. Senate. Report of the Senate Committee on Commerce on S. 39. Report No. 93-13, 93rd Cong., 1st sess., February 2, 1973.

U.S. Department of State. Aviation: Offenses and Certain Other Acts Committed on Board Aircraft. Treaties and Other International Acts Series 6768. Publication 0-36-139, 1969.

__________. Bulletin. Washington, D.C.: U.S. Government Printing Office, 1960-1973.

__________. "The Role of International Law in Combating Terrorism." Department of State Publication 8689. General Foreign Policy Series 270 (January, 1973).

U.S. Department of Transportation. Federal Aviation Administration, Office of Aviation Medicine. Master List of All Hijacking Attempts, World Wide Air Carrier, and General Aviation. Washington, D.C.: Government Printing Office. Updated periodically.

U.S. Department of Transportation. Federal Aviation Administration. Chronology of Hijackings of U.S. Registered Aircraft. Washington, D.C.: Government Printing Office. Updated February 1, 1973.

U.S. President. Message from the President of the United States, transmitting to the Senate the Convention for the Suppression of Unlawful Acts Against the Safety of Civil Aviation. Executive T, 92nd Cong., 2nd sess., 1972.

Legal Citations

An Act Further to Provide for the Collection of Duties on Imports and other Purposes. Statutes at Large. Vol. 12 (1861).

Blackmer v. United States. 284 U.S. 421 (1932).

Bonnet's Trial. 15 Howell's State Trial 1231 (1718).

Charlton v. Kelly. 229 U.S. 447 (1913).

Coumas v. Superior Court of San Joaquin Co. 31 Cal. 20 682 (1948).

The Cutting Case, Mexico, Bravos District Court (1886).

Dole v. New England Mutual Marine Insurance Co. 2 Cliff. 394 (1st Circ., 1864).

Factor v. Laubenheimer. 290 U.S. 276 (1933).

Great Britain. An Acte for punysshement of Pyrotes and Robbers of the See, 1536. 28 Hen. 8. ch. 15, The Statutes (3rd Revised Edition), Vol. 1.

In Re Kavic, et al. 80th Annual Digest 371 (Federal Tribunal Switzerland, 1952).

Marienna Flora. 11 Wheaton 39 (1826).

The Paquete Habana (The Lola) 177 U.S. 677 (1900).

The Prize Cases. 2 Black 635 (1862).

Regina v. Dawson. 13 Howell's State Trial 45 (1596).

United States v. Arizona. 120 U.S. 484 (1887).

United States v. Baker (Savannah Privateers). 5 Blatchford 6 (1861).

U.S. Constitution, Art. III, Sec. 2.

United States v. Palmer. 3 Wheaton 610 (1818).

United States v. Pirates. 5 Wheaton 184 (1820).

United States v. Smith. 5 Wheaton 153 (1820).

Unpublished Materials

Joyner, Christopher C. "Obligation and Authority viz-à-viz International Law in Hans Kelsen's 'Pure Theory': A Critical Interpretation." (Unpublished manuscript, Florida State University, 1972).

Zavoina, William and McKelvey, Richard. "A Statistical Model for the Analysis of Legislative Voting Behavior." (Unpublished American Political Science Association Convention paper, 1969).

Other Sources

Airline Pilot. 1960-1973.

Aviation Daily. 1960-1973.

The Economist. 1960-1973.

IATA *News Review*. 1960-1973.

ITF *News Letter*. 1960-1973.

New York *Times Index*, 1960-1973.

Personal interviews with Ambassador Richard Kearney, U.S. Member, International Law Commission, Washington, D.C., April 14, 1973.

Personal interviews with officials of the U.S. Department of State, Office of the Legal Adviser, Washington, D.C., February 13-15, 1973.

Wall Street *Journal*. 1960-1973.

Washington *Post*. 1960-1973.

INDEX